Banning them, securing us?

MANCHESTER
1824

Manchester University Press

Banning them, securing us?

Terrorism, parliament and the ritual of proscription

Lee Jarvis and Tim Legrand

Manchester University Press

Published by Manchester University Press
Altrincham Street, Manchester M1 7JA
www.manchesteruniversitypress.co.uk

British Library Cataloguing-in-Publication Data
A catalogue record for this book is available from the British Library

ISBN 978 1 5261 4492 8 hardback

First published 2020

Typeset by Newgen Publishing UK
Printed in Great Britain
by TJ International Ltd, Padstow, Cornwall

For Ami, Sukie, Artie and Piali

Contents

Figures

Acknowledgements

Although we didn't realise it at the time, this book's gestation began nearly ten years ago during a late-night conversation in a small flat in Swansea. In the course of that conversation, we managed to agree on two things. First, we agreed that the outright banning of specific organisations from liberal democratic states is potentially troubling, almost certainly illiberal, and, clearly, open to politicking and misuse. Second, despite a shared unease with this practice (which seemed fundamental to other aspects of the UK's counter-terrorism regime), we also agreed that our knowledge of proscription was rather more limited than it might have been. So, we set out to sate this curiosity and began to explore the political, historical and discursive dynamics of the listing or proscribing of terrorist organisations. Neither of us expected the journey that followed to be quite as long or provocative, or as interesting, as it has been. And, as we find ourselves looking back from the end of that project, it is appropriate that we take a few words to offer our thanks to some of those who have helped us. As always, it was the encouragement, support and love of very many people that meant we were able to finish this book, and we would like, therefore, to acknowledge some of those people explicitly (and to offer our apologies to many others we have no doubt omitted).

First, we would like to thank all of our academic colleagues and interlocutors at our current and former universities and beyond, many of whom have been extremely generous with feedback, comments and criticism at various points during this and related projects. Amongst very many important people these include Simon Bronitt, Elizabeth Cobbett, Suzanne Doyle, Alan Finlayson, Adam Henschke, Alexandria Innes, Richard Jackson, Michael Lister, Lee Marsden and Michael Stohl, as well as all of the contributors to the special issue of *Terrorism and Political Violence* (Volume 30, Issue 2) on the global politics of proscription which we co-edited while developing our ideas. We would like also to thank all of those who kindly attended, organised or invited us to present on the ideas within this book (often when those ideas were still very much a work in progress), including at Edith Cowan University, Fondation Maison des Sciences de L'Homme, Nottingham Trent University, Queen's University Belfast, the University of East Anglia, the University of Leeds, the University of Sydney, the University of Tübingen, and the University of Warwick, as well as at two of BISA's Annual Conferences in Edinburgh and London. Much of the book's initial planning was completed during periods of study leave we received, and for which we gratefully acknowledge the Australian National University and the University of East Anglia. At Manchester University Press we are grateful, too, for the support and encouragement we received from Robert Byron, Jonathan de Peyer, Tony Mason, Gail Welsh and the anonymous reviewers of an earlier draft.

Given that the argument that we make in this book has been under development for some time, earlier versions of some passages have appeared in article form. It is also appropriate, therefore, that we thank the various journal editors and peer reviewers for their feedback along the way, and that we acknowledge their publishers for permission to reproduce these works and their arguments thus:

An earlier version of arguments made in Chapters 1 and 2 of this book was published as an article under the title, 'Enemies of the State: Proscription powers and their use in the United Kingdom', https://doi.org/10.1057/bp. 2014.8. The final, definitive version of this paper has been published in *British Politics* 9/4, December 2014, published by Palgrave Journals. All rights reserved.

An earlier version of arguments made within Chapter 5 was published as an article under the title, 'I am somewhat puzzled: Questions, audiences and securitization in the proscription of terrorist organizations', https://doi.org/10.1177/0967010616686020. The final, definitive version of this paper has been published in *Security Dialogue* 48/2, April 2017, published by SAGE Publishing. All rights reserved.

An earlier version of arguments made within Chapter 6 was published as an article under the title, 'Legislating for Otherness:

Proscription powers and parliamentary discourse', https://doi.org/10.1017/S0260210515000509. The final, definitive version of this paper has been published in *Review of International Studies*, 42/3, July 2016 published by Cambridge University Press. Reprinted with permission.

An earlier version of arguments made within Chapter 7 was published as an article under the title, 'Preaching to the converted: Parliament and the proscription ritual', https://doi.org/10.1177/0032321717694049. The final, definitive version of this paper has been published in *Political Studies* 65/4, December 2017 published by SAGE Publishing, All rights reserved.

Finally, and most of all, our thanks and our love go to our wives, Aya and Sunita, to our children Ami, Sukie, Artie and Piali, to our parents, our wider families, and to our friends. All of you have been there for us in exciting, challenging and frustrating times and we could not have finished this project without you. Thank you!

Introduction: banning them

The imagination of politicians and publics around the world was captured in 2014 when a new terrorist organisation thrust itself violently and a little unexpectedly upon the world stage. Videos of Western hostage beheadings, the seizure of significant territory in Iraq and Syria, and – to cap it all – a declaration of statehood, thrust what became known, variously, as the Islamic State of Iraq and the Levant (ISIL), the Islamic State in Iraq and Syria (ISIS), Islamic State (IS) or, more pejoratively, Daesh, into the global limelight.

Politicians in the United Kingdom rushed to denounce the organisation's barbarisms. In a speech to the United Nations General Assembly, Prime Minister David Cameron (2014) spoke to 'the mortal threat we all face', denouncing 'ISIL's sick extremist world view ... [and] murderous plans to expand its borders well beyond Iraq and Syria, and to carry out terrorist atrocities right across the world'. Cameron's then political rival Ed Miliband spoke similarly, if more cautiously, on the need to respond to this threat, arguing in a newspaper editorial around the same time: 'In the face of this danger I am clear we cannot ... simply shrug our shoulders and hope it goes away' (Grice 2014). Such was the threat posed by ISIS that the British response quickly escalated to support for air strikes against Islamic State targets following parliamentary authorisation in August 2014 (in the case of Iraq), and again in December 2015 (in the case of Syria).

Less newsworthy, but no less important, was Parliament's decision – in June 2014 – to outlaw 'the Islamic State of Iraq and the Levant, also known as the Islamic State of Iraq and al-Sham' (Brokenshire 2014a) by adding it to the United Kingdom's list of proscribed terrorist organisations.[1] In so doing, Parliament exercised one of its oldest and most fundamental powers: the power to outlaw those deemed an enemy of the state. Today, this power is contained within the Terrorism Act 2000 (hereafter TA 2000) and is typically applied against groups designated as terrorist threats to the United Kingdom or its interests: the cases that form the focus of this book. Proscription casts a criminal shroud over membership of and support for banned groups, with the aim of diminishing their capabilities and signalling society's 'communal condemnation' thereof (Walker 2018, 238). Throughout Britain's long political history, its monarchical and democratic institutions have maintained a proscription power – in one form or another – in order to punish, criminalise or exclude individuals and organisations who have fallen out of favour or are deemed to resemble a threat. Indeed, one of the earliest recorded acts of the post-Civil War 'Rump' Parliament (see Chapter 1), was to outlaw each of the leaders of the routed Royalist movement by name. Proscription has since been preserved as one of Parliament's most severe powers, though – as we shall see – its use has shifted away from outlawing individuals *as* individuals, in favour of banning groups and membership thereof.

The June 2014 proscriptions constituted the fifteenth extension of the UK's list of banned terrorist groups since the passage of the TA 2000. In seeking parliamentary approval for this, the UK's Minister for Security and Immigration, James Brokenshire, emphasised the threat posed by the Islamic State and outlined the need for new, targeted action following this group's recent split from al Qaeda in Iraq. In his words to the House of Commons at the time:

> The Islamic State of Iraq and the Levant is a brutal Sunni Islamist terrorist group active in Iraq and Syria. The group adheres to a global jihadist ideology, following an extreme interpretation of Islam that is anti-western and promotes sectarian violence. ISIL aims to establish an Islamic state governed by sharia law in the region and uses violence and intimidation to impose its extremist ideology on civilians. ISIL has previously been proscribed as part of al-Qaeda. However, steps taken by al-Qaeda's senior leadership to sever ties with ISIL have prompted consideration of the case to proscribe ISIL in its own right. (Brokenshire 2014a)

Drawing on arguments within the accompanying explanatory memorandum[2] Brokenshire pressed on with the government's case for proscription by listing ISIL's outrages, reflecting on the risk that 'foreign fighters' would seek to join the organisation, and highlighting that the organisation is already 'designated as a terrorist group by both Canada and Australia, and as an alias of al-Qaeda by the US, New Zealand and the United Nations' (Brokenshire 2014a). The Shadow Minister for Foreign Affairs, Diana Johnson, was one of those who responded to the government's request. Following a brief but pointed complaint that the government had shared its intentions with the media beforehand,[3] Johnson nevertheless confirmed that the government would have the opposition's total support for this action:

> The Opposition do not have access to the same intelligence as the Home Secretary and the Minister. However, on the basis of the assurances that the Minister has given the House and the information that he has set out clearly today, the Opposition are happy to give the motion our full support. (Johnson 2014b)

So it happened that, following a House of Lords debate on 19 June, ISIL and the four other groups named on the proscription order were successfully added to the UK list. From that point on – as detailed further in Chapter 1 – it has been a criminal offence within the United Kingdom, to: belong to ISIL; invite support for the organisation; arrange or manage meetings on behalf of it; support its activities; or wear clothing indicating membership of the group. The fate of Shamima Begum – who had her British citizenship revoked by the Home Office in 2019 having travelled to join ISIL as a fifteen-year-old child – indicates the very real, and very significant, consequences of such designations.

ISIL – or Daesh as it is now more commonly known – serves in many ways as the poster child of contemporary terrorist organisations. Widely depicted as brutal and uncompromising, motivated by a religious fanaticism, unconstrained in its ambitions by national borders, and drawing support from individuals around the world, it stands as the archetype of what some have taken to describing as 'new terrorism' (e.g. Neumann 2009). It is, therefore, noteworthy that the British government's immediate response to this organisation was to draw on a political power – proscription – that has been honed across many centuries of confrontation with various (identified) enemies: from the foes of King Alfred in the ninth century, to the Jacobite rebels of the seventeenth and eighteenth centuries, and numerous republican and unionist groups associated with the Northern Ireland 'Troubles' far more recently.[4] In this sense, at least, ISIS is merely the latest target of a power with ancient roots.

Other echoes of the past may also be seen in more recent proscriptions such as the listing of the extreme right-wing organisation National Action and its aliases Scottish Dawn and NS131. National Action was finally banned in the UK in December 2016 after publicly celebrating the murder of the MP Jo Cox. This celebration – and its public enthusiasm for other atrocities on social media and beyond – were deemed to constitute glorification of terrorism: an offence that had been grounds for proscription in the UK since 2006.[5] This decision was important, first, for again highlighting historical continuities in the practice of excluding organisations: Oswald Mosley's British Union of Fascists, for instance, had been similarly banned by the UK government in May 1940 amid concerns with actual or potential fifth-columnists. The banning of National Action was also, moreover, important as it emerged – at least in part – from widespread public outrage at this organisation and its attempt to instrumentalise Jo Cox's murder for its own (widely reviled) ends. This matters because it indicates the importance of public, political and media involvement in proscription debates and decisions which should not – and cannot – be taken as automatic or objective responses to external threats.[6] The role of specific publics and interest groups was, for instance, widely seen to be prominent again in the later, March 2019, listing of Hezbollah in its entirety by the UK state.

That the listing of terrorist organisations might be subject to political or other considerations encourages us to reflect, briefly, on the value of this power for its proponents. As we shall see in Chapter 1, proscription is often seen to serve multiple purposes that relate to, but extend beyond, counter-terrorism. Indeed, as the Home Office argues:

> In addition to the proscription offences, proscription can support other disruptive activity including the use of immigration powers such as exclusion, prosecution for other offences, encouraging removal of on-line material, messaging and EU asset freezes. The resources of a proscribed organisation are terrorist property and are, therefore, liable to be seized.

Such outcomes are far from hypothetical, and proscription offences have been employed in a number of high-profile cases in recent years. Perhaps most notable is the 2016 prosecution of notorious preacher Anjum Choudhary who was sentenced to five years and six months in prison for inviting support for the Islamic State. Proscription, in this instance, provided a mechanism for prosecuting an individual who had frustrated political and police efforts to bring him to justice over a number of years. As the head of the Metropolitan Police's Counter-terrorism Command, Commander Dean Haydon, argued of Choudary and his co-conspirator following their prosecution:

> These men have stayed just within the law for many years, but there is no one within the counter-terrorism world that has any doubts of the influence that they have had, the hate they have spread and the people that they have encouraged to join terrorist organisations. (Grierson *et al.* 2016)

Given the significance of proscription's outcomes, which extend to lengthy prison sentences and heavy fines, proscribed groups often commit considerable resources in order to remove themselves from the United Kingdom's list. To date, only three organisations have been successful to this end – the Mujaheddin e Khalq, also known as the Peoples' Mujaheddin of Iran, in June 2008; the International Sikh Youth Federation in March 2016; and, most recently, Hezb-e Islami Gulbuddin, in June 2017. The loyalist paramilitary organisation Red Hand Commando submitted its own (unsuccessful) application for deproscription in the autumn of 2017. Such efforts speak to the power's undoubted importance for its targets and their members. At the same time, the successes and, more frequently, the failures of attempts to get de-listed point to the role of multiple factors in the make-up of the UK's list; factors that are often exogeneous to the threat posed by such groups and include public and political pressure and interests, geopolitical developments, the variable capabilities and resources of proscribed organisations, and the presence of interested diaspora communities.

Proscription, outlawry and exclusion: the power of naming

Proscription is a tool situated within a family of instruments of political exclusion, blacklisting and outlawry. While such terms are often used interchangeably, not least because they often work toward similar outcomes of expulsion, they are not entirely synonymic. What they share is the designation of a specific entity (typically an individual or group) as unlawful or illegitimate within a particular jurisdiction, and the construction of a climate in which that entity cannot meaningfully exist. All of these instruments, in other words, work to exclude newly designated others from an established community. As Jason Sharman therefore argues of financial blacklists, 'blacklisting as a declarative is a self-contained action (speech act) sufficient to produce new institutional facts' (2009, 580). This observation is true, too, of outlawry and proscription which again both produce and communicate a designated entity's new status through declaration. In ancient Rome this operated through a painted sign; in Britain's colonial administration of Ireland it was a 'proclamation' printed on a broadside poster; and today this takes place via press releases and electronic addenda to Schedule 2 of the TA 2000.

In its earliest form, 'proscription' was yet another Roman innovation. It surfaces during the reign of the dictator Lucius Cornelius Sulla Felix (known as 'Lucky'). Sulla's brutal reign involved the remorseless pursuit and execution of his enemies within ancient Rome, buttressed by the liberal use of *Lex Cornelia de proscription*. The word was borrowed from the older practice of posting a public notice (*tabulae publicae*) of citizens whose assets had been forfeited and auctioned off (*proscriptio bonorum*). From here we derive our modern usage of the proscription of individuals: the Latin roots *pro-* and *scribere-* produce the verb *proscribere* (and the past participle: *proscriptus*). Sulla extended this practice such that a formal proscription removed a person's status as a citizen (the *proscripti*), making said citizen's killing now lawful.

The orator and statesman Cicero was amongst those to have met their fate through proscription. Having fallen into Mark Antony's disfavour, he was proscribed and killed in 43 BC. In *The Hand of Cicero*, Shane Butler (2002) chronicles how, after Cicero's arrest and execution, a macabre public display was made of his body. Citing Plutarch, Butler relates the following: 'When Cicero was butchered, Antony ordered that his head be cut off, along with his right hand, the hand with which he had written the speeches against him' (cited in Butler 2002, 1–2). For Butler, the proscription list contained its own peculiar form of power over life and death:

> The list's beguiling familiarity, its formal order and ordinariness, stood in uncanny contrast to the violence it commanded. Was it really possible to kill a man simply by writing his name? Here was something else uncanny, for the Romans were used to the association of death with proper names in the guise of the epitaph – what made the proscription different was that it announced a death that had yet to occur. But perhaps the most striking feature of the proscription was the way in which it displaced and diffused responsibility for the slaughter. Who was the real murderer? Sulla? The state? The law? The informants? The *percussores*? Was even the sign-painter in some way responsible? For a few days at least, it was the list itself that ruled Rome. (Butler 2002, 7–8)

As this suggests, the Roman use of proscription applied to individuals, and in subsequent iterations and forms across the world this mode of exclusion came to be known as *outlawry*. Chapter 1 explores outlawry in pre-modern Britain in detail, but in almost all its forms outlawry refers to the public exclusion of an individual, removing their status as a legitimate member of a community.

Blacklisting is a related instrument of exclusion. In popular usage, a blacklist refers to an inventory of entities – organisations, groups, individuals, objects or practices – that are deemed illegitimate or unwelcome in order to publicly announce the curtailing of their rights, privileges or dealings. The term 'black list' stems from the reign of Charles II, who in 1681 produced a list of all those who had voted for the execution of his father, Charles I:

> Those in this foregoing list are they (I dare not say) who are the worst of their country's enemies … If any innocent soul be found in this black list, let him not be offended at me, but consider whether some mistaken principle or interest may not have misled him to vote.[7]

The contemporary era has seen widespread use of such blacklists. In late 1947, for instance, and prior to McCarthy's public pursuit of communists in the US State Department, the US Attorney General published a List of Subversive Organizations (AGLOSO), which operated as an effective blacklist, though ostensibly its purpose was to help federal agencies determine the loyalty of staff or potential job applicants. In fact, the AGLOSO had been in secret use by the federal government since 1940 (see the Hatch Act

1939). The European Union today employs a blacklist to specify entities considered terrorist (see Chapter 2), while the United States maintains a 'no fly' blacklist of individuals suspected of association with terrorism.

The modern practice of proscription, as it operates within the UK, intersects with both blacklisting and outlawry. It differs from the Roman use of proscription insofar as it is applied to *organisations* not individuals. Yet, like blacklisting and outlawry, it involves a public declaration of an entity's illegitimacy. The sanctions against the designated entity – the group or organisation – are similar to those of the blacklist, involving the limiting of interactions with lawful entities and the freezing of assets. The sanctions for individuals, however, are criminal. Importantly, as suggested above, the instruments of proscription, outlawry and blacklisting are all fundamentally performative. They confer a new status on an entity by the act of adding a name to a list. In so doing, the list constructs the entity anew by transforming its relationship with the state and society. Notwithstanding contemporary calls for the stripping of citizenship from individuals such as Shamima Begum, outlawry is, largely, obsolete in the modern world – the UK, for instance, abolished the practice in 1879. Yet proscription and blacklisting, as we shall see, remain in active and widespread use today.

Lacunae and arguments

Given (i) the significance of proscription decisions for national security, (ii) the implications such decisions pose for citizenship and rights of speech, association, movement, and (iii) the potential of all of this to shed light on wider political dynamics and developments, the academic community has been surprisingly slow to engage with this power. As we argue in Chapter 2, although there is a small, if growing, body of legal literature on national proscription and listing regimes there has been remarkably little scholarship within fields such as International Relations, Security Studies or Political Science. This caution is especially surprising given the amount of academic ink spilled on terrorism and counter-terrorism in the post-9/11 period. Alex Schmid (2011, 460), for instance, identifies the publication of 2,281 new books on terrorism between 2001 and 2008, with another study finding that 54 per cent of 14,006 surveyed academic and popular articles on terrorism were published in 2002 and 2003 alone (Lum *et al.* 2006).

The literature on this power that does exist, we argue in Chapter 2, offers important critical insights into the consequences of proscription. This includes reflection on proscription's role in reducing important civil liberties, analysis of the ways in which proscription may impede peace processes or conflict resolution initiatives, discussion of the risk that listing organisations may criminalise individuals by association, as well as commentary on this power's (limited) impact on national security. This scepticism is unusual – even refreshing – within research around terrorism and counter-terrorism, much of which tends towards a relatively sympathetic reading of government efforts and arguments (Jackson *et al.* 2009, 2011).

Leaving aside, for the moment, the undoubted importance of recent scholarship on proscription, our argument in this book is that its emphasis on proscription's *outcomes* (for security or citizenship) has led to the overlooking of equally important questions relating to the politics and performances of proscription *processes*. Addressing the latter, we show, involves shifting our focus a little and setting aside the two questions that have tended to dominate debate thus far, namely: (i) does the banning of specific terrorist organisations make 'us' safer from the threat posed by terrorism; and (ii) can the banning of specific terrorist organisations be justified (on security grounds) given the potential implications of such decisions for citizens, communities, their rights and liberties? Although those two questions are important, our argument is that asking these questions means we have already assumed, and perhaps even conceded, too much regarding proscription's possibility, legitimacy and utility.

Key themes

This book has been written in an attempt to move beyond a focus on proscription's consequences and to engage, instead, with two related questions. First, what is it that renders the proscription or banning of specific organisations by the British state possible? How, in other words, has this power come to be so widely understood and accepted as a legitimate, appropriate and necessary tool in the state's (extensive) counter-terrorism armoury, and why do we not see more contestation around its usage?[8] Second, what, in turn, is made possible through the process of proscription itself? What work is done by this power within broader politics, performances and discourses; such as performances and discourses of identity, political authority and national security?

In order to engage with these questions, we focus our attention upon the debates that take place within the United Kingdom's two Houses of Parliaments each time one (or typically more than one) organisation is added to the UK's list. Although we explore the formal, legal process of proscription more fully in Chapter 1, it is worth noting here parliamentary assent must be sought by the Home Secretary or her delegate any time the UK government seeks to extend its list of proscribed organisations. This is significant, for our purposes, for three reasons. First, it renders Parliament an important site in which the politics of proscription decisions play out. As we argue in the book, parliamentary debates on the banning of new organisations are not only characterised by cross-party acquiescence and agreement – although there is much of this. There is, at the same time, much evidence of dissent, disagreement, distraction and questioning within the legislature's response to the executive's actions. This dissent and disagreement is shaped, facilitated and constrained, of course, by particular rules and norms, and takes place within specific parameters according to which the participants conduct themselves. A key aim of this book is to shed light on some of these, and to explore their importance to wider performances of security decision-making.

Second, Parliament's authority in confirming proscription decisions also – at least in principle – provides it with a significant public scrutiny role in this process. As we shall see in Chapters 4 and 5, there are many examples of legislators using these debates as an opportunity not only to query the appropriateness of specific proscription orders, but also to challenge the validity of proscription more generally, and, indeed, to ask a whole host of additional questions of the executive, including, frequently, why specific *other* organisations, who might be equally deserving of this sanction, are not being considered for listing. Such discussions often see invocation of constituent and community interests, indicating that the politics of proscription is not limited, in these debates, to the specific organisations under consideration.

Where the above two points speak to the constitutional status of Parliament within the separation of powers central to the

Westminster model, Parliament – and this is the third reason – is also an important bearer of British political values that have become sedimented in traditions, processes and protocols over centuries. These traditions and protocols reflect, construct and reproduce ideas about political authority and conduct within and beyond Parliament, with proscription debates forming an important part of this process. So, at a micro-level, proscription debates serve to reflect and reproduce conventions of parliamentary behaviour in relation to national security issues: MPs, for instance, are often chastised in these for poor behaviour, political point-scoring or absenteeism. At a macro-level, these debates also reproduce hierarchies of political issues (with national security concerns seen to have especial importance) and (geo-)political imaginaries, confirming the authority of parliamentarians to distinguish inside from outside, or self from other, in banning or designating foes. Proscription debates, in short, contribute to the (re)production of (ideas around) parliament, parliamentarians, the state, its enemies, and the worlds inhabited by all of the above.

Our analysis of these debates in this book employs an interpretivist sensibility that draws upon broadly constructivist literature within Security Studies, International Relations and beyond. This provides for a discursive reading of the politics of proscription and the work that is done by specific narratives, arguments and questions therein for performances of security, identity and authority. Empirically, our analysis focuses upon each of the thirty-eight debates that took place between the passage of the TA 2000 from which the UK's contemporary proscription regime emerged, and the writing of this book. This focus, we argue in Chapter 3, provides a completeness to our analysis given that it engages every one of the relevant debates around this power, as well as generating sufficient textual material for a meaningful exploration of what we come to conceptualise – in Chapter 7 – as the proscription ritual (see Milliken 1999; Dunn 2006).

In focusing our attention thus, we are not seeking to argue that parliamentary debates are the only moment (that matters) in the proscription process. Nor are we arguing that these debates are limited to their linguistic content. In terms of the former, these debates are, clearly, situated within political processes that might begin far earlier with closed-door discussions between the Home Office and representatives of the intelligence community, or, indeed, with representatives from other states. That said, these debates do, we suggest, have especial political significance precisely because they host the performance of democratic scrutiny and decision-making which is so central to proscription's legitimacy. Not only is their content publicly available – through the parliamentary record, Hansard – providing an accessibility lacking in behind-the-scenes decision-making processes. But their accessibility – to publics, researchers, and importantly to parliamentarians – is an important dimension of their reproduction as evidence of democratic decision-making and, therefore, of proscription's legitimacy.

On the latter point, proscription debates – like all debates – involve numerous extra-linguistic decisions, activities, habits and architectures. Amongst many others, these include conscious and unconscious signals and gestures within participants' body language; norms regarding appropriate conduct; the scheduling of these debates within particular parliamentary calendars; and the physical materialities of the debating chambers. Our primary focus on the language of these debates is, therefore, partial, but emerges out of our discursive approach, which builds directly on a body of existing scholarship within and beyond critical security studies (Campbell 1992; Jackson 2005; Browning and McDonald 2013; Hansen 2013), and has a methodological compactness. We do, however, reflect on the interaction between linguistic and non-linguistic aspects of these debates in the book's final chapter and conclusion as we move to arguing that these constitute a very particular form of political ritual. Such an approach, we suggest, provides scope for analysing performativity within the proscription process, and its significance for proscription's (constructed) necessity and legitimacy.

Arguments

The book's overarching argument, alluded to above, is that the process of proscribing terrorist organisations within the United Kingdom – and, indeed, in countries beyond the United Kingdom – serves as a form of political ritual. Parliamentary debates on additions to the UK's list are less interesting for any decision-making power they may hold, we will argue – and, to risk a spoiler here, organisations that are debated are *always* added to the list – than they are for their constitutive role. This constitutive role is multiple, and contributes, we suggest in the chapters that follow, to the (re) production of at least five phenomena.

First, the proscription ritual contributes to the constitution of specific organisations as 'terrorist', and as a significant threat to the British state and/or (on occasion) its allies or the international community. Second, the ritual serves to reproduce terrorism, more generally, as anathema to the British political system, and a security threat capable of address by this modern form of banishment. Third, it contributes to the construction of the British national identity as a space of liberal, democratic and responsible politics, and, fourth, to the construction of Parliament as both representative and guardian of that space (of liberal, democratic, responsible politics) in which important decisions are taken only after appropriate consideration and reflection. Fifth, the proscription ritual also, we argue, works to position proscription itself as a reasonable, appropriate, necessary and legitimate tool for the defence of national security. In short, the act of proscription and the debates that stage specific decisions under this regime therefore contribute to the (re)production of (British) self, (terrorist) other, and the relationship between the two.

Approaching the process of proscription in this way is useful, we argue, for reflecting on the seemingly surprising importance of the disagreement and debate which takes place within Parliament before the decision to list additional organisation(s) is confirmed. As indicated above, disagreement within such debates is hardly substantive, in that it has little discernible bearing on their outcome, which is – at least in the British case – effectively a foregone conclusion. Neither, however, is it trivial or irrelevant. Rather, our argument is that the act of debating proscription orders, or questioning the executive, is central to the performance of liberal democratic politics – wherein accountability is provided by a separation of powers and agonistic political debate – that both sustains (by helping to justify) and is sustained by the proscription process. The proscription ritual, in other words, has to *look like* a decision-making enterprise, with at least the potential for uncertainty of outcome, in order for it to remain persuasive. This is despite – as we shall see – widespread agreement on the stakes, processes and necessities of proscription.

This importance of contestation to the proscription ritual, which operates as something other than a decision-making enterprise, may help to explain three further features of these debates that appear, at first glance, paradoxical. The first relates to proscription's seriousness, in which parliamentary debates around a power widely described – by its critics and advocates – as serious and weighty, are frequently commandeered for the discussion of issues beyond their immediate focus. This includes demands that organisations beyond those specified on a relevant proscription order be considered for the UK's list (typically because of their past actions or the current threat that they pose); indulgence in apparent trivialities, such as joking and political point-scoring; as well as the use of these debates for discussion of disconnected and irrelevant topics, both historical and contemporary.

A second and potentially surprising aspect of proscription is that it works to concretise, perhaps even reify, the very phenomenon it seeks to vanquish. One need not be an advocate of the 'new terrorism' thesis mentioned above to have some scepticism about the organisational coherence of some of the groups presently listed by the United Kingdom and other states. Indeed, the history of terrorism is – as we argue in Chapter 2 – in part a history of fracture and transformation. Yet, by identifying and naming specific organisations that may or may not exist as such in the minds of their supporters, the ritual of proscription serves to bring those organisations into being *as* proscribed terrorist organisations. Just as graduation ceremonies produce graduates, coming of age rituals produce adults, and the writing of constitutions produces peoples, the proscription ritual, perhaps paradoxically, produces its own subjects – terrorist organisations – at the very moment it attempts to vanquish them.

Third, as we demonstrate in Chapter 5, the proscription ritual also embodies something of a performative contradiction. As we shall see, parliamentary debates around the banning of terrorist organisations are saturated with reference to the British identity as a liberal, democratic, moderate and tolerant space. Depicted thus, proscription emerges as a regrettable but necessary measure to safeguard the British political system and associated way of life. It is undertaken – in this articulation – only as a last resort, following the expert advice of intelligence communities and others (advice which cannot be shared with parliamentarians on security grounds, it is frequently claimed), and after an appropriate level of deliberation and debate to ensure the credibility of any decision reached. And, yet, this construction of Britain as a liberal democratic haven is precisely that which makes it possible to take the quite illiberal – and arguably anti-democratic – decision to proscribe an organisation following questionable scrutiny, with all of the implications this entails.

Some of these features may be found in other debates within the UK Houses of Parliament and beyond; our claim here is not that these are unique to this particular power. Rather, our claim is that approaching proscription as a ritual that is constitutive of its multiple realities – Britain as a liberal democratic space; Parliament as the defender of that liberal democratic space; terrorist groups as a threat meriting banishment, and so forth – is useful, because it helps us to *recognise* these dynamics, and to bring them forward for question and critique. This, we suggest, takes debate around proscription some distance beyond questions surrounding the power's ethics and effectiveness, and opens a series of – equally pressing – questions around its reality-making potential. Doing so, in the process, offers additional opportunities for reflection on the distinctiveness or otherwise of proscription, vis-à-vis other security mechanisms, other political rituals, and other articulations of threat and danger.

Contributions

In making the above argument, our analysis of the proscription ritual attempts to make four immediate contributions to existing understandings of this power, and the contexts in which it operates. In the first instance, at a descriptive level, this book develops a detailed empirical case study of the politics of security that spans almost twenty years of British parliamentary life. These twenty years, moreover, take in governments from across the mainstream political spectrum, including the centre-left Labour Party, the centre-right Conservative Party, and a coalition between the Conservative and Liberal Democrat parties. Our analysis, which builds on and updates some of our earlier research, is the first to engage with these proscription debates in any systematic way, which offers, we hope, a rich and detailed excavation of their unfolding and importance. In doing the above, the book also offers a second, analytic, contribution, which is to shed some light on the workings of Parliament in this context. This includes, amongst other things, reflection on the specific types of topic and question that are voiced by contributors to these debates, as well as consideration of the importance of verbatim repetition between the two Houses of Parliament, and even between debates. By exploring such dynamics, we reflect in this book on who speaks, how and when in this context, and – in so doing – seek to address existing studies of parliamentary and political discourse in the UK and beyond.

Third, conceptually, the book progresses towards – in Chapter 7 – a new heuristic of political ritual that has wider applicability, we hope, for making sense of institutionalised forms of security politics relating to and extending beyond our focus here. Our heuristic builds on, and re-assembles, insight from anthropological, sociological and other scholarship, in order to highlight four key components of political rituals: orchestration, constitutivity, sedimentation and performativity. Finally, the book also offers a wider theoretical contribution by approaching its analysis of this specific ritual as an opportunity for reflection on broader dimensions within British politics. These include historical trends of continuity and change – within the time period under study, but also in relation to proscription's antecedents – as well as the workings of power in a system that seeks to outlaw both 'real' organisations with material assets, and the ideational structures that offer ideological sustenance to those organisations and their members.

In making the above contributions, the book attempts to push forward at least four important contemporary literatures. First, and most obvious, is existing scholarship on proscription itself (see Jarvis and Legrand 2018 for an overview). Our emphasis on processes rather than outcomes, and on proscription's constitutive rather than causal dynamics, offers an attempt – indicated above – to ask a different set of questions of this power, while working within the spirit of critique shared by much recent research. Second, the book contributes to another small, but again growing, body of scholarship on parliamentary security politics (e.g. Huysmans and Buonfino 2008; Neal 2012, 2019). By highlighting the importance of ritualised dynamics therein, and by bringing a relatively neglected case study to this debate, we attempt both to deepen and broaden this research which has already begun to make significant inroads into our understanding of the work done by security professionals that are not political executives or members of the intelligence or policing communities.

Third, the book contributes to contemporary debate on political rituals and their role in creating, sustaining and transforming social, political and other forms of life (e.g. Kertzer 1989; Rai 2014). It does so, in part, via our new heuristic through which to analyse political ritual and the constitutive significance thereof, and through the application of existing approaches to this particular case study. And, finally, the book also seeks to contribute more broadly to ongoing debate within critical security studies and critical terrorism studies around the construction, implications, significance and exclusions of discourse on security and (counter-)terrorism (e.g. Campbell 1992; Jackson 2005; Jarvis and Lister 2015).

Chapter overview

The book begins by tracing the historical roots of various powers which have facilitated the designation and/or exclusion of specific enemies of the state or society. This is a partly genealogical exercise in which we return to the murky origins of outlawry on these isles, before there was even a 'Britain' of which to speak, reflecting on proscription's gradual displacement of such powers as the principal means of political exclusion. We commence by exploring the importance of outlawry to early medieval society as an instrument of social control, criminal justice and monarchical power, before showing how proscription is woven through Parliament's history as a means of consolidating authority: first, in the proscription of Royalists and Jacobites and later in the prohibitions of reformist groups in the eighteenth and nineteenth centuries. The chapter then turns to twentieth-century expressions of proscription: first, as a means of control employed by colonial authorities; second, in response to the spectre of fascism in the 1930s and 1940s; and, third, as a precursor and reaction to the maelstrom of violence throughout the Northern Ireland conflict. The chapter ends by reflecting on the contemporary deployment of proscription under the regime introduced through the TA 2000. Here we explore proscription powers, the process of their enactment and the manner in which proscription has unfolded since 2000. We conclude by sketching the core principles of political exclusion as these have evolved through the British state's encounters with diverse political foes over the centuries.

In Chapter 2 we situate the British experience in international context. Our core argument is that the increasingly expansive global deployment of proscription and blacklisting powers in the contemporary period is a product both of desperate legislative responses to al Qaeda's precipitous emergence in the late 1990s and 2000s, and – at the same time – a continuity of long-standing precedents of political control. The chapter, in its first part, explores the use of proscription by colonial authorities in the early twentieth century, especially in attempts to contain emancipatory movements, and the increased hardening of political processes to communism in the post-war period which involved preclusions of local communist movements across core states in the global North. In its second part, the chapter sets out the prevailing proscription frameworks employed by the UN and EU along with those of a selection of important states. This, we suggest, underscores the influence of the United Kingdom's proscription laws on other countries. In the final part of the chapter, we consider how scholars have responded to the contemporary wave of blacklisting laws. Here we engage with a range of scholarships including in law, political science and sociology to unpack prominent criticisms of proscription's efficacy and ethics.

Chapter 3 builds on this discussion by sketching the theoretical and methodological framework for the book's empirical research. We begin by making the case for a move from causal to constitutive questions in analysing this power, arguing that this entails greater reflection on proscription's processes than outcomes. Upon this we situate our research within broadly constructivist approaches to the political, before elaborating on our understanding of discourse, identity and political ritual: the key concepts that structure the analysis that follows from Chapter 4.

Chapter 4 begins our analysis of parliamentary proscription debates by outlining the diverse ways in which this power is positioned politically and normatively therein. We demonstrate, first, that proscription is consistently depicted as a power of significance that merits a certain seriousness. For proscription's advocates, this significance comes from its contribution to national security via the prevention, deterrence and disruption of terrorist ambitions, as well as its symbolic value in communicating British or parliamentary resolve. Parliamentary critics of proscription, on the other hand, see the power as important because of its deleterious implications for social and political life. These include issues around its effectiveness; its potentially counter-productive implications; the civil liberty consequences of listing organisations; and the impact of proscription upon democratic processes more broadly. In reflecting on these arguments, the chapter highlights some of the rhetorical strategies upon which politicians draw within these debates, as well as a not uncommon tendency for distraction and diversion.

Chapter 5 builds on this discussion by shifting our attention away from concrete statements about proscription's significance, and towards the type of questions that are asked within these debates. It argues that these questions help to demonstrate the legislature's discursive role in shaping proscription's meaning; a role that includes appealing for – and perhaps even demanding – justification, explanation, elaboration and clarification from the executive on this power's application. The questions asked by parliamentarians in this context matter, we argue, for at least three reasons. First, they provide a significant component of the content of these debates – occupying a lot of the time taken by this ritual – and taking them seriously therefore provides a fuller understanding thereof. Second, they illustrate the importance of contestation, dispute and debate that we see as central to the proscription ritual and its performance of liberal democratic accountability. Third, these questions also have wider conceptual significance for helping us to think through the temporalities and fixedness of specific roles within security dramas, as well as the heterogeneity of participants therein.

Taken together, Chapters 4 and 5 argue that parliamentary debates on proscription are characterised, amongst other things, by diverse perspectives on proscription's significance, and a wide range of questions regarding proscription's mechanics, consequences and implications. These perspectives and questions, we argue, help to make proscription meaningful (for national security, citizenship and so forth), and shed light on a more complex politics of security than that assumed by prominent understandings and theorisations of the workings of security discourse. In Chapter 6 we build on this argument by suggesting that these debates perform a further constitutive function in contributing to a process of identity formation in which the UK self – or components thereof such as Parliament and parliamentarians – is distinguished from various terrorist others. Proscription debates – and the banning of terrorist groups – are, therefore, performative in that they confer illegitimacy on their target(s): producing particular organisations and their members as 'unacceptable in this country' (Hughes 2002). In doing this, moreover, they (re-)produce the United Kingdom as a particular type of political entity with specific – and, very explicitly, liberal, democratic – attributes and characteristics. This sets up a relatively straightforward antagonism between, on the one hand, a liberal, open and responsible UK self which is mindful of cultural and religious difference, and both cautious and moderate in its actions, and, on the other, a series of illiberal, irrational and extremist terrorist others who remain steadfast in their determination to wage immoral violences against states such as the UK and their publics. Importantly, although there are – again – examples of genuine dissent in these debates, critics of proscription or its application tend to reproduce rather than contest this binary relationship, in effect by appealing for the UK to be truer to its own self-identity.

In Chapter 7 we bring the book's analysis to a close by focusing on some of the core characteristics of these debates. These include: a remarkably standardised and repetitive framing; the existence of a core script which is often repeated, with minor alterations, across parliamentary debates, including those separated by several years; a set of established and identifiable roles that are taken up by participants (participants who, of course, come and go with the passage of time); repeated arguments around the importance of respecting these debates and their outcomes; and – perhaps most significant of all – a predictable, near-inevitable, outcome which is known in advance to those present. These characteristics indicate that proscription debates should be approached not – or, at least, not only or not primarily – as a decision-making exercise in which the outcome is genuinely to be decided. Rather, as a form of contemporary political ritual that reinforces the identities of its subjects by performing that which it claims to represent: liberal democracy. Vital within this, we suggest, is the appearance of dissent amidst broader cross-party consensus on proscription's necessity and legitimacy.

In the Conclusion, we reflect on the UK's use of proscription and the implications of this for national security today. The historical and relational contexts explored in the book demonstrate the ongoing relevance of proscription, and particularly the international influence of the UK's proscription traditions, in shaping state administration. The multiplicity of uses assigned to this power, moreover, also exposes proscription as a versatile tool of political convenience for regulating ideas and political symbols. Here we suggest that central to proscription is the British state's preoccupation – justified or otherwise – with symbolic power, whether displayed through the flying of flags, the wearing of uniforms, the performance of rituals or the recitations of oaths. On this analysis, proscription is concerned with denying symbolism to illegitimate entities even though, or perhaps because, citizenship itself is a symbolically constituted status. This, we argue, has wider implications for security scholars insofar as it potentially renders visible other security moves by state institutions: a development with real potential significance for our understanding of the political more broadly.

Notes

1 As is common, four other organisations were listed for proscription at the same time: Turkiye Halk Kurtulus Partisi-Cephesi; Kateeba al-Kawthar; Abdallah Azzam Brigades including the Ziyad al-Jarrah Battalions; and the Popular Front for the Liberation of Palestine-General Command.

2 www.legislation.gov.uk/uksi/2014/1624/pdfs/uksiem_20141624_en.pdf. (accessed 18 December 2019).

3 As Johnson (2014b) argued: 'on this occasion, the shadow Home Secretary and the Chairman of the Home Affairs Committee were not the first people to be briefed. It appears that journalists were briefed before the order was even laid in Parliament.'

4 Fourteen organisations connected to Northern Ireland are still proscribed in the United Kingdom under legislation preceding the 2000 Terrorism Act.

5 The group's tweets included 'Only 649 MPs to go' and 'Jo Cox would have filled Yorkshire with more subhumans!'.

6 Political is not used here as a synonym for either nefarious or self-serving. It is reasonable to assume that the public and elite response to National Action's activities was genuine.

7 Calendar of state papers, Domestic series of the reign of Charles II. Longman, Green, Longman & Roberts, 1968. Available at: https://catalog.hathitrust.org/Record/100824302 (accessed 1 March 2019).

8 On the utility and importance of 'how possible' questions see Doty (1993) and Holland (2013).

1 Proscription in the United Kingdom: a tough but necessary measure?

We begin our exploration of proscription in the UK with a brief genealogy of the development, use and application of banning powers from the medieval to the modern era. As we shall see, radicalism, terrorism and political violence have been central concerns of almost all local and national authorities through the rocky political history of the British Isles and its dominions.[1] From Saxon Britain to the Rump Parliament to the British Empire, suppression of the threat posed by individuals and political movements has made use of a gamut of precipitous initiatives that ban, outlaw, banish, demonise, ostracise and proscribe. Such actions cast the person – at times as an individual, at others through affiliation to designated groups – as *a priori* criminal, traitor, usurper or terrorist.

Understanding this genealogy is important because proscription powers remain a crucial plank in the UK's counter-terrorism architecture today (see Donohue 2008). In the UK government's framing, the consequence of proscription is that 'an organisation is outlawed in the UK and that it is illegal for it to operate here'. Moreover, it is 'a criminal offence to belong to, support, or display support for a proscribed organisation' (Bassam, 2005). This power of proscription, in keeping with historical precedents, is therefore something of an extraordinary measure. At a stroke, and with limited parliamentary oversight, the Home Secretary is able to criminalise the members and associates of organisations designated 'terrorist' and, in so doing, trigger a suite of ancillary sanctions and policing powers. In the UK today, seventy-four 'international' terrorist organisations are proscribed under the TA 2000, which also continues the proscription of a further fourteen organisations in Northern Ireland banned under earlier legislation.

The proscription provisions of the TA 2000 emerge from a lineage of powers to ban, exclude and criminalise that has proved remarkably consistent through two periods spanning more than a thousand years. In the first period, in the practice of outlawry in Anglo-Saxon and medieval Britain, the individual was outlawed as a *punishment*; the targets, therefore, tended to be felons, debtors or itinerant court delinquents. In the second period, from the mid-1600s onwards, exclusion evolves into proscription as a form of *preventative* security measure. Now, we see the individual being criminalised for the threat they pose, or for their association with a movement that is deemed to pose a danger to the state or the public. The two periods are inextricably linked insofar as outlawry and proscription, at least in the British experience, each render their subject's presence unlawful through a unilateral process in which the subject is neither in attendance nor represented, nor able to register prior objection thereto.

The chapter begins by reaching back to the eighth century in pursuit of the roots of contemporary exclusions. It traces how the logics of this severe power gradually move from the exclusion of individuals to the exclusion of political groups over a millennium or so. It then explores responses to the Jacobite rebellion and nineteenth-century British radicalism to identify antecedents to today's proscription laws, and to set out the circumstances of their deployment. In the second section, the chapter addresses the consolidation of proscription powers in the regulation of domestic and overseas dissent during the twentieth century. Here the chapter engages with the British state's handling of the fascist movements of the 1930s and 1940s, the challenge of Irish republicanism, and emancipatory movements in its overseas colonies. A third section then turns to today's proscription powers and their deployment against international terrorism. This sets out in detail the reach of contemporary legal powers and their application since 2001. The chapter concludes by discussing the core threads of proscription powers across this lengthy history, drawing attention to key features thereof including how proscription operates as a symbolic performance of sovereignty and a mechanism for regulating competing political allegiances and symbols.

A brief history of outlawry and proscription

> For when it is now clear beyond all dispute, that the criminal is no longer fit to live upon the earth, but is to be exterminated as a monster and a bane to human society, the law sets a note of infamy upon him, puts him out of it's [*sic*] protection, and takes no farther care of him than barely to see him executed. He is then called attaint, attinctus, stained or blackened. He is no longer of any credit or reputation; he cannot be a witness in any court; neither is he capable of performing the functions of another man: for, by an anticipation of his punishment, he is already dead in law. (Blackstone 1769 (4), 374)

The outlawry of individuals has been a mainstay of power and control in the British and Irish isles for centuries. There are few more damning punishments than exclusion from the protections of the law, as William Blackstone vividly describes above. Though its precise origins are unknown, Bryan Carella (2015) finds evidence of 'the earliest legal expression of outlawry' in an archive of papal papers, the Legatine Capitulary, sent to Britain in 786.[2] The phrase 'utroque iure caruerunt' ['and they have been deprived of both laws'] suggesting some form of outlawry, in practice if not name, existed in 'secular and ecclesiastical justice in Anglo-Saxon law' (Carella 2015, 143).[3] The explicit terminology of 'outlawry', it seems, becomes only apparent much later in Anglo-Saxon law. Seal finds 'outlawry' in the legal codes of King Alfred (871–899) and King Æthelstan (924–927), deriving from the Saxon word *Utlah*[4] (see Seal 2011, 35). Van Houts, however, dates this slightly later:

> A chronological inventory of the occurrences of *laga*, the Scandinavian loanword for 'law', and its cognates *utlah*/*utlagu*/*utlaga* would show that word entered the [Old English] written language in *ca*. 970 and that it rapidly rose to a peak during the 990s and early eleventh century, after which it became the dominating vocabulary for outlawry though never entirely replacing indigenous vocabulary of *fliema* (fugitive) or *adrifen* (banning). (2004, 15)

Etymological ambiguities aside, there can be little disagreement as to the implications of outlawry for its targets. In the early medieval epoch, the judicial system was heavily provincial with few enforcement resources, and so outlawry was used to sanction accused individuals who failed to appear in court, to punish persistent law-breakers by depriving them of the law's protection, or as retribution for those attracting the monarch's displeasure. A punishment of outlawry could be imposed by county courts in civil cases[5] on debtors. In criminal cases, treasonous, seditious or severe criminal acts could result in outlawry. Holding to the gendered norms of the day, outlawry was a punishment reserved for men: 'a woman could not herself be outlawed, not because of any special leniency towards women but simply because in law she did not exist. Like a child, she was outside the law' (Stewart 2016, 45).

Outlawry within the UK and indeed across medieval Europe carried significant repercussions. Most obviously, it was common across outlawry practices for law-abiding citizens to be given legal indemnification for killing an outlaw. In early Nordic society, for example, the outlawed man was dubbed *skógarmaour* – literally 'forest man', to depict one who had been banished to the uninhabited forests. Such a banishment was typical in stripping the individual of all rights, which included exclusion from society, the confiscation of his assets, the rendering of his children illegitimate, and the legalisation of his killing (see Whaley 2002; Barraclough 2010). Those found to provide assistance to an outlaw – perhaps by offering shelter or food – were subject to the same punishment. The Icelandic law code, *Grágás*, provided for similar consequences, equating the status of the newly outlawed to that of a wolf: 'hann skal sva vida vargr heita, sem vidast er verold byggd, ok vera hvarvetna raekr ok rekinn um allan heim' ['he shall be known as a wolf, as widely as the world is inhabited, and be rejected everywhere and be driven away throughout all the world'] (Barraclough 2010).

The use of animalistic metaphors to communicate the status of the outlaw is significant and persists through outlawry's history. Outlaws during the reign of King Edward the Confessor (1042–1066) were designated *woolferthfod*: literally, a wolf's head (Harward 1896, fn22).[6] The purpose of this 'figurative metamorphosis' (Jones 2010, 27) was to signal a metaphorical moral and legal equivalence: that the outlaw could be lawfully killed by anyone as though a dangerous animal (see Richards 1902, 298). Outlawry continued throughout and after the Norman Conquest of Britain, with the term *woolferthfod* giving way gradually to the Latin legal synonym of the same meaning: *Gerere caput lupinum* [may his be a wolf's head] (Jones 2010, 27).

Though outlawry still manifested largely as a punishment for murder or felonies, it was also employed by monarchs to deal with those suspected of treason in Britain. By 1215, however, the signing of the Magna Carta curtailed the monarch's power to summarily and arbitrarily outlaw individuals, enshrining the principle of *habeas corpus* into the British legal code:

> No free man shall be seized or imprisoned, or stripped of his rights or possessions, or outlawed or exiled, or deprived of his standing in any way, nor will we proceed with force against him, or send others to do so, except by the lawful judgment of his equals or by the law of the land.[7]

Though Magna Carta ensured that exclusion could only result from a judicial process, outlawry remained integral to criminal justice. Renowned thirteenth-century jurist Henri De Bracton records in *De Legibus et Consuetudinibus Angliae* [*On the Laws and Customs of England*] that a man who fails to respond to a fourth court summons, 'first forfeits the country and the realm and is made an exile' and becomes 'lawless' or a 'friendless man' (1968, 361).[8] Bracton sets out in detail the consequences of being outlawed. The most striking, of course, is the threat of lawful killing: 'For it is a just judgment that he who has refused to live by the law should perish without law and without judgment' (1968, 363). The loss of rights extended to all of the target's property, for the outlaw now 'forfeits everything pertaining to right and possession' (1968, 363). On top of this, 'obligations and homages, fealties and oaths, and all other things contracted by mutual agreement are dissolved', such that the outlawed was obliged to 'forfeit their inheritances and tenements', any 'actions [grievances pursuable through the legal system] available to him before the outlawry', and 'gifts and sales made after the felony committed'. Finally, Bracton writes, upon outlawry, the outlaw's 'chattels' and any 'free land' was to be 'taken into the lord king's hand at once' (1968, 363). Outlawry's most severe consequence – being killed – was not, however, an inevitability, as this account of thirteenth-century pleas in Somersetshire, taken from the 'Rolls of the Itinerant Justices' published in the late nineteenth century, indicates:

> The extent to which resort was made to the process of outlawry will be manifest from an examination of these rolls. For one man hanged, many were outlawed. Let us take the great roll of a.d. 1242–3 (No.

756) for example. We find that on that eyre there were 15 persons hanged to upwards of 100 actually ordered to be outlawed or waived, and 45 who took sanctuary and abjured the realm. This is a large proportion, and is not a little suggestive of the opportunities which a criminal had of escape. On the Gloucestershire eyre of a.d. 122 [a] complaint was made of 330 acts of homicide. One man was mutilated and about 14 were hanged, while about 100 orders for outlawry were given. (Chadwyck Healey 1897)

The practices and penalties of outlawry remain apparent into the fourteenth and fifteenth centuries, preserved in the British National Archives' collection of petitions to the king for the restoration of property following the expiry or pardon of an outlaw. For example, one petitioner asks the king to restore family property following his outlaw father's death (as described by the National Archives):

Henry Nicholas requests the restoration of property in the parish of All Hallows Staining in the City of London. He traces the descent of the property through his family from Laurence Nicholas in the time of Edward II, and states that Richard II seized the property following the outlawry of his father, William, for the death of Hornere. His father is now dead.[9]

Moving forward to the seventeenth century, we see outlawry and religious prohibitions[10] again employed to suppress threats to the crown, especially as the 'Rump' Parliament asserted its supremacy in the midst and aftermath of the English Civil War of 1642–51. After defeat in this war, those loyal to the crown – the Royalists – found themselves subject to proscription.[11] A 1649 Order of Parliament, for instance, decreed that 'all such as who have been acting in the plotting, designing, or assisting in, the Irish rebellion, shall be proscribed, as enemies and traitors to the Commonwealth, and shall die without mercy wheresoever they shall be found within the limits of this nation'. As such, it was now:[12]

Resolved, That the Persons hereafter named; *viz. Charles Stuart*, Eldest Son of the late King; *James Stuart*, Second Son of the late King; *John* Earl of *Bristoll, Wm.* Earl of *Newcastle*, Sir *William Widdrington, George* Lord *Digby*, Sir *Philip Musgrave*, Sir *Marmaduke Langdale*, Sir *Richard Greenvile*, Sir *Francis Doddington*, the Earl of *Worcester*, Sir *John Winter*, Sir *John Culpepper*, Sir *John Byron*, and *George*

> Duke of *Buckingham*; and all that have been plotting, designing, or assisting, in the *Irish* Rebellion; and all such Persons as now do hold out any Castle, Fort, or Island, against the Parliament; shall be proscribed, as Enemies and Traitors to the Commonwealth; and shall die without Mercy, where-ever they shall be found within the Limits of this Nation;[13] and their Estates shall be confiscate, and forthwith employed for the Use of the Commonwealth. (House of Commons Journal Volume 6, 14 March 1649, p. 165)

This response to 'enemies and traitors to the Commonwealth' represents a bridging of outlawry and proscription: the Order 'proscribes' the individuals, under threat of death, *as* individuals but also for their association as a movement, in keeping with the subsequent practice of proscribing groups or causes.

Outlawry survived within the British legal code until the nineteenth century, though it became less useful over time. Mark Howe decries the 'intricate confusion to which English courts had, by the 18th century, brought the process of outlawry' (1937, 564). Outlawry in England was abolished by the Criminal Code (Indictable Offences) Act of 1879 and in Scotland in December 1949 by the Criminal Justice (Scotland) Act.[14] Although it was effectively obsolete by the time of its formal removal, the power had persisted for an extraordinary period in the British Isles: around a millennium.

Elsewhere in the Commonwealth, however, outlawry had not yet run the course of its usefulness. In late nineteenth-century colonial Australia, for instance, violent gangs of bandits – 'bushrangers' – had become an urgent problem for local authorities with very limited law enforcement capacity, especially in the outback's dense and remote bushland. The solution was to introduce a form of outlawry in the Felons Apprehension Acts that bore close resemblance to the ancient powers of medieval Britain. Speaking in support of outlawry legislation in the state of Victoria, for example, an MP offered a uniquely Australian version of the *caput lupinum* metaphorical device: 'But under this Bill a person may stalk [the outlaw]; he may steal upon them, and shoot them down as he would shoot a kangaroo'[15] (see Eburn 2005).

1746 and the era of proscription

The first traces of the proscription powers that we see in Britain today – and, specifically, the outlawing of *groups*, rather than *individuals* – emerge in the 1746 legislation introducing the Act of Proscription. The English Civil War had not decisively settled the question of secession. When Charles II died without an heir to the throne, his brother James II – a Catholic convert – assumed the throne for three years before his ousting by English nobles and replacement with his Protestant daughter, Mary. Those supporting the claim to the throne of James II, who had since fled to France, assumed the name Jacobites, from the Latin spelling of James. James II died in 1701, but his son James 'the Old Pretender' maintained the claim of the Stuart right to the throne. Though James was never to mount a serious challenge – an attempted Jacobite rebellion in 1715 was quashed quickly – in 1745 his son, 'Bonnie Prince Charlie', led a Jacobite rebellion that threatened the Union.

The Jacobite army was defeated eventually at Culloden, yet Parliament determined that the rebellion amongst the Scottish Clans remained a powerful threat, given its underpinning by an ideological set of demands, traditions and identity claims. Passing the Act of Proscription 1747 (introduced in 1746), in which the rebellion was described as 'wicked' and 'unnatural', Parliament sought the 'effectual disarming [of] the highlands' by outlawing 'warlike' weapons.[16] This Act also sought to eradicate any Clan fealty, by introducing education regulations that required school teachers to attest 'their good affection to his Majesty's person and government' and, moreover, 'as often as prayers shall be said in such school, to pray, or cause to be prayed for, in express words his Majesty, his heirs and successors, by name, and for all the royal family'. Within the legislation was a section, which came to be known as *The Dress Act*, that further introduced a ban on 'Highland Clothes' under threat of imprisonment or transportation to a colony:

> no man or boy within that part of Britain called Scotland, other than such as shall be employed as Officers and Soldiers in His Majesty's Forces, shall, on any pretext whatever, wear or put on the clothes commonly called Highland clothes (that is to say) the Plaid, Philabeg, or little Kilt, Trowse, Shoulder-belts, or any part whatever of what peculiarly belongs to the Highland Garb; and that no tartan or party-coloured plaid of stuff shall be used for Great Coats or upper coats.

Thus, we already see by the mid-eighteenth century a number of elements of proscription that have continued through to the present day, including the regulation of education and educators, and the prohibition of certain uniforms, styles of dress and symbols.

Preclusionary proscription

Towards the end of the eighteenth century, the British Parliament found cause to commit to a second wave of proscriptions. The 1790s was a decade of fundamental political transformation. The French Revolution of 1789 (from which, of course, the language of terrorism to us comes) had alerted European rulers to the risk of popular revolt and 'forced the complacent British to rake over their ideological coals' (Davies 2000, 615). This era saw the term 'radical' enter the political lexicon[17] to disparage the groundswell of discontent sweeping across Britain. Inspired particularly by Thomas Paine's *The Rights of Man* (1791), a series of 'corresponding societies', prominently the Friends of the People and the London Corresponding Society, were established by artisanal workers dedicated to achieving political and parliamentary reform.

An apprehensive government headed by Pitt the Younger moved to suppress these movements with a series of preventive laws. These would criminalise, suppress or preclude activities that made possible an organisation's existence, and were backed by specific proscriptions of those groups of greatest concern to the government. Two initial pieces of legislation were introduced. The first, *The Seditious Meetings and Assemblies Act 1795*, made unlawful any gathering of fifty or more persons:

> That all Meetings, of any Description of Person, exceeding the Number of fifty Persons (other than and except as aforesaid,) which shall be holden without such previous Notice as aforesaid, for the Purpose or on the Pretext of considering of or preparing any Petition, Complaint, Remonstrance, Declaration, or other Address to the King, or both Houses, or either House of Parliament, for Alteration of Matters established in Church or State, or for the Purpose or on the Pretext of deliberating on any Grievance in Church or State, shall be deemed and taken to be unlawful Assemblies.[18]

The second, *The Treasonable and Seditious Practices Act 1795* (repealed in 1998), condemned 'the continued attempts of wicked and evil disposed persons' disturbing the 'tranquillity' of the kingdom with a 'multitude of seditious pamphlets and speeches daily printed, published and dispersed with unremitting industry and with a transcendent boldness' that contain 'contempt' for the king threatening 'overthrow of the laws, government and happy constitution of these realms'.[19] The Act outlines various traitorous activities – attempts to injure or kill the king, waging war against the state, inducing foreign attacks, and so on – and introduces punishments for those who:

> by Writing, Printing, Preaching, or other Speaking, express, publish, utter, or declare, any Words or Sentences to excite or stir up the People to hatred or Contempt of the Person of his Majesty, his Heirs or Successors, or the Government and Constitution of this Realm.[20]

Because they throttled speech and pamphlets, stifled radical ideas and criminalised large gatherings, these two Acts were together dubbed 'the Gagging Acts' (Scrivener 2000, 69–70). With the new powers in hand, state authorities charged three prominent English radicals – Thomas Hardy, John Thelwall and John Horne Tooke – with seditious libel and treason: crimes punishable by the death penalty. Much to the irritation of the government, however, the trial jury found all three not guilty. Shortly thereafter, two naval mutinies at Spithead and Nore in March and May 1797 deepened the Pitt government's resolve to quash radical or seditious sentiment. Parliament quickly passed the *Seduction from Duty and Allegiance Act* and the *Act against Administering Unlawful Oaths*: the purpose of both pieces of legislation was to render unlawful certain forms of political association and the swearing of oaths of allegiance. The latter Act was used to prosecute a group of Dorset agricultural workers in 1934, whose case became a *cause célèbre* with reformers who christened them the Tolpuddle Martyrs.

Despite the acquittals of leading radicals, the Pitt government pressed on, introducing the Societies Act 1799[21] to target corresponding societies, seen as stemming from a 'traitorous conspiracy' and representing 'a new and dangerous nature, inconsistent with publick tranquillity, and with the existence of regular government'. The Act accused the societies of operating in secret, with 'unlawful oaths and engagements of fidelity and secrecy', and of using 'secret signs'. And so the Act defined 'unlawful combinations and confederacies' as any society with members that were 'required or admitted to take any oath' and whose membership was 'kept secret from the society at large'.[22] Thus the Act 'hereby utterly suppressed and prohibited' the 'Societies of United Englishmen, United Scotsmen, United Britons, United Irishmen' and 'The London Corresponding Society'.

This appetite for outlawing radical groups continued unabated into the nineteenth century. The economic and social tensions arising from the unpopular Corn Laws and the long-running Napoleonic wars fomented widening popular demands for political reform in Britain. Friction between the government and reformists came to a head in St Peters Field, Manchester, in 1819 where around 80,000 people had gathered to listen to Henry Hunt, a renowned orator speaking in support of the reform of parliamentary representation. In a heavy-handed attempt to break up the crowd and arrest Hunt and other speakers, the local authorities called in a force of cavalry and yeomanry, killing fifteen people and injuring hundreds more (for a comprehensive account, see Reid 2017). The Peterloo Massacre, as it came to be known, sparked a wave of protests across the country. Fearful of the continuing surge in radicalism, the government then introduced the so-called Six Acts to further constrict the conditions under which political groups could operate: the Unlawful Drilling Act 1819 (repealed 2008); Seizure of Arms Act; Misdemeanors Act; Blasphemous and Seditious Libels Act; Seditious Meetings Act; and Newspaper and Stamp Duties Act. Of these, the latter two represented the most worrisome intrusion on public political debate. The Seditious Meetings Act outlawed large meetings, while the Newspaper and Stamp Duties Act increased the cost of selling political pamphlets by adding government duty to each copy. Debating the proposed legislation, the then Leader of the House of Commons, George Tierney, expressed his apprehension at the effect of the proposed laws:

> every page and every corner of every page of our history showed that assemblies had been convened, where men were allowed to harangue in any times of alarm. Mr. Burke had well called them the safety-valve of the constitution, by which all the foul air was permitted to escape. (Tierney 1819)

This was an era, in short, in which the government showed persistent willingness to narrow the sphere of political engagement to protect an increasingly contested status quo. Legislation was the primary instrument for excluding unwelcome sorts of politics where it was used, first, to designate and outlaw 'corresponding societies' for their radicalism; second, to create a chilling environment for irregular or ad hoc political groups by criminalising large gatherings for the purpose of airing 'any public grievance' or dispute connected to labour rights; and, third, in an attempt to limit their circulation, to increase the price of political pamphlets. Continuing his speech denouncing the Bills, Hansard reports Tierney's remarks thus:

> Would not the new bills rather exasperate than repress? If there were these large bodies of men in a state of dangerous effervescence, which he [Tierney] much doubted, would not the peril be doubled, when they wore told that they must expect nothing but coercion—that new laws[23] should be invented to put them down, and that none of their grievances, whether real or imaginary, should receive a moment's attention? (Tierney 1819)

Before turning, in the next section, to the twentieth century it is worth emphasising two features within the provisions of the Six Acts. First, the Seditious Meetings Act 1819 (as with antecedent legislation) which outlawed meetings of fifty or more people also made it unlawful for those attending an illegal meeting to possess 'any flag, banner, or ensign, or displaying or exhibiting any device, badge or emblem'.[24] Second, the language of these laws signalled both metaphorical and literal denunciation. The new popular order of politics was 'seditious', 'treasonable', 'dangerous', 'wicked and evil', antithetical to the national interest, and responsible for causing 'terror and alarm'. These traits were in lexical contrast to the normalised 'regular government' and the 'loyal subjects' of His Majesty. Importantly, the government's resolve to counter the new radicals was underlined by a provision in *The Seditious Meetings Act* that echoed the practices of pre-modern outlawry: justices of the peace who were involved in ordering the break-up of illegal meetings were permitted to main or kill attendees resisting an order.

UK proscription in the twentieth century

Turning now to the twentieth century, we encounter a UK government and its agents deploying proscription or banning powers across domestic and commonwealth jurisdictions alike. As demonstrated below, this incorporates: designations in the 1930s and 1940s intended to counter the growing spectre of fascism at home; second, the use of proscription as a prominent manifestation of exclusion within Britain's administrative colonies; and, third, perhaps most prominently, its employment to attenuate or head off the possibility of political violence associated with the Northern Ireland conflict – particularly in the years between the Easter Rising of 1916 and the Good Friday Agreement of 1998.

The Public Order Act 1936

Banning powers, in application if not in name, returned to the fore in 1930s Britain. Fascist parties, under the charismatic leadership of Hitler, Franco and Mussolini, had gripped Italy, Spain and Germany. The British Union of Fascists (BUF) seemed to threaten the same in the UK under the stewardship of Sir Oswald Mosley. A rally by the BUF and fronted by Mosley at Olympia in London in June 1934 provoked particular concern amongst parliamentarians and the public. The rally was punctuated by bursts of violence between Mosley's black-shirted followers and anti-fascist protesters. A reporter for the British *Guardian* newspaper provided this contemporaneous account:

> There were catcalls and booing and cheering, and in a scuffle one could catch sight of a yelling demonstrator being dragged off by the police. It was what has so often before, and with much less justice, been described as an 'ugly scene.' Inside the great hall it was seen that Sir Oswald Mosley had nothing of theatricalism to learn from either Hitler or Mussolini. There was a massed band of Blackshirts, there were flags, the Union jack, and the black and yellow flag of the British Union of Fascists. (*Guardian* 1934)

Scenes such as these prompted fears of a rising fascist paramilitarism of the Blackshirts, prompting Parliament to pass the Public Order Act 1936. The Act, which remains in force today, banned the wearing of uniforms in public with the aim of promoting or advocating a political cause. The Act prohibits groups that are 'organised and trained or organised and equipped either for the purpose of enabling them to be employed for the use or display of physical force in promoting any political object'.[25] It stipulates that 'any person who in any public place or at any public meeting wears uniform signifying his association with any political organisation or with the promotion of any political object shall be guilty of an offence'.[26]

The Public Order Act signalled the government's concerns over the BUF's rising popularity, especially as war increasingly looked inevitable. A second set of powers, drafted in 1937, granted the Home Secretary broad powers to detain any persons representing a threat to national security. These powers, contained within Defence Regulations 18b, were rapidly passed by Parliament on 1 September 1939. The emergency measures of Defence Regulation 18b(1a) empowered the Home Secretary to detain anyone 'he has reasonable cause to believe a person to be of hostile associations'. By 1940, the government position against the BUF, which was openly opposing the war, hardened amidst the retreat of the British Expeditionary Force at Dunkirk. A memorandum by the British Home Secretary, Sir John Anderson, *Invasion of Great Britain: Possible Co-operation by a 'Fifth Column'* noted that while the BUF were not openly advocating 'assisting the enemy', the government had nonetheless prepared a list of BUF leaders to be detained in the event of a more open threat.[27] On 18 May 1940, the Home Secretary addressed a meeting of the War Cabinet, underlining the absence of any behaviour with which to action a prosecution:

> In regard to British Fascists, the Home Secretary explained at length the difficulty of taking any effective action in the absence of evidence which indicated that the organisation as such was involved in disloyal activities.[28]

Yet by 22 May, and against the very real prospects of German invasion, the Home Secretary's recommendation had changed to favouring action against the BUF:

> The Home Secretary said that he realised that the War Cabinet might take the view that, notwithstanding the absence of such evidence, we should not run any risk in this matter, however small.[29]

And so the very next day, 23 May 1940, Sir Oswald Mosley and thirty-four of the senior movement leaders were arrested, with around 750 further arrests following in June and July. On 10 July, the government actioned powers under Defence Regulation

18b(AA), to declare the BUF an illegal organisation (Linehan 2000, 174–175).

Although the emergency powers contained within the Defence Regulations expired at the end of the war, the Public Order Act 1936 not only survived the end of the war but has remained in force ever since. Far from passing into obsolescence, the Act has been used in prosecutions against the flying pickets of the 1984–85 Miners' Strike, and most recently against leaders of the far-right group 'Britain First' – Paul Golding in 2016 and Jayda Fransen in 2017 – for their wearing of green jackets with their organisation's emblem. Doubtless, there is parallel – if not homage – between this latter organisation and Mosley, who wrote in his book *Fascism Explained*, 'The watchword of Fascism is "Britain First". We love our country' (Mosley 1933, s.1).

Proscription in colonial administration

Organised political opposition to British colonial rule became increasingly pronounced in the twentieth century, especially after the Second World War.[30] To contain the widening unrest, colonial governors – perhaps cognisant of the extensive use of proscription in Ireland – resorted to banning organisations at the forefront of local struggles. This was an era in which proscription was widely deployed by non-Soviet states against communist parties (see Chapter 2) and by European colonial administrations to quell emancipatory voices. It is reasonable to assume that the British government devolved proscription powers to colonial administrators. Indeed, in 1956, in response to a question in Parliament (Butler 1956), the Secretary of State for the Colonies had to write to all colonial governors seeking information on all uses of the power across colonial territories.[31]

In the case of Kenya, for instance, opposition to oppressive British rule had been evident throughout the twentieth century. Longstanding antipathy towards the coercive land seizures by European settlers were steadily compounded by growing inequality, anger at colonial rule and economic and social inequalities (Kanyinga 2009). In the wake of the Second World War, Kenyan nationalist sentiment was given a fillip by the return of Jomo Kenyatta, the Kikuyu leader of the Kikuyu Central Association (KCA) who had been resident in the UK during the war (see Van der Bijl 2017, 29–30). The KCA had been formed to organise resistance to land appropriations by settlers, and was proscribed by colonial authorities in 1940 (Grob-Fitzgibbon 2015, 194). Kenyatta, who would go on to become Kenya's first post-independence leader, took over the leadership of the Kenya Africa Union (KAU) in 1947. The group's agitation against the precepts of colonial rule earned Kenyatta and the KAU's senior officials close attention from colonial authorities.

Violent resistance against British rule broke out in the guerrilla war of 1952–56 led, ostensibly, by the 'Mau Mau' nationalist movement. The name had uncertain provenance – some suggested that 'mau mau' came from the Swahili phrase *Mzungu aende ulaya Mwafrica apete uhuru*: 'let the White Man go home so that Africa can have its independence' (Alao 2006, 5). Others claim the British government used the moniker 'Mau Mau' to homogenise all resistance movements (including the KCA and KAU) into a single, violent, illegitimate, evil and uncivilised entity. In his memoirs, Secretary of State for the Colonies, Oliver Lyttelton, described the nominal leader of the Mau Mau movement, Jomo Kenyatta, as 'a demonic figure with extreme left wing views', writing:

> The driving force of the Mau Mau movement was, nakedly, power, and the expulsion of the white man: its methods of gaining adherents were the methods of African witchcraft. The Mau Mau oath is the most bestial, filthy and nauseating incantation which perverted minds can ever have brewed ... I can recall no instance when I have felt the forces of evil to be so near and so strong. As I wrote memoranda or instruction, I would suddenly see a shadow fall across the page – the horned shadow of the Devil himself. (Lyttelton 1963, 380)

In a drive to decapitate the Mau Mau uprising, Kenyatta and several of his associates were seized and put into detention in 1952. Reflecting on KAU's position as a memberless organisation, Lord Ogmire noted:

> The position of the Kenya African Union is a peculiar one. All officials have been arrested, but the Union is not proscribed. That must give great satisfaction to the members, but it leaves the Union rather in the position of the Cheshire cat, with only the grin left. (Ogmire 1952)

Speaking to Parliament in the same year, Lyttelton denounced the Mau Mau as an offshoot of the KCA while connecting the group to a violent ideological and political praxis:

> Mau Mau is a secret society confined almost entirely to the Kikuyu tribe. It is an off-shoot of the Kikuyu Central Association, which was proscribed for subversive activities in 1940. It encourages racial hatred and is violently anti-European and anti-Christian. It pursues its aims by forcing secret oaths upon men, women and children and by intimidating witnesses and law-abiding Africans. It resorts to murder and other brutal and inhuman methods. (Lyttelton 1952)

In their commitment to decisively ending the uprising, a suite of repressive measures – including a brutal programme of internment, torture and forced 'brainwashing' of kikuyu dissidents – was employed by the colonial authorities. In particular, the 'Mau Mau oath' caught the notice of authorities and received special attention. In January 1953, using emergency powers announced in 1952, Sir Evelyn Baring, governor of Kenya, banned oath-taking under penalty of death (Van der Bijl 2017, 51). Lyttleton later claimed in Parliament:

> At least four forms of categories of Mau Mau oaths have now been uncovered. Apart from this fact, nearly all Mau Mau oaths include undertakings to burn houses, to kill and to commit or assist in other forms of violence against both Europeans and loyal Africans. It is noticeable that by the increasing bestiality of the third and fourth-oath-taking ceremonies the Mau Mau is attempting to drive groups of adherents outside the civilized and tribal pale. Thirty-nine persons in the Meru district have recently been convicted not merely of oath-taking but of attempting unnatural offences as part of that ceremony. Such practices are held in peculiar odium by the Kikuyu and other Tribes. (Lyttelton 1953)

The KAU was ultimately proscribed entirely in 1953, despite British intelligence concluding that year (irrespective of Lyttleton's assertions) that its leader, Jomo Kenyatta, had no links to the 'Mau Mau' uprising (McGarr 2010, 454). And, while these colonial measures did eventually quell some violence in Kenya, Kenyan nationalist sentiment had become irrepressible such that the country gained full independence from the UK in December 1963. In a noteworthy postscript to Kenya's independence, Jomo Kenyatta subsequently assumed control of the country by proscribing, in 1969, the main opposition to his authority: the leftist Kenyan People's Union.

The Kenyan experience speaks to the use of proscription against nationalist movements as a common act of last resort for colonial authorities facing unrest. Elsewhere in Africa, for example, authorities in Uganda had proscribed Dini Ya Musambwa (1948), the Bataka Party (1949), the Uganda African Farmers' Union (1949) and 'the Society known as the Mau Mau' (1954). In Tanzania, the KCA and Mau Mau were outlawed alongside the Ukamba Members Association and the Teita Hills Association. Here authorities also made use of the Societies Ordinance 1954, mirroring laws enacted elsewhere across the Commonwealth, to deny the registration of nine organisations thus making their operation unlawful.[32]

Something similar emerges in the short-lived, white-settler ruled, Federation of Rhodesia and Nyasaland, established by the UK in response to growing calls for independence. Under this Federation – which was to dissolve in 1963 – the government of the self-governing colony of Southern Rhodesia (now Zimbabwe) passed the 1959 Unlawful Organizations Act, which proscribed the prominent nationalist group, the Northern Rhodesian African National Congress,[33] and empowered the government to outlaw groups that were deemed 'likely to disturb public order, prejudice the tranquility of the nation, endanger constitutional Government, or promote feelings of ill will or hostility between the races' (Weitzer 1990, 70). The legislation, which was not subject to judicial review, banned any organisation that acted in support of 'the opinions of any organisation outside the colony' and made it an offence to attend the meetings of, or produce or distribute materials in support of, any such group.[34] The apartheid government of South Africa was emboldened sufficiently by this proscription to enact its own legislation of the same name – the Unlawful Organizations Act No. 34 of 1960 –to outlaw the African National Congress and the Pan Africanist Congress. In his political history of 'settler states', Weitzer (1990, 51) observes that 'Rhodesian settlers (like those in South Africa and Liberia) depended on rigid, de jure exclusion of the majority'.

Across significant parts of the British Empire, we therefore see proscription – or prohibition by refusing the registration of groups as societies – practised by multiple authorities anxious to contain local impulses for liberation from colonial rule. In Cyprus, similarly, numerous groups were outlawed, including the Pancyprian Trade Union Committee, the Pancyprian Nationalist Youth Organisation,

Reform Party of the Working People and National Organisation of Cypriot Combatants (EOKA) alongside TMT, a Turkish resistance organisation. In what is now modern Yemen, the National Liberation Front was banned during the 'Aden Emergency' (1965).[35] In Malaysia, in the midst of the 'Malaya Emergency', colonial authorities banned the Malayan Communist Party in 'an attempt to restore confidence in the colonial regime' in 1948 (Stockwell 1993, 85) with bans also extended to the 'New Democratic Youth League' and five other prohibited groups. And, in the post-war period, Singapore undertook similar prohibitions. The city-state did not have legislation mandating proscription per se. Instead, authorities made use of the Societies Ordinance of 1931, which rendered registration of all groups of ten or more individuals mandatory, and, if deemed antithetical to the peace of the state, allowed the Governor General to declare them illegal (see Yong and McKenna 1990, 200). Between 1948 and 1956, three organisations were excluded under the Ordinance: the 'New Democratic Youth League', the Malayan Communist Party and the Malayan People's Anti-Japanese Army Ex-Comrade's Association.

These were the years in which the dying spasms of colonial rule had repercussions for the policing of political violence in the UK. The same civil servants – as administrators and police or military officials – acting in colonial administrations returned to the UK, being posted, at times, to positions of responsibility for Northern Ireland. It is unsurprising, then, that we see similar anti-dissent strategies and forms of exclusion being practised there too, including internment and proscription.

A century of proscription in (Northern) Ireland

Proscription is woven through the historical course of the Northern Ireland conflict. At the end of the nineteenth century, in an effort to exert greater control over unrest in Ireland, the British government passed the Criminal Law and Procedure (Ireland) Act, 1887. This served to extend the criminal code to allow the senior administrator, the Lord Lieutenant of Ireland, the power to declare organisations 'dangerous' and thereby to ban them. The Irish National League was the first such group to be 'proclaimed' under the legislation. The order, when put before Parliament, prompted an (unsuccessful) opposition motion to set aside the proclamation on the grounds that 'no information has been furnished to Parliament to justify the issue of the said Special Proclamation' for which individuals may be 'punished as criminals without judicial inquiry into the nature of their acts'.[36] The powers were used again in 1918 by Britain's administrator of Ireland, Sir John French, to ban a cluster of groups associated with Irish nationalism (see Heartfield and Rooney 2015). The proclamation was publicised on a broadside poster:

> By the Lord Lieutenant and Privy Council in Ireland.
>
> French,
> Whereas, by our special proclamation, dated the 3rd day of July, 1918 in pursuance and by virtue of the 'Criminal law and Procedure (Ireland) Act, 1887,' we declared from the date thereof certain associations in Ireland, known by the names of
>
> The Sinn Fein organization
> Sinn Fein Clubs
> The Irish Volunteers
> The Cumann na m-Ban,[37] and
> the Gaelic League,
>
> to be dangerous:
> And whereas said associations now exist in the County of Clare: Now we ... do hereby by this our order prohibit and suppress within the said county of Clare, the Associations.[38,39]

Following the formal establishment of Northern Ireland as a recognised administrative jurisdiction in 1920, the new Parliament of Northern Ireland passed the Civil Authorities (Special Powers) Act (Northern Ireland) 1922. Using the powers specified in Regulation 24A of the legislation, the new government proscribed five groups: the Irish Republican Army (IRA), the Irish Republican Brotherhood, the Irish Volunteers, Cumann na m'Ban and Fianna na h'Eireann.[40] Intended as a short-term emergency measure, the legislation empowered the Northern Ireland Minister of Home Affairs – Sir Richard Dawson Bates was first to commence in this role – to make new regulations without parliamentary approval. The Act empowered the government to outlaw membership of, or support for, 'unlawful organisations' and to prohibit – in echoes of the Seditious Meetings Act 1819 – 'uniforms or badges indicating membership of any association or body specified in the order'. In the same legislation, provisions were made to censor political opposition to the British government's rule in Northern Ireland:

> 25. No person shall by word of mouth or in writing, or in any newspaper, periodical, book, circular, or other printed publication —
>   (a) spread false reports or make false statements; or
>   (b) spread reports or make statements intended or likely to cause disaffection to His Majesty, or to interfere with the success of any police or other force acting for the preservation of the peace or maintenance of order in Northern Ireland. [...]
>
> 26. The civil authority may by notice prohibit the circulation of any newspaper for any specified period, and any person circulating or distributing such newspaper within such specified period shall be guilty of an offence against these regulations.

Though the Civil Authorities (Special Powers) Act (Northern Ireland) 1922 initially contained a requirement for its annual review and renewal, this was quickly stretched to three-year renewals and, eventually, made permanent: indeed, this 'emergency' legislation remained in force in Northern Ireland for fifty years. During that time, several republican groups found themselves outlawed, including Saor Eire (1931), Sinn Féin (1956), the Republican Clubs (1967), Cumann Poblacta na h'Eireann (1936) and Fianna Uladh (1956), though the only loyalist organisation proscribed was the Ulster Volunteer Force (see Bourne 2015, 5).

Northern Ireland: 1972–2000

At the height of the Troubles in 1972, Lord Diplock was appointed to head a commission to review the counter-terrorism law applicable to Northern Ireland and Britain, especially the exceptional internment laws, with a view to discarding ineffective or bad law and producing a 'normalised' suite of anti-terrorism legislation. The years preceding the commission had seen unprecedented levels of fighting. The conflict had been in a state of escalation since the deployment in August 1969 of the British Army to the streets of Northern Ireland to quell widespread rioting. The next two years saw blood-letting on both sides, such that in 1972 alone 497 people were killed and countless maimed amid running gun battles and bombings. 1972 was also the year of the Bloody Sunday killings in which British paratroopers shot dead thirteen unarmed civilians. The spiralling violence led to the Stormont government's suspension, and the introduction of Direct Rule from Westminster in March 1972.

The 'Diplock Report' recommended suspending the right to trial before a jury, and empowering the Home Secretary to outlaw organisations involved in terrorism. The resulting Northern Ireland (Emergency Provisions) Act 1973 (EPA: re-enacted in 1976, 1984, 1989) applied solely to Northern Ireland and was closely followed by the Prevention of Terrorism (Temporary Provisions) Act 1974 (PTA: re-enacted 1978, 1991, 1996) which applied separately to Great Britain (see Blackbourn 2014, 76–77). During these debates, at various times, objections were raised, including around the meaningful existence of organisations:

> while membership of the UDA is not illegal, some members of that organisation have been detained, and others convicted of crimes as serious as that of murder. The instance of the UDA makes the point clear. The law should be directed at individuals and not at organisations, and on that basis the policy of proscription, as a principle, is little short of worthless. (Rees 1973)

Though intended to be temporary, the PTA and EPA remained in force for more than two decades before their extensive consideration by Lord Lloyd in *The Inquiry Into Legislation Against Terrorism 1996*. The scope of the Inquiry was to review anti-terrorism legislation and make recommendations to the government on the need for a permanent, consolidated anti-terror statute removing the distinction between Northern Ireland and mainland Great Britain (Walker 1997). In recommending retention of the proscription provisions of the PTA and EPA, Lord Lloyd stipulated their rationale thus:

> First, it will furnish a conclusive presumption that an organisation which is for the time being proscribed is a terrorist organisation. This will facilitate the burden of proof in terrorist cases. Secondly, proscription will be the starting point for the creation of a number of fundraising and other offences, especially fundraising for terrorism overseas. (1996, 6.12)

Two years later, in a consultation paper, the government made clear its intention to maintain proscription as a mechanism for challenging an organisation's fundraising capacity and, crucially, its claim to legitimacy:

> Whilst the measures may not in themselves have closed down terrorist organisations, a knock on effect has been to deny the proscribed groups legitimate publicity and with it lawful ways of soliciting support and raising funds … perhaps more importantly the provisions have signalled forcefully the Government's, and society's, rejection of these organisations' claims to legitimacy. (Home Office 1998, 4.7)

These two aims of proscription were supplemented by a third, associated most often with Margaret Thatcher's government; that is, 'to deprive terrorist organisations of the "oxygen of publicity"' (Home Office and Northern Ireland Office 2000): a principle that led to the contentious ban on the broadcast of the voices of those connected to terrorist organisations in Northern Ireland between 1988 and 1994.

In a coda to this era, it is telling that the UK government was hesitant to extend proscription laws to capture overseas organisations. A 1998 Home Office consultation paper stated: 'the Government recognises that the arguments are finely balanced for and against including in future counter-terrorist legislation a power for the Secretary of State to proscribe or designate terrorist organisations connected with domestic or international terrorist activities'. Amongst its reasons to refrain, the paper suggested that:

> The practical and policy difficulties involved in drawing up and then maintaining an up to date list of international and domestic groups to be covered would be formidable. For a start the potential scope of the list would be very wide (literally scores of groups could be possible candidates) and there would be a real risk of the list quickly becoming out of date – particularly if, as now, additions to, or deletions from, the list could only be made after debate by, and with the explicit agreement of, Parliament. Moreover the Government might be exposed to pressure to target organisations that it might not regard as terrorist or to take action against individuals whom it would not regard as terrorists. (Home Office 1998)

Proscription in the UK today

The British use of proscription in the contemporary period has, of course, been influenced by post-9/11 fears of a new type of terrorist threat marked – as Tony Blair subsequently reflected – by 'an intent, a purpose and a scope beyond anything we had encountered before' (Blair 2010). Against this background, successive British administrations have repeatedly affirmed the need for an uncompromising, multifaceted counter-terrorism paradigm, including contribution to significant military operations in Iraq, Afghanistan and beyond. Domestically, the UK re-structured its counter-terrorism framework around a new CONTEST Strategy, introduced in 2003, to cohere policy in this arena. Moreover, despite the prior existence of quite significant anti-terrorism legislation – including that discussed above, these developments have been accompanied by a concerted push for enhanced powers to interdict violent extremist activity at earlier stages of preparation (McCulloch and Pickering 2009; Macdonald 2012). Such powers have made use of a broader range of offences (Saul 2005), more expansive definitions of terrorism (Fenwick 2002) and – crucially, for us – a wider latitude for banning organisations (Legrand and Jarvis 2014).

It is, however, the TA 2000 – which, of course, narrowly predated 9/11 – that was key for the emergence of the contemporary proscription regime. This Act removed the territorial distinction between Great Britain and Northern Ireland and, importantly, was applicable to all forms of international and domestic terrorism. Three core public policy objectives seated in the proscription provisions of the TA 2000 derive directly from those of the PTA and EPA discussed above: (1) the facilitation of law enforcement and prosecution; (2) the symbolic demonstration of the incompatibility of a particular organisation with established UK values; and (3) suffocation of the organisations' rhetoric through denial of 'the oxygen of publicity' (Wilkinson 1997).

In the eyes of the UK Home Office, proscription today serves instrumental, cooperative, symbolic and communicative functions. First, it contributes to making the UK a hostile environment for terrorists and their supporters. Second, it signals condemnation of proscribed groups. Third, it allows the UK to support its international partners in their own counter-terrorism efforts. And, fourth, it sends 'a strong message' regarding UK intolerance of terrorism.

As Home Secretary Charles Clarke (2000) argued of proscription before a House of Commons Standing Committee during the introduction of the Terrorism Bill in 2000:

> First, it has been, and remains, a powerful deterrent to people to engage in terrorist activity. Secondly, related offences are a way of tackling some of the lower-level support for terrorist organisations ... Thirdly, proscription acts as a powerful signal of rejection by Government – and indeed by society as a whole – of organisations' claims to legitimacy ... It is important for society to state that certain activities are simply ... beyond the pale ... The legislation is a powerful symbol of that censure and is important.

Clarke's imputation of proscription as 'powerful' offers an example of proscription's frequent framing as a matter of national significance. This framing, discussed further in Chapter 4, often makes use of verbatim language, for instance:

> I have today laid an order which will proscribe al-Muhajiroun, Islam4UK, and a number of the other names the organisation goes by ... *Proscription is a tough but necessary power to tackle terrorism and is not a course we take lightly.*[41]

> I have today laid an order which, subject to parliamentary approval, will proscribe Al Shabaab. *Proscription is a tough but necessary power to tackle terrorism and is not a course of action we take lightly.*[42]

> [Proscribing the 'Pakistan Taliban' under the name Tehrik-e Taliban Pakistan]: *Proscription is a tough but necessary power to tackle terrorism and is not a course of action we take lightly.*[43]

At other times, in addition to its 'toughness', proscription is described as 'a heavy power' (Bassam 2000) or 'at best a fairly blunt instrument'.[44] This language becomes increasingly important, as we shall see, in the performance or presentation of proscription to public and parliamentary audiences.

Proscription today enjoys broad and, importantly, bipartisan support within the British political system, with the introduction of the TA 2000 in July 2000 seeing a discernible acceleration in its usage. In the first instance, this Act continued the proscription of fourteen organisations[45] connected to Northern Ireland under the PTA 1989 and EPA 1996 (see Figure 1.1).

Figure 1.1 Terrorism Act 2000, Schedule 2: Proscribed Organisations

- The Irish Republican Army
- Cumann na mBan
- Fianna na hEireann
- The Red Hand Commando
- Saor Eire
- The Ulster Freedom Fighters
- The Ulster Volunteer Force
- The Irish National Liberation Army
- The Irish People's Liberation Organisation
- The Ulster Defence Association
- The Loyalist Volunteer Force
- The Continuity Army Council
- The Orange Volunteers
- The Red Hand Defenders

In the first order after the TA 2000 came into force, an additional list of twenty-one organisations was presented to Parliament (see Figure 1.2).

Between 2001[46] and the time of writing, a further fifty-five 'international terrorist organisations' have been added to the United Kingdom's list, two of which are proscribed for the glorification of terrorism under powers contained in the Terrorism Act 2006 which followed the '7/7' bombings in London of July 2005. The list includes enduring and well-known groups such as the Islamic State of Iraq and the Levant (ISIL), Basque Homeland and Liberty (Euskadi ta Askatasuna) (ETA), and al Qaeda, as well as a host of less familiar counterparts such as Asbat Al-Ansar ('League of Partisans' or 'Band of Helpers') – 'a group seeking to enforce its extremist interpretation of Islamic law within Lebanon and, increasingly, further afield' (Home Office 2017), or Babbar Khalsa (BK) – a 'Sikh movement that aims to establish an independent Khalistan within the Punjab region of India' (Home Office 2017).

The proscription process under the Terrorism Act 2000

The UK's current proscription laws are codified in Section 3 of the TA 2000. The Act empowers the executive, with Parliament's assent, to outlaw specific associations that the Home Secretary believes to be 'concerned in terrorism'. This includes (although is not confined to) organisations which: commit or participate in acts of terrorism; prepare for terrorism; promote, encourage (or unlawfully glorify)[47] terrorism; or are 'otherwise concerned in terrorism'.[48] In addition to this statutory test, the Home Secretary may take into consideration

Figure 1.2 The Terrorism Act 2000 (Proscribed Organisations) (Amendment) Order 2001 (No. 1261)

- Al-Qa'ida
- Egyptian Islamic Jihad
- Al-Gama'at al-Islamiya
- Armed Islamic Group (Groupe Islamique Armée) (GIA)
- Salafist Group for Call and Combat (Groupe Salafiste pour la Prédication et le Combat) (GSPC)
- Babbar Khalsa
- International Sikh Youth Federation [*delisted 2016*]
- Harakat Mujahideen
- Jaish e Mohammed
- Lashkar e Tayyaba
- Liberation Tigers of Tamil Eelam (LTTE)
- Hizballah External Security Organisation
- Hamas-Izz al-Din al-Qassem Brigades
- Palestinian Islamic Jihad—Shaqaqi
- Abu Nidal Organisation
- Islamic Army of Aden
- Mujaheddin e Khalq [*delisted 2008*]
- Kurdistan Workers' Party (Partiya Karkeren Kurdistan) (PKK)
- Revolutionary Peoples' Liberation Party—Front (Devrimci Halk Kurtulus Partisi-Cephesi) (DHKP-C)
- Basque Homeland and Liberty (Euskadi ta Askatasuna) (ETA)
- 17 November Revolutionary Organisation (N17)

a range of discretionary criteria, including: the 'nature and scale' of an organisation's activities; the threat an organisation poses to the UK or its citizens overseas; the extent of an organisation's presence in the UK; and the 'need to support other members of the international community in the global fight against terrorism'.[49]

The process of laying a proscription order adheres to a strict template. Where the Secretary determines that an organisation should be proscribed, she must lay an order before both Houses of Parliament and secure approval in full through the affirmative procedure.[50] Importantly, while the order must be debated by Parliament, *it may not be amended* in any way. And, because the Secretary of State is under no obligation to lay orders on a case-by-case basis, proscription orders for multiple organisations may be – and typically are – presented to Parliament. Once Parliament affirms an order[51] – and no orders have been resisted by Parliament to date – organisations are added to the list of proscribed organisations in Schedule 2 of the TA 2000, upon which the proscription takes effect.

Change of name or alias of a proscribed group

In the fissiparous world of political groups, it is not uncommon for an organisation to split, splinter or reform under a new name. Where the Secretary of State believes an organisation listed on Schedule 2 has begun to operate under an alternative name, Section 22 of the Terrorism Act 2006 empowers her to add those additional names to an existing proscription order. While the initial order to proscribe an organisation must be voted affirmatively by Parliament, any orders specifying alternative names are only subject to the negative procedure.[52] In practice, this means that such amendments to register an alias inevitably proceed. Parliament rarely moves to block Statutory Instruments (SIs) or amendments thereto: the last occasion the House of Commons opposed a draft SI was in 1978; the House of Lords in 2012, and before that on two occasions in 2007 and 2000. In addition, for an individual to be prosecuted for membership of a proscribed organisation operating under a different name, it is not necessary for that alias to be added to Schedule 2: the police or crown need prosecution simply to demonstrate that the alias organisation 'is for all practical purposes the same as the proscribed organisation listed in Schedule 2' and that the individual has committed any of the offences relating to the proscribed organisation.

Consequences and penalties of proscription

Proscription triggers a range of penalties for those subject to this power, including around membership (s11), support and advocacy (s12), and the wearing or carrying of uniforms and articles. Specifically, as mentioned in the Introduction, proscription makes it a criminal offence to:

- belong, or profess to belong, to a proscribed organisation in the UK or overseas (section 11 of the Act);
- invite support for a proscribed organisation (not restricted to the provision of money or other property) (section 12(1));
- arrange, manage or assist in arranging or managing a meeting in the knowledge that the meeting is to support or further the activities of a proscribed organisation, or is to be addressed by a person who belongs or professes to belong to a proscribed organisation (section 12(2)); or to address a meeting if the purpose of the address is to encourage support for, or further the activities of, a proscribed organisation (section 12(3)); and

- wear clothing or carry or display chapters in public in such a way or in such circumstances as arouse reasonable suspicion that an individual is a member or supporter of the proscribed organisation (section 13).

Proscription also prompts a range of supplementary powers allowing, for example, agencies to deny entry to the UK, to seize or freeze an organisation's assets, and to disrupt an organisation's online communications. The implications of proscription for an organisation and its supporters are significant, with the range of available penalties extending from fines of up to £5,000, through to prison sentences to a maximum of ten years (Home Office 2017, 3).

Deproscription

Where organisations believe they have been unfairly or inappropriately proscribed, the TA 2000 provides a mechanism to apply to the Home Secretary for deproscription. The Home Secretary has discretion to allow or refuse the application, although resort to a further appeal to the Proscribed Organisations Appeal Commission (POAC) exists if refused. The TA 2000, Section 5(3) sets out the POAC's powers thus:

> The Commission shall allow an appeal against a refusal [by the Secretary of State] to deproscribe an organisation or to provide for a name to cease to be treated as a name for an organisation if it considers that the decision to refuse was flawed when considered in the light of the principles applicable on an application for judicial review.

The 'principles applicable' are 'points concerning those rights under the European Convention on Human Rights which are "Convention rights" under the 1998 [Human Rights] Act' (TA 2000 Explanatory notes). As noted in the introduction, only three organisations have successfully applied for deproscription in the UK to date: Mujaheddin e Khalq (MeK), also known as the Peoples' Mujaheddin of Iran (PMOI) in 2008; the International Sikh Youth Federation (ISYF) in March 2016; and Hezb-e Islami Gulbuddin (HIG) in December 2017.

Locating the present

The lens of antecedent and ancient outlawry practices with which we began our discussion sharpens analysis of today's proscription regime. As this chapter has shown, we can trace the growing prominence of this bold power through pre-modern practices of Saxon criminal justice, the English Civil War of the seventeenth century, the Highlands clearances, Jacobin revolutionary fervour of the eighteenth century, the struggle for labour rights in the nineteenth century, the twentieth century's emancipatory struggles of colonised peoples, and the Irish republican and loyalist movements. What emerges from this brief genealogy is the arresting conclusion that the march of time has done little to curb the appeal and arbitrary harshness of proscription; indeed, the severity of the power remains as important to national security politics in the twenty-first century as it was in the eighth.

The genealogy also reveals how, in Parliament's efforts to vanquish the ideas and organisations of political antagonists, proscription emerges as an ancient locus of authority, power and control. Looking across the British state's efforts to vanquish its ostensibly illegitimate political foes by exclusion, we can begin to elicit a series of connected principles of exclusion that seem pivotal to its place in national security politics. Through Britain's history, the proscription of political organisations is exercised where the proscribing agent holds – or claims to hold – the authority to do so in sovereign territory. In so doing, proscription operates to signal its target's subjugation to that sovereign authority. That is, the act of proscription is symbolically constitutive of sovereignty. In the recital of proscription orders – as posters or oration – we therefore encounter appeals of necessity to safeguard the legitimate community (which is denoted by adherence to lawfully prescribed processes of political engagement and moral political aims) from illegitimate groups denoted by their unlawful subversion of prescribed processes and pursuit of malevolent political aims.

These features of proscription might be presented, in simplified form, as a series of binaries organised around:

(i) Situated proscribing actors, claiming 'our' authority, who:
lay claim to a singular sovereign authority

on behalf of a legitimate political or cultural community
circumscribe the values, beliefs and identity of that community, and,
pronounce on moral and political rectitude

and

(ii) Specified proscribed actors, who:
represent an illegitimate political cause,
constitute a current, future or potential threat to the self
with a precarious supporting community of 'others', and are constitutive of moral and/or political turpitude.

This constitutive function of proscription is evident in the proscriptions ordered by the Pitt government, the Lord Lieutenant of Ireland, the Governor Generals in Britain's colonies; and in those of twenty-first-century Home Secretaries. As an act of power, it operates as an assertion of the proscriber's sovereign authority and of the subjugation of the proscribee in a literal act of *ad hominum*. This dynamic is discernible, for instance, in the resolution of the nascent 'Rump' Parliament, where the proscription of the Royalists was enacted in a fit of sovereign fiat. In the words of the order we see the conflation of: (1) a threat to the state ('Commonwealth'); (2) a specified group of individuals with a political cause; (3) their *a priori* and extrajudicial criminalisation (of *caput lupinum* in this instance); (4) the confiscation of their resources ('Estates'); and (v) clear delimitation of the territory in which they are persona non grata. These five principles of proscription are mirrored in today's Terrorism Act, under which proscription may proceed based on: (1) the threat posed to the UK; by (2) an organisation 'concerned in terrorism'; (3) who then become criminalised *a priori*; (4) which empowers the seizure of assets; (5) and facilitates the denial of their existence in the UK.

Notes

1 We cannot avoid an early coda. Tracing the chronology of outlawry and proscription through the history of what, today, is called the United Kingdom of Great Britain and Northern Ireland (shortened to the UK) necessarily requires some jagged jurisdictional deviations. The United Kingdom has, as is well known, only been 'united' since 1707. Before

then, its boundaries have ebbed, flowed, fractured and expanded. For the sake of clarity, we use the periodisation very helpfully assembled by Norman Davies in his book, *The Isles: A History* (2000). The Anglo-Saxon period, where we commence, is followed by the Kingdoms of England and the Scots; then the Kingdom of England and Wales, alongside the Kingdom of Ireland; the Commonwealth and Free State of England, Wales and Ireland; the Commonwealth of Great Britain and Ireland; the United Kingdom of Great Britain; the United Kingdom of Great Britain and Ireland; the United Kingdom of Great Britain and Northern Ireland.

2 The Legatine Capitulary is: 'a collection of canons promulgated ostensibly by a papal legation sent to England in order to address unspecified abuses' (Carella 2015, 111).

3 Carella argues that the principle of outlawry is represented in the Saxon phrase '*utroque iure caruerunt*' which appears in the Legatine Capitulary.

4 Sometimes spelled *Utlagh* or *Uthlagh*.

5 Towards the late medieval period, outlawry in county courts was displaced by central courts who would issue writs of exigent against those accused of crimes, which specified that their repeated failure to attend court would result in a declaration of outlawry.

6 Harward offers this account: 'Woolferthfod is the condition of such who were outlawed in the Saxons' time, for not submitting themselves to justice: for if they could be taken alive, they should be brought to the king; and if they in fear of apprehension did defend themselves, they might be slain, and their heads brought to the king; for they carried a Woolf's Head, that is to say, their head was no more to be accounted of than a Woolfs Head. Being a beast so hurtful to a Man.'

7 English translation taken from G.R.C. Davis (1963) *Magna Carta*. London: British Museum. pp. 23–33, cited by the British Library and available at: www.bl.uk/magna-carta/articles/magna-carta-english-translation (accessed 18 December 2019).

8 Henri de Bracton's *De Legibus Et Consuetudinibus Angliæ* ['On the Laws and Customs of England'] was written in the 1220s or 1230s, and translated by Samuel E. Thorne in 1968. We can access this work thanks to the Harvard Law School Library, where a digital version is maintained at: http://amesfoundation.law.harvard.edu/Bracton/index.html Volume 2, p. 361.

9 UK National Archives, Calendar of Close Rolls, Hen IV, vol. III, 1405–1409. *Petitions to the king; to the king and council; to the council; to the parliament; and the like*. Reference: SC 8/188/9358.

10 Notably, prohibitions against Catholicism were rife during the Reformation of the sixteenth century; indeed, the 1701 Act of Settlement included a provision against the British throne being occupied by a Catholic: a provision which persists today.

11 In a painting entitled 'The Proscribed Royalist', John Everett Millais depicts a Puritan women protecting a Royalist concealed in a hollow tree after the Battle of Worcester in 1651.

12 The Journals of the House of Commons. Vol. VI. 14 Martiii, 164. *A.* 1648. Reprinted 1803.

13 This precise sentiment is repeated almost verbatim with all proscriptions made by Parliament in this period. In 1661, for example: 'That his Sacred Majesty, that now is, and his Highness the Duke of York his Brother, should be proscribed as Enemies to the Commonwealth, and die without Mercy, wheresoever they should be found within this Nation'. 'House of Commons Journal Volume 8: 11 July 1661', in *Journal of the House of Commons: Volume 8, 1660–1667* (London, 1802), pp. 297–299. *British History Online*, www.british-history.ac.uk/commons-jrnl/vol8/pp297–299 (accessed 20 February 2018).

14 Criminal Justice (Scotland) Act, 1949, 12, 13 & 14 Geo. 6, c. 94, 15(2).

15 Victoria, *Parliamentary Debates*, Legislative Assembly, 30 October 1879, 1589 (Dr Madden): cited in Eburn (2005).

16 The text of the Act is available at: www.electricscotland.com/history/other/proscription_1747.htm (accessed 18 December 2019).

17 From the beginning of the nineteenth century, 'radical' was an established neologism of British politics. The term 'connoted a plebeian reformer, or a proponent of ambitious democratising schemes, or a materialist utilitarian rationalist; someone who aligned themselves with the intellectual legacy of the radical Enlightenment' (Innes and Burns 2003, 33).

18 1795: 36 Geo.3 c.8: An Act for the more effectually preventing Seditious Meetings and Assemblies. Available at: http://statutes.org.uk/site/the-statutes/eighteenth-century/1795–36-geo-3-c-7-treasonable-and-seditious-practices-act/ (accessed 18 February 2018).

19 *An Act for the Safety and Preservation of his Majesty's person and Government against Treasonable and Seditious Practices and Attempts 1795*. In The History of Two Acts, Entitled, an Act [36 Geo. III. Cap. 7] London: G.G. and J. Robinson, Paternoster Row. p. 772 (accessed 20 February 2018).

20 *Ibid.*

21 The Societies Act (*The Act Against Unlawful Combinations and Confederacies*) 1799 introduced the requirement, which remains in

force today, that printers include their name and address on the first or last leaf of a printed document.

22 *Act Against Unlawful Combinations and Confederacies* (1799) 39 Geo. III, c.79.

23 The recorded text in Hansard uses 'Jaws' instead of 'laws'.

24 'An Act for more effectually preventing Seditious Meetings and Assemblies 1819'. *The Statutes of the United Kingdom of Great Britain and Ireland. 60 Geo III & Geo IV 1819–1820*. London: Her Majesty's Statute and Law Printers.

25 *Public Order Act 1936*, in Robert G. Lee (ed.) *Blackstone's Statutes on Public Law and Human Rights 2015–2016*, p. 18.

26 The Act adds the proviso that uniforms may be permitted if 'the chief officer of police is satisfied that the wearing of any such uniform as aforesaid on any ceremonial, anniversary, or other special occasion will not be likely to involve risk of public disorder'.

27 War Cabinet. Invasion of Great Britain: Possible Co-Operation by a 'Fifth Column'. WP (G) (40) 131. 17th May 1940. Held by the UK National Archives: CAB-67–6–31.

28 War Cabinet 128 (40). Conclusions. Held by the UK National Archives: CAB-65–7–23.

29 War Cabinet 133 (40). Conclusions. Held by the National Archives: CAB-67–7–28.

30 As the foregoing discussion shows, the post-Second World War proscriptions had clear antecedents drawn from British experiences of the eighteenth and nineteenth centuries. For example, facing growing political unrest in India, the colonial administrators – the British Raj – introduced the Prevention of Seditious Meetings Act 1907, legislation adopted almost wholesale from laws passed immediately after the French Revolution.

31 CO 1035/131 'Organisations proscribed or prohibited on colonial territories'. 'Extract of file contains responses of Colonial Governors to a request from the Colonial Office for a list of proscribed or prohibited organisations in their territories. Includes responses from North Borneo, Sarawak, Singapore, Malaya, Brunei, Hong Kong'.

32 Correspondence with the Secretary of State for the Colonies, June–July 1956. Accessed via National Archives.

33 Similarly, the administrators of the British protectorate Nyasaland (now Malawi), suppressed the Nyasaland African Congress in March 1959, though its senior cadres circumvented the ban by reforming as the Malawi Congress Party in September of that year.

34 What is more, the UOA reversed the burden of proof: the onus of proof was anyone prosecuted on the basis of these offences to show that they were *not* acting in support of the outlawed group.
35 In the Middle East, a violent and more crude programme of 'aerial proscription' was also enacted. Unable to effectively detain or intern problematic populations, instead declaring an entire area 'proscribed' the colonial authorities sent aerial patrols over those areas with the authority to bomb or shoot anyone at will.
36 HC Deb 26 August 1887 vol 320 cc33–152.
37 Cumann na mBan, 'The Women's Council', is an Irish paramilitary women's nationalist group, formed in Dublin in 1914. The group remains an active organisation and are proscribed under the TA 2000. Cumann na mBan has the distinction of being the longest proscribed organisation in the UK: it has now been banned for more than a century.
38 French, J.D.P., Macpherson, J.I. & Glenavy, J.H.M.C. (1919). Text taken from image of the poster held at the National Library of Ireland. Accessible at: http://catalogue.nli.ie/Record/vtls000511960 (accessed 18 December 2019).
39 The proclamation was laid before the UK Parliament the next day: HC Deb 04 July 1918 vol 107 c1818.
40 *The Belfast Gazette*, 26 May 1922, pp. 445–446. Available at: www.thegazette.co.uk/Belfast/issue/46/page/445/data.pdf (accessed 18 December 2019).
41 Statement by the Home Secretary, Alan Johnson, 12 January 2010. Reported in 'Islam4UK Islamist group banned under terror laws', http://news.bbc.co.uk/2/hi/8453560.stm (accessed 19 December 2019).
42 Statement by the Home Secretary, Alan Johnson, 1 March 2010. Reported in 'Britain to ban militant Somali Islamist group', http://uk.reuters.com/article/idUKLDE6201IA (accessed 19 December 2019).
43 Statement by the Home Secretary, Theresa May, 2011. Reported in 'Britain moves to ban Pakistani Taliban under terror law', http://uk.reuters.com/article/us-britain-taliban/britain-moves-to-ban-taliban-under-terror-law-idUKTRE70H2CV20110118 (accessed 19 December 2019).
44 Lord Carlile of Berriew (2010, 16).
45 It is worthy of note that several of these organisations connected to Northern Ireland were not added to the EU's blacklist, which was agreed on 27 December 2001 (see 2001/931/CFSP). Absent from the EU blacklist were: Cumann na mBan; Fianna na hEireann; Saor Eire; The Continuity Army Council; The Red Hand Commando; The Irish

National Liberation Army; The Irish People's Liberation Organisation; and the Ulster Volunteer Force. This is possibly because the UK government saw them as defunct, pseudonymous or possibly as aliases. Alternatively, their placement on the UK Schedule 2 served a different purpose to that of the EU blacklist. Not present on the UK list but added to the EU list were the Continuity Irish Republican Army and the Real IRA.

46 The Anti-Terrorism, Crime and Security Act 2001 amended the TA 2000 to empower the government to detain any non-UK national deemed a terrorist threat until they could be deported or leave the UK.

47 The provision to include 'unlawful glorification' of terrorism was added in the Terrorism Act 2006, Section 21 (5a, b & c).

48 Terrorism Act 2000, Section 3 (5).

49 Explanatory Memorandum to the Terrorism Act 2000 (Proscribed Organisations) (Amendment Order) 2011, 7.2.

50 Under this procedure, both Houses of Parliament must expressly approve proposed amendments to statutory instruments. They are not, however, able to change any element of proposed amendments.

51 To be removed from Schedule 2 – to be deproscribed – requires an organisation to make an application directly to the Secretary of State. If the Secretary agrees, she may lay an order to remove the organisation from Schedule 2 before Parliament for approval. Should the Secretary refuse, the organisation may appeal to the Proscribed Organisations Appeals Commission (POAC), which may only allow the appeal if it considers the Secretary's determination flawed, subject to judicial review principles. Either the organisation or the Secretary may appeal POAC's decision at the Court of Appeal, the decision of which is binding (House of Commons Library 2014).

52 Under the affirmative procedure, proscription orders require a majority of votes to pass. Under the negative procedure, the order is made unless either House proposes and passes a motion disapproving the order.

2 Proscription in context: historical, geographical and political dynamics

The UK is far from alone in its history of proscription: global politics is littered with efforts to ban non-state and anti-state groups, especially those with communist, anarchical and anti-colonial provenance. The continuing deployment of proscription by parliamentary democracies, dictatorships and oligarchies alike is testament to its enduring appeal for those in power; an indicator, perhaps, of a fear that popular revolt, or the dismantling of the state by other means, remains plausible. Today, proscription powers are deployed widely by states in the international system, either by the domestic commission of unilateral legal powers or through the multilateral blacklisting mechanisms of international organisations (IOs) such as the United Nations and the European Union.[1] Importantly, the considerable variance between national legal systems and political imperatives means that banning powers are idiosyncratic in their application, and uneven in their consequence.

The aim of this chapter is two-fold. First, to situate our case study – the deployment of proscription through one of the world's oldest democratic institutions, the UK Parliament – in its broader contemporary context. The chapter's second aim is to reflect on a number of important existing criticisms of proscription powers. We begin by considering proscriptions levelled against movements seeking emancipation from the yoke of colonial rule, and then against communist entities in the post-war period. Next, we turn to the array of anti-terrorism laws hurriedly introduced after al Qaeda's attacks on the United States in 2001. Here we consider, first, the proscription regimes implemented and promulgated by the United Nations and the European Union, and, second, a selection of national proscription regimes that, in interesting ways, interact with the UK's apparatus. Finally, we turn to an array of issues identified by academics, activists, policymakers and others around the effectiveness and ethical implications of this power.

Proscription in the twentieth century

Woven throughout the twentieth and twenty-first centuries is an assortment of struggles for national or ethnic liberation, particularly amongst colonised countries but also in states with long-standing internal antagonisms. A common response to such struggles has seen prevailing authorities designating such entities as a threat to the state or national community, and using existing or newly granted powers to outlaw opposition and criminalise material or symbolic support. As shown in Chapter 1, this logic is centuries old, but it found particular purchase in the post-war period amongst European colonial administrations confronted by local political organisations that were gaining in strength, sometimes (but not always) urged ideologically onwards by the emancipatory rhetoric of socialism. To counter such threats, proscription offered a simple expedience. For example, in the midst of growing popular unrest, France's colonial authorities banned the Étoile Nord-Africaine, Parti Communiste Algérien, Front de Libération Nationale (FLN), the Organisation Speciale in French Algeria and Le Ressemblement Democratique Africain in French West Africa. Likewise, to head off insurgency in its colonial territories, British authorities banned the Kikuyu Central Association and the Kenya Africa Union and many other organisations including in Rhodesia, India, Cyprus, Aden and Malaya (see Chapter 1).

Crudely installed postcolonial settlements gave rise to continuing intra-state antagonisms, especially in cases witnessing subsequent secessionist campaigns. In South Asia, for example, after independence from Britain, the Tamil Tigers (LTTE) fought a campaign for Tamil independence from the Sinhala-majority Sri Lanka. The Sri Lankan government's use of proscription against the LTTE, for critics, further entrenched the state's long-standing hostility towards the Tamil community:

> The deliberate conflation of 'terrorism' with the Tamil political project by successive Sri Lankan governments has produced a political culture in which the main (Sinhala) parties routinely vie to adopt more hard-line positions on the 'ethnic question' a practice which began as long ago as 1956. (Nadarajah and Sriskandarajah 2005, 98)

A similar dynamic of postcolonial discomfit remains in India where the state has variously clashed with localised secessionist groups including Maoist Naxalites in northeast India and the Khalistan movement in the Punjab. In the Middle East, too, a litany of armed groups, prominently the Palestinian Liberation Organization (PLO) and Hamas, have sought to carve out an independent Palestine in an ongoing conflict with Israel since the post-war expiry of the British Mandate.

Crucially, then as much as now, the (political) use of violence per se by a non-state organisation was neither a necessary nor sufficient condition for proscription. Indeed, throughout the twentieth century, states have frequently tolerated and often backed violent non-state groups, usually when those groups have furthered the interests of those in power, including, amongst others: the Death Squads of El Salvador; Antiterrorist Liberation Groups (GAL) backed by the Spanish government; Pemuda Pancasila (Pancasila Youth) in Indonesia; the Black Cats vigilante group in South Africa; the United Self Defence Forces of Colombia (AUC); and Loyalist movements in Northern Ireland (see Stohl and Lopez 1984, 1988; George 1991; Byman 2005; Stokes 2005; Blakeley 2009; Jackson *et al.* 2010; Jarvis and Lister 2014).

The proscription of communist parties

From the early years of the twentieth century, communism was portrayed by its opponents as a boundless threat to prevailing systems of authority across the world. In the years leading up to and following the Second World War, democracies, theocracies and monarchies alike took pre-emptive action to outlaw communist organisations (see Figure 2.1). In some states, high court or electoral tribunal decisions determined the illegality of a communist party, such as in Brazil and West Germany. In others, such as Guatemala and Peru, the national constitution included provisions incompatible with the existence of a political entity with foreign links, thus acting as a de facto ban. For the most part, however, states banned communist parties either via proscription laws enacted by national assemblies or, in authoritarian regimes, through presidential or monarchical fiat. A contemporaneous analysis by the US Central Intelligence Agency wrestled with the conundrum democracies faced in keeping communist groups at bay: 'It is difficult to devise laws and administrative orders', the author argues, 'that strike at the Party and yet do not interfere with the activities of non-Communist opposition groups'.[2]

In public, communist parties were often portrayed as simple instruments of Soviet foreign policy, and therefore posing an existential threat to the state. Indeed, the United States Congress used the text of the US Communist Control Act of 1954 to declare:

> The Congress hereby finds and declares that the Communist Party of the United States, although purportedly a political party, is in fact an instrumentality of a conspiracy to overthrow the Government of the United States. It constitutes an authoritarian dictatorship within a republic, demanding for itself the rights and privileges accorded to political parties, but denying to all others the liberties guaranteed by the Constitution. Unlike political parties, which evolve their policies and programs through public means, by the reconciliation of a wide variety of individual views, and submit those policies and programs to the electorate at large for approval or disapproval, the policies and programs of the Communist Party are secretly prescribed for it by the foreign leaders of the world Communist movement. (US Communist Control Act of 1954)[3]

A declassified CIA analysis, *Legal vs. Illegal Status: Some Considerations relevant to Banning a Communist Party* (1957), submits an equivocal evaluation of the effectiveness of the pre- and post-war proscriptions of the communist movement. 'Outlawry', the document asserts in one heading, 'Is Usually Detrimental but not Fatal'. The document goes on to suggest advantages accrued by a ban: the party 'is reduced to a hard-core of militants, who are prepared to serve obediently' as 'dedicated revolutionaries' who are 'willing to undertake hazardous assignments'; the leadership is able to focus their efforts on 'building the underground apparatus', 'subversion, espionage and subversion'; and finances can be 'expended on a limited number of objects' and not wasted on unproductive activities. The document concludes: 'Repression requires lopping

Figure 2.1 Proscription of communist parties around the world: 1922–62[a]

Australasia and South Pacific	Australia (1950, set aside 1951)
Europe	Greece (1947); Spain (1939/40); Portugal (1926); West Germany (1956)
Africa	Algeria (1962); Ivory Coast (1963); Morocco (1952); Tunisia (1963); Union of South Africa (1950); Sudan (1958)
Middle East	Lebanon (1939); Syria (1939); Turkey (1922); United Arab Emirates (1954); Iran (1949); Iraq (1960); Jordan (1957)
South and South East Asia	Pakistan (1954); East Bengal (1954); Burma (1946 and 1953); Thailand (1952); Federation of Malaya (1947); Singapore (1948); South Korea (1949); Philippines (1957)
North, Central and South America	Argentina (1959 and 1962); Guatemala (1961); Haiti (1948); Dominican Republic (1961); El Salvador (1961); Nicaragua (1945); Costa Rica (1948); Panama (1953); Brazil (1947); Chile (1948); Paraguay 1936; the United States (1954)[b]

a Bureau of Intelligence and Research (1963) 'World Strength of the Communist Party Organizations', *US Department of State*. Intelligence Report No.4489 r-15.
b Many other countries introduced *de facto* rather than *de jure* proscriptions against communist parties; others used constitutional conditions precluding the existence of political parties linked to foreign political groups. Here we have listed instances where specific laws banning a group were introduced.

off all arms of the octopus-like organisation', and – remarkably – that 'Nazi Germany offers probably the best example of the successful extirpation of Communism's multi-armed organization' (pp. 21–23).

The worldwide proscriptions of communist groups were an outward expression of an anxiety – similar to that of European states in the aftermath of the French Revolution – that a radical ideology could gain a foothold in the public political imagination. Those who questioned the merit of proscribing political groups in a democracy were countered by arguments that communism was anti-democratic. A West German court, for instance, ruled a communist organisation was incompatible with the tenets of liberal democracy (McWhinney 1956). Communism, depicted thus, presented an existential threat – even though, crucially, the movements tended to be non-violent – that *ipso facto* merited special or emergency powers to preserve national security. This sentiment, once accepted, cemented as a precedent for proscription – the parameters of which were later to be expanded.[4]

The 1991 collapse of the Soviet Union relieved Western countries of the need to reflect too deeply on the merits of continuing proscriptions against communism. Yet as the Soviet Union disintegrated, an apparent upturn in 'international' terrorism persuaded several states to revise existing legal prohibitions and powers against violent groups. A spate of bombings and armed attacks in the 1980s and 1990s prompted both the United States and United Kingdom to begin revising, consolidating and updating existing anti-terrorism powers. Bombings that struck the World Trade Center in 1993 and Oklahoma City in 1995 helped convince the United States to institute the Terrorism Prevention Act 1996, while the UK government hurriedly put in place the Criminal Justice (Terrorism and Conspiracy) Act 1998 after an August 1998 bombing in Omagh that killed twenty-nine people.

The post-9/11 landscape of proscription

The attacks on 11 September 2001 were a pivotal moment in global counter-terrorism policy generally and proscription specifically. Within weeks of the attacks, the United Nations produced a resolution calling for a global legislative offensive against terrorism, prompting urgent legislative drafting throughout 2002. The European Union followed the UN's lead, mirroring its sanctions lists and issuing its own blacklist. Individually, states strengthened their existing laws to meet the UN injunction, or developed new ones in line with the UN recommendations.

United Nations

The United Nations blacklisting powers stem from a series of resolutions passed between 1998 and 2002 after a spate of attacks on the United States and other states. Together, these resolutions formed, on the one hand, a sanctions regime targeting al Qaeda and the Taliban quite specifically and, on the other, a broader regime enjoining member states to introduce measures to tackle the scourge of terrorism.

The first was established after al Qaeda's attacks on the US embassies in Nairobi and Dar es Salaam in 1998. In response, the UN passed Resolution 1189 (1998), which called for states to 'adopt practical and effective measures to prevent, combat and eliminate all forms of terrorism affecting the international community as a whole'. The subsequent UN Security Council Resolution (UNSC) 1267 – passed in October 1999 – gave teeth to that injunction, condemning the Taliban regime in Afghanistan 'for the sheltering and training of terrorists and planning of terrorist acts' and announcing a package of financial and travel sanctions on the Taliban leadership. The Resolution established a UN Security Council committee that was tasked with the oversight of sanctions against a blacklist of individuals. In December 2000, UN Resolution 1333 extended the sanctions regime to include Osama Bin Laden and associates. In January 2002, just three months after the 9/11 attacks, the UN introduced Resolution 1390, which widened the criteria for inclusion upon the sanction list to include any individual, group or entity associated with Bin Laden or the Taliban.

Together these resolutions form the basis of a continuing global blacklist of specified individuals and entities. The 'targeted' sanctions of this blacklist oblige UN member states to freeze or seize assets, restrict the travel of, and otherwise level 'appropriate penalties' against, designated individuals, entities and groups. Notably, under this regime, entities and individuals may be added to the UN's consolidated sanctions list with little oversight: any member state may propose an addition to the list, for any of the reasons given in an expansive set of listing criteria, though Security Council members retain a right to object. The first consolidated list containing seven entities and 162 individuals was published in March 2001. Today the Consolidated United Nations Security Council Sanctions List contains 386 listed entities, and 686 individuals.[5]

A second regime was created in response to the 9/11 attacks. Resolution 1373, passed in December 2001, called on member states to introduce into domestic law measures to 'prevent and suppress, in their territories, the financing and preparation of any acts of terrorism'. In the absence of a definition of terrorism, 1373 acted as an imprimatur granting UN member states extraordinary latitude in how they interpreted their task, since no specific individuals or organisations are specified by the Resolution. The UN set up a Counter Terrorism Committee and required states to report on their actions within ninety days, underlining the expected pace of legislative response. So far-reaching was the injunction that *all* states found they needed to amend their domestic anti-terror laws to comply with the Resolution (Stiles 2006, 47–48). Preferring a collaborative approach, the UN CTC undertook not to use its enforcement powers, preferring 'a non-confrontational, collaborative spirit' (Stiles 2006) to assisting states.

The UN CTC's model proscription law drew, amongst other influences discussed below, from a common law tradition, fitting with the sixty-eight common law jurisdictions of the UN's 192 members states. The urgency to comply with Resolution 1373 precipitated a profound sea change in global counter-terrorism legislating and, indeed, in the diffusion of proscription laws. A 1996 review of counter-terrorism powers by Lord Lloyd found only 25 per cent of twenty Western countries employed proscription powers – today they may be found in *90 per cent* of the same states. We return to the implications of this below.

Europe

The Council of the European Union followed the lead of the UN in establishing two lists: one which adopted the UN list of terrorist entities in its entirety, and a second which stands as the EU's own autonomous terrorist blacklist. The European Community Treaty established an effective, and legal, 'Common Foreign and Security Policy' of the bloc (see Cardwell 2015). Under Article 301 of the treaty, the Council affirms its commitment to take 'necessary urgent measures' for economic sanctions against specified non-EC countries, which are implemented by member states via EC Regulations. This provision forms the basis for the adoption of the two UN regimes: (1) On 27 May 2002, the EC adopted Common Position 2002/402/CFSP, which explicitly gave effect to the UN Resolution 1390(2002) and adopted the UN lists administered under 1267(1999), and 1333(2000), which specified sanctions against al Qaeda and the Taliban. (2) The second UN regime – established by Resolution 1373 and calling for a broader introduction of anti-terrorism laws – was given effect by the EU (2001/931/CFSP) on 27 December 2001. Under the Common Position, 'terrorist group' was defined as:

> a structured group of more than two persons, established over a period of time and acting in concert to commit terrorist acts. 'Structured group' means a group that is not randomly formed for the immediate commission of a terrorist act and that does not need to have formally defined roles for its members, continuity of its membership or a developed structure. (2001/931/CFSP: para. 3)

Under 2001/931/CFSP, 'competent authorities' were the key decision-makers on which individuals or entities may be included on the EU blacklist, understood to be 'a judicial authority, or, where judicial authorities have no competence in the area covered by this paragraph, an equivalent competent authority in that area':

> The list in the Annex shall be drawn up on the basis of precise information or material in the relevant file which indicates that a decision has been taken by a competent authority in respect of the persons, groups and entities concerned, irrespective of whether it concerns the instigation of investigations or prosecution for a terrorist act, an attempt to perpetrate, participate in or facilitate such an act based on serious and credible evidence or clues, or condemnation for such deeds. Persons, groups and entities identified by the Security Council of the United Nations as being related to terrorism and against whom it has ordered sanctions may be included in the list.

This second regime is operated entirely by the EU and given legal effect by EC Regulation 2580/2001. Under the 2001/931/CFSP listing (hereafter, the EU blacklist), an initial set of groups were designated, outlined in Figure 2.2.

As Figure 2.2 demonstrates, the initial EU blacklist included organisations connected to domestic conflicts in Spain, Greece and Northern Ireland. These were provided by relevant member states without review by European partners. Curiously, several of the Northern Ireland organisations proscribed under the UK's TA 2000 were not selected – Cumann na mBan and Fianna ma nHireann, for instance, remain proscribed in the UK today (see Chapter 1), yet do not appear on the EU list. One possible explanation is that the UK government regard these organisations as defunct, but maintain a UK listing either symbolically, or to pre-empt any attempt at their resurrection.

Figure 2.2 Groups blacklisted by the EU in 2001: 2001/931/CFSP

Continuity Irish Republican Army (CIRA); Euskadi Ta Askatasuna/Tierra Vasca y Libertad/Basque Fatherland and Liberty (ETA) (The following organisations are considered part of the terrorist group ETA: K.a.s., Xaki; Ekin, Jarrai-Haika-Segi, Gestoras pro-amnistía.); Grupos de Resistencia Antifascista Primero de Octubre/Antifascist Resistance Groups First of October (G.R.A.P.O.); Hamas-Izz al-Din al-Qassem (terrorist wing of Hamas); Loyalist Volunteer Force (LVF); Orange Volunteers (OV); Palestinian Islamic Jihad (PIJ); Real IRA; Red Hand Defenders (RHD); Revolutionary Nuclei/Epanastatiki Pirines; Revolutionary Organisation 17 November/Dekati Evdomi Noemvri; Revolutionary Popular Struggle/ Epanastatikos Laikos Agonas (ELA); Ulster Defence Association/Ulster Freedom Fighters (UDA/UFF)

National approaches

States often unilaterally institute their own proscriptions in addition to those mandated by treaties. In Australia, for example, the Charter of the United Nations (Anti-Terrorism Measures) Regulations 2001 was passed, which imported wholesale the UN's list of individuals and entities designated as terrorist. Subsequently, the Australian government assumed the right to unilaterally declare organisations as terrorist in the Criminal Code Amendment (Terrorist Organisations) Act 2004 (Cth) (see also McGarrity and Williams 2018). The Canadian government responded to the post-9/11 context similarly promptly. Where the UN list of designated entities was already enacted by the United Nations al Qaida and Taliban Regulations (UNAQTR) (1999) and the Regulations Implementing the United Nations Resolutions on the Suppression of Terrorism (RIUNRST), in December 2001 the capacity to unilaterally designate terrorist entities was added to the Canadian Criminal Code by the Anti-Terrorism Act 2001 (see also Forcese and Roach 2018).

Perhaps most prominent amongst national proscription lists, however, are the US designated terrorist lists. The US administers a raft of legal instruments used to sanction terrorist activity by restricting travel and funds transfer, criminalising material support from third parties, and imposing other economic penalties or embargoes. These include the 'Terrorist Exclusion List', the 'Specially

Designated Terrorists' (SDTs) list, the 'Specially Designated Global Terrorists' (SDGT) list, and the state-sponsors of terrorism list, all of which are subsumed into the list of 'Specially Designated Nationals and Blocked Persons' (SDN). Terrorist groups are designated within the Foreign Terrorist Organization (FTO) list under Section 219 of the Immigration and Nationality Act. The Act provides that the Secretary of State may add an organisation to the FTO list if it meets three statutory criteria: first, 'the organization is a foreign organization'; second, the organisation is currently engaged in terrorism or 'retains the capability and intent to engage in terrorist activity'; and, third, 'the terrorist activity or terrorism of the organization threatens the security of United States nationals or the national security of the United States' (Sec 219 (1) a,b,c).[6] The process involves the Secretary of State notifying Congress of her decision, allowing seven days to register any objection to the proposed listing. If none are forthcoming, the decision to designate the group as a foreign terrorist organisation takes effect and is published in the Federal Register. At the time of writing, there are sixty-eight groups on the US FTO list, while thirteen organisations – including the Japanese Red Army and the Abu Nidal Organisation – have been delisted.

There are a range of other proscription regimes maintained worldwide. Accessing these presents a challenge for researchers, since there is no public consolidated list describing all international and national lists of proscribed terrorist organisations. In addition, several private sector companies offer what amounts to a 'risk management' service for clients anxious to avoid transacting business with groups designated terrorist. On one estimate,[7] globally there are 179 ongoing listing regimes – all of which are liable to amendment or addition at any time. Amongst those that are public, in addition to those noted above, are those maintained by India,[8] Pakistan,[9] Israel,[10] Russia,[11] Turkey[12] and – collectively – Saudi Arabia, the United Arab Emirates, Egypt and Bahrain.[13]

The influence of UK proscription and membership offences as 'best practice'

One consequence of UN Resolution 1373 was to induce states to rather quickly adopt similar approaches, with but ninety days to write and institute the requisite laws and regulations. To assist, the UN provided guidance on 'best practices' under a 'Directory of International Best Practices, Codes and Standards'. This directory lists a combination of legal and policy instruments from international organisations and states.[14] Proscription and membership offences are described in the implementation of UN Resolution 1373 2(d)[15] – which calls for states to deny the use of their jurisdiction by terrorists – and a single document compiled by the Commonwealth Secretariat: 'Model Legislative Provisions on Measures to Combat Terrorism', which recommends the following:

> For the prohibition on making funds available and the general support offences under para 1(d) of the Security Council resolution, it is also useful to adopt a domestic process by which persons and entities can be proscribed as terrorists or terrorist groups by executive action. This will avoid the requirement to establish a link to terrorist acts in each individual case. The requirements for and process adopted for the 'listing' of individuals and groups will be dependent upon the requirements of domestic law in this regard.[16]

It is significant that the recommended process of proscription, which was developed in a report of experts drawn from across the Commonwealth, is one which draws quite directly from the UK TA 2000 (see Figure 2.3). In brief, the guidance suggests a process by which the minister – acting on the advice of the government's most senior law official – declares an entity to be terrorist. Provision for judicial review of that decision is also recommended (after an appeal to the minister), and membership offences appear taken almost verbatim from UK law.

As Figure 2.3 shows, the lexical similarities between the UK legislation (which was authored in 1999) and the UN recommended best practice are striking. The definitions of the offences of membership (and the defence thereof), and supporting or organising a meeting are, to all intents and purposes, identical.[17] Detecting this cross-national law transfer is useful for it helps track the influence of UK and UN anti-terrorism law-making. So, the UK's provision of membership of proscribed organisations is found verbatim in anti-terrorism laws passed post-2001 by, *inter alia*, Bangladesh,[18] The Gambia, India,[19] Tanzania,[20] Nigeria,[21] Mauritius,[22] Brunei Darussalam,[23] Ghana,[24] Swaziland,[25] the Seychelles[26] and Kenya.[27] These are all, notably, members of the Commonwealth that legislate in English.

Figure 2.3 Comparison of 'Model Legislative Provisions on Measures to Combat Terrorism' and the UK Terrorism Act 2000

Arrangements of Meetings in Support of Terrorist Groups 18. (1) Every person who arranges, manages or assists in arranging or managing a meeting which he **or she knows is –** **(a) to support a terrorist group,** **(b) to further the activities of a terrorist group,** **(c) to be addressed by a person who belongs or professes to belong to a terrorist group,** commits an offence and shall on conviction be liable to imprisonment for a term not exceeding ( ) years. **In this section 'meeting' means a meeting of 2 or more persons, whether or not the public are admitted.**	**Support.** (1) A person commits an offence if— (a) he invites support for a proscribed organisation, and (b) the support is not, or is not restricted to, the provision of money or other property (within the meaning of section 15). (2) A person commits an offence if he **arranges, manages or assists in arranging or managing a meeting which he knows is—** **(a) to support a proscribed organisation,** **(b) to further the activities of a proscribed organisation, or** **(c) to be addressed by a person who belongs or professes to belong to a proscribed organisation.** (3) A person commits an offence if he addresses a meeting and the purpose of his address is to encourage support for a proscribed organisation or to further its activities. (4) Where a person is charged with an offence under subsection (2)(c) in respect of a private meeting it is a defence for him to prove that he had no reasonable cause to believe that the address mentioned in subsection (2)(c) would support a proscribed organisation or further its activities. (5) In subsections (2) to (4)— (a) **'meeting' means a meeting of three or more persons, whether or not the public are admitted, and** (b) a meeting is private if the public are not admitted. (6) A person guilty of an offence under this section shall be liable— (a) **on conviction on indictment, to imprisonment for a term not exceeding ten years, to a fine or to both, or** (b) on summary conviction, to imprisonment for a term not exceeding six months, to a fine not exceeding the statutory maximum or to both.

As the primary referent for the majority of post-2001 anti-terrorism law reforms across the world, including the EU's blacklist and the African Union's (stalled) listing, Resolution 1373 represents a sea change in global anti-terrorism legislating. The injunction on states to introduce competent anti-terrorism measures within ninety days naturally led states to seek out and adopt existing legal frameworks, especially those backed by 'expert' and international organisation endorsement. With UN backing for the Commonwealth's Expert Group recommendations, it is therefore little surprise that states took the opportunity to import the text almost wholesale. In so doing, however, these states adopted laws developed over the UK's idiosyncratic, and mixed, experiences of confronting anti-state violence across – as we saw in Chapter 1 – a period of centuries. Understanding the lineage of the ideas underpinning the UN's resolution is important, for it offers one way into making sense of the remarkable tapestry of laws and regulations that ban or sanction designated terrorist organisations, further underscoring the necessity for exploring the operation of UK proscription powers.

Proscription: impacts and consequences

Since the UN's 2001 injunction that member states enact legislation to counter violent extremism, we have seen extraordinary variation globally in who is, and is not, considered 'terrorist', even between allied countries.[28] The consequences of this inconsistency are considerable: global counter-money-laundering initiatives have been stymied by a failure to adequately agree *between* states which groups do, and do not, fall within national and/or international (UN) designation provisions, and states have routinely used terrorist designation lists to deny the claims of asylum seekers. Movements seeking national self-determination or liberation from oppressive governments have been lauded – funded in some cases – by some governments, yet condemned as terrorist by others.[29] Perhaps of greatest concern, however, is the growing evidence that some forms of proscription are counter-productive, galvanising support for violent extremist groups in some states and giving much-wanted profile to otherwise unknown organisations.

These are amongst the critiques forwarded by scholars on the effects and effectiveness of proscription. There is widespread agreement that proscription is a power of some importance. Yet, despite its growing use for counter-terrorism globally, surprisingly limited scholarly attention has yet been afforded to its mechanisms, outcomes and significance. Moreover, aside from work on the normalisation of emergency powers (Flyghed 2002; Blackbourn 2008), and the creation of 'precursor crimes' (Macdonald 2012), the sociology, public administration and political science literatures have been relatively muted here (although see Walker 2006), especially compared to the volume of critical reflection on related developments, such as powers of detention and offences relating to the glorification of terrorism (Barendt 2005).

Legal scholars have, to date, led the way in exploring proscription's ambitions, achievements and implications for liberal democracy. Australian legal scholarship has been most active (especially, Hocking 2003; Tham 2004; Goldsmith 2007; Douglas 2008; Hogg 2008; Lynch *et al.* 2009; McCulloch and Pickering 2009), yet there is comparatively little political science research on this power's symbolic and performative dimensions (though see de Goede 2011, 2018). Looking beyond the immediate causal story to be told about proscription is important since, as Mark Muller indicates, 'Proscription regimes are not simply legal tools against terror but ideological and political ones as well' (2008, 128; see also Jarvis and Legrand 2016, 2017; Legrand and Jarvis 2014). In this final section, we therefore draw attention to five primary concerns emanating from the power of proscription itself. First, the challenges associated with designating terrorist organisations. Second, the ubiquity of political interests, considerations and manoeuvrings in proscription decisions. Third, normative tensions between this power and established principles of liberal democracy. Fourth, questions of the effects and effectiveness of proscription. And, fifth, questions relating to the antagonisms that emerge between the lists maintained by different states.

Issues of designation

The manner in which states designate organisations as terrorist is rife with challenges. A first clear problem is the assumption of coherence and boundedness that the act of naming an organisation conveys. Whatever one's view of the 'new terrorism' thesis – and the claim therein that the late twentieth century witnessed a radical transformation in the structure of terrorist organisations (see Burnett and Whyte 2005; Spencer 2006) – groups today labelled 'terrorist' often lack anything approaching the institutional stability connoted by their designation thus. Goldsmith (2007), for example, argues that jihadist groups are constituted via 'shared values, common socialisation, effective bonds and modern communication technologies' rather than formal organisational structures. Hogg (2008, 304) notes similarly that the major terrorist threat today emerges from 'local, self-starter individuals and groupings' acquiring 'motivation, training technical knowledge and support' from new communications media. As a result, attempts to define a 'terrorist organisation' – as in the Australian Crown's recent court case (NSW Supreme Court 2007) – may fail to capture the 'fluid and elusive forms of organisational activity' of international terrorism. 'Organisation' is thus understood by some critics of proscription to operate as little more than a symbol 'to provide illusory comfort by imposing a familiar shape on a formless threat' (Hogg 2008, 304).

There is, perhaps, no better example of this than al Qaeda, which was discussed as a coherent organisation within US intelligence discourse for many years before it constituted anything approaching such a form (Gerges 2011, 29). As Jason Burke (2003, 9) persuasively argues, investigators were 'very keen to find a group, led by an identifiable figure, and give it a name', long before al Qaeda existed in any concrete sense. This was, not least, due to the constraints of existing conspiracy laws which had been constructed to deal with criminal organisations possessing a more coherent sense of boundedness (Burke 2003, 11). Thus, although the phrase 'al Qaeda' had been in use by radical Islamist groups before the late 1990s (Burke 2003; Gerges 2011, 43), its status as a moniker for a distinct militant organisation was applied almost entirely exogenously until approximately five years before the 11 September 2001 attacks.

A second issue of designation – referenced in Chapter 1 – is the frequency with which organisations designated 'terrorist' either change their operating name, or employ multiple names in the conduct of their activities (Pedahzur *et al.* 2002, 143). A useful example is the May 19th Communist Organization which was active in the United States during the 1980s:

> On January 28, 1983, the group used the name 'Revolutionary Fighting Group' to claim credit for damage in the bombing of the federal building on Staten Island, New York. In three subsequent bombings in 1983, they used the name 'armed Resistance unit' when they sent communiqués to the media. The National War college, the Washington Navy Yard, and the U.S. Capital Building were all bombing victims of the armed Resistance unit. In 1984, they again changed their name, this time to the 'Red Guerrilla Resistance.' Three more targets were hit that year: the Israeli aircraft Industries Building in New York city, the Washington Navy Yard Officers' club, and the South African consulate in New York were all bombed before the spree ended … It was not until their indictment in 1988 that the public learned that all three groups were actually one and the same. (Smith and Damphousse 2009, 476–477)

To move to the present, Aum Shinrikyo has multiple alternative names listed by the US State Department: A.I.C. Comprehensive Research Institute; A.I.C. Sogo Kenkyusho; Aleph; and Aum Supreme Truth; while the Iraq-based group, Ansar Al-Islam, has thirteen (US Department of State 2012). And, similar issues emerge, of course, in the UK, as illustrated by Schedule 2 of proscribed organisations:

> The Government laid Orders, in January 2010 and November 2011, which provide that Al Muhajiroun, Islam4UK, Call to Submission, Islamic Path, London School of Sharia and Muslims Against Crusades should be treated as alternative names for the organisation which is already proscribed under the names Al Ghurabaa and The Saved Sect. (Home Office 2014, p.4)

Third, terrorist groups tend not to enjoy a lengthy existence: indeed, one analysis found that only 53 of 100 groups survived beyond one month, with nationalist, leftist and religious groups averaging a lifespan of 35–38 months (Vittori 2009). One reason for this short shelf-life is the tendency of terrorist groups to splinter or factionalise from within. The Continuity Irish Republican Army (IRA) and the Real IRA, for example, represent only two of the most prominent splinter groups within Irish republicanism: splitting from the Provisional IRA in 1986 and 1997 respectively (Horgan and Morrison 2011). In the Palestinian-Israeli conflict factionalism has been a similarly perennial feature such that, for example, 'the Popular Front for the Liberation of Palestine (PFLP), Democratic Front for the Liberation of Palestine (DFLP), and the Popular Front for the Liberation of Palestine-General Command (PFLP-GC) split with the [Palestine Liberation Organization] PLO over the Israeli-Palestinian peace process' (Cronin 2009, 67–68). This possibility of disintegration again renders proscription a far more challenging prospect that requires the identification and naming of successor organisations by Home Secretaries or their international equivalents.

Fourth, even in those cases where a terrorist organisation might be discernible as such, there are additional challenges associated with the identification of individual members. Part of the issue here is the fluid structure of (some) contemporary groups, in which 'membership' has become increasingly diffuse (Hoffman 1997, 2). In the most decentred of organisations today, membership can effectively consist of little more than distant identification (Jarvis 2012).The Madrid train bombings of 2004 by individuals inspired by al Qaeda offers one well-known example. As Lia (2010, n.p.) remarks of al Qaeda: 'membership … is open to virtually everyone … As long as one is willing to accept its extremist ideology, anyone can, in principle, become an al-Qaida member'. Another factor here, however, can be the transitory commitment of individuals belonging to violent organisations. As Smith and Damphousse (2009, 477) illustrate:

> some group members affiliate with several groups over time, which makes it difficult to identify a stable membership base within a terrorist group from which to trace the group's life course. Within the extreme right, a good example is the Order. While maintaining some affiliation with the Covenant, Sword, and Arm of the Lord (CSA), many members drifted from the CSA to the newly formed Order. Additional Order members emerged from the Aryan Nations and some participants in the Order (particularly those indicted for seditious conspiracy in the aftermath of the Order's demise) maintained primary membership in the CSA and Aryan Nations and only loosely affiliated themselves with the Order.

In short, proscription regimes require political executives to successfully narrate the existence of an identifiable and coherent 'organisation' committed to a discernible and illegitimate political motive. Yet, as the above indicates, it is far from apparent that this can meaningfully be accomplished. Extremist groups elude authorities and evade designation by assuming different guises, splitting, reforming or allying with other causes. Indeed, even where an 'organisation' can be distinguished for the purposes of proscription, proving and prosecuting membership remains a sizeable challenge. In this sense, there is a widening gulf between the government's proscription apparatus, which requires the possession of 'fixed' identities by designated organisations, and the reality of porous, rapidly evolving, multiplying and fragmenting political movements.

Political issues

A second set of concerns relates to the ubiquity of political interests within the construction and implementation of proscription decisions. In the first instance, internal political considerations and discourses are often central to the identification and outlawing of organisations deemed 'terrorist' by the state. As the European Union Anti-Terror Coordinator suggested of the Kurdistan Workers' Party's (PKK) proscription, 'The reasons are political. You say that it is a criminal organization, not a political organization. That is the message' (Van de Kerckhove 2009, cited in Casier 2010). Yet, as he continued, the designation was instrumental as much as it was symbolic: 'The list can be a means to leverage, to pressure Turkey to respect its minorities and human rights' (Van de Kerckhove 2009, cited in Casier 2010). Such concerns are also, at times, tied to the opposite outcome where – as Iain Cameron (2003, 237) argues of the EU's regime – 'there can be, cynical, political reasons for not wanting to blacklist [a group]', even if regarded as 'mainly terrorist'. Although we might not be surprised to see politics intrude upon proscription regimes, it is important to bear in mind that such decisions exceed assessments of empirical threats.

A well-known example of such concerns is the criticism received by the US Foreign Terrorist Organisations list for becoming 'increasingly politicized' and shaped by the prevailing political environment (Shapiro 2007, 548), rather than by threats to US security (Nadarajah and Sriskandarajah 2005, 96). As Julie Shapiro (2007, 579) puts it: 'the only distinction between freedom fighters and terrorists may be the Executive Branch's predilection for that group or not'. Selectivity in proscription's deployment (Muller 2008, 128–129), therefore, has considerable power to shape the outcome of political struggles by depriving designated groups of recognition and support. On this view, proscription may impede peace processes (Hogg 2008, 312; Gross 2010; Sentas 2010, 17; Haspeslagh 2013) and, potentially, even shore-up oppressive regimes (Sentas 2010, 16). What is more, the politicised deployment of proscription can thereby operate in ways that appear contrary to the desired ends:

> [T]here should be no illusion about how the infusion of politics into law by this process has degraded the legal integrity of a number of proscription regimes and actively hindered the ability of third parties and the international community to resolve certain conflicts through peaceful means. (Muller 2008, 128)

Second, where internal political considerations impact heavily upon proscription decisions, so too do external, international, relationships. In the lead-up to the 2003 war in Iraq, for example, the US State Department acquiesced to Moscow's request that three Chechen groups be designated terrorist organisations amidst fears of a Russian Security Council veto on the former issue.[30] Similarly, the People's Mojahedin of Iran (PMOI) was proscribed by the United States and EU as a bridge-building attempt with President Khatami following his 1997 election in Iran (Muller 2008, 125). In that case, though, the political undertones of the designation were demonstrated rather conclusively in 2004 negotiations in Vienna aimed at limiting Iran's nuclear ambitions. Amongst several proposals to the Iranian government, EU diplomats offered to 'continue to regard the PMOI as a terrorist organization' if Iran suspended its nuclear programme.[31]

The risk, in short, is that proscription regimes effectively become pawns in broader foreign policy games, employed and adjusted for purposes other than preventing terrorism. And, as Mark Muller (2008, 125) points out, there is a real danger of this temptation towards instrumentality generating hostility amongst those caught up in these manoeuvrings:

> That is why many legal commentators have argued that whether a group is on or off a proscription list has more to do with geo politics and diplomatic relations between states than with genuine threats to a particular country's national security and the strict application of law in relation to terrorism. The UN stricture to member states to

> co-operate in countering terrorism in practice has become intertwined with a whole set of other foreign, military and strategic objectives that govern relations between states. The temptation to offset any strict application of the law relating to fighting counter terrorism in favour of achieving other desirable foreign policy goals is huge. This temptation fundamentally affects the integrity of counter terror legislation and creates real resentment and further resistance within dissident groups who are caught by measures taken on broader policy grounds.

A third political issue concerns the differential levels of influence possessed by groups at risk of proscription. The designation of the Liberation Tigers of Tamil Eelam (LTTE) as a terrorist organization by various Western states, for example, met with considerable opposition from the global Tamil diaspora, which 'lobbied hard in support of the LTTE, especially in the lead-up to the US and UK bans, even going as far as mounting a legal challenge in the USA' (Nadarajah and Sriskandarajah 2005, 97). Conversely, the Nigerian diaspora campaigned with similar gusto in the United States and beyond to *have* Boko Haram listed as a Foreign Terrorist Organisation.[32] In some instances, sustained lobbying by listed organisations led to their successful removal from lists of proscribed groups. The case of the PMOI (see above) is an instructive example: following a campaign that included reported payment of over $1.5 million to Washington lobby firms, the PMOI managed to secure removal from the US FTO list in 2012 (McGreal 2012), and from the UK and European Union terror lists in 2008 and 2009 respectively. This experience contrasts markedly with that of groups that would likely appeal their proscription but lack the financial or political resources to do so.

Where the above examples are all marked by the intrusion of politics into proscription decisions, a fourth concern relates to the absence thereof. Specifically, this refers to the lack of consultation, due process, and parliamentary oversight in a regime predicated upon a presumption in favour of the executive's proposals. In the UK, unless sufficient opposition is mobilised in Parliament, proscriptions sought by the Home Secretary are, effectively, automatically approved. Thus, when twenty-one proscribed organisations were laid before Parliament in March 2001 in a 'take it or leave it' list (Muller 2008, 125), Lord Archer protested that

Parliament could not 'oppose the inclusion of any one organisation without opposing the entire order' (*HL Hansard*, 27 March 2001, col 148). The political hazard in opposing the ostensible designation of terrorist organisations is not inconsequential. For example, Diane Abbott MP was one of a handful of MPs who had voted against the order in 2001, a decision that was raised in a BBC interview in May 2017 with Andrew Marr:

> **Andrew Marr:** Let me come onto your bit, you said, nobody votes against these kinds of things without a lot of thought. Shortly before 9/11 you voted against proscribing Al Qaeda as an organisation. That was a huge mistake on your part was it not?
>
> **Diane Abbott:** Have you actually read the legislation we were voting on?
>
> **Andrew Marr:** I have read the legislation and I've looked at the addendums as well.
>
> **Diane Abbott:** And what the legislation called for was a whole list of –
>
> **Andrew Marr:** Which I have here.
>
> **Diane Abbott:** – organisations, some of which some people would argue were not terrorist organisations but dissident organisations. And to say that because I –
>
> **Andrew Marr:** Which ones, because I've got the list here. Al Qaeda, Egyptian Islamic Jihad, the Armed Islamic Group, Harakat Mujahideen, the Liberation Tigers of Tamil, the Palestinian Islamic Jihad Group, Islamic Army of Aden, the Abu Nidal Organisation, the Kurdistan Workers Party, which of these should not be proscribed?
>
> **Diane Abbott:** Titles are one thing, but the reality of some of those groups were that they were dissidents in their country of origin, and that's why some of us were not – had they taken Al Qaeda as one thing, that would have been something. But you know –
>
> **Andrew Marr:** This is a group of really dangerous organisations from all around the world, many of whom have killed a lot of people. Lashkar-e-Taiba carried out the 2008 Mumbai attacks which killed more than 170 people. That was on the list. No list is perfect but it was a pretty good list and you voted against proscribing those groups.

Diane Abbott: Because there were groups on that list which I deemed to be dissidents rather than terror organisations. You have to give people credit for thinking about how they vote. As I said to you earlier, we're hearing about all this anti-terror legislation that Jeremy and I voted against, but we're not hearing that the Tories voted against some of the self-same legislation, particularly control orders and detention without trial.

Andrew Marr: Well, there is the list. Which of those organisations do you think should not have been proscribed? Because you know, you voted against the whole lot being proscribed because presumably some of them you thought were okay. I'm just wondering which ones you think are okay.

Diane Abbott: It's not that I thought they're okay. I thought that they were dissident organisations.[33]

The interviewer's heavy criticism of Abbott's judgement illustrates the political ramifications of the process designed for proscription, and represents a blow for the scrutiny role played by Parliament. This subjugation of parliamentary scrutiny drew further criticism from Lord McNally, who voiced concern that the sweeping powers afforded the executive by the TA 2000 had been deployed cynically:

> those who dealt with the original [Terrorism] Bill did not envisage that secondary powers would be used to hoover up, as it were, 21 organisations in a single instrument. By any standard of natural justice, that does not make sense. It means that the good, the bad and the ugly are put together … I believe that in approaching the matter in this way the Home Office has discredited the procedure from the outset. (*HL Hansard*, 27 March 2001, col 152–153)

As this suggests, the scrutiny afforded by Parliament is diminished by a process that presents a spectrum of political organisations (domestic and international) for MPs to endorse or reject *en masse*. The process is constructed to grant one individual the power to make a proscription order, without any external oversight or validation except the POAC's ability to request the Home Secretary review a decision after the fact. Each order, moreover, is put before Parliament with little or no public evidence to justify or substantiate the Home Secretary's claims that an organisation is concerned in terrorism. For some, such as Lord Marsh, the good faith of decision-makers may be sufficient to justify this sidestepping of scrutiny and oversight. As he asked in relation to the March 2001 controversy noted above:

> We know the people involved in the production of this list in this place. In addition to the noble Lord, Lord Bassam, they include Jack Straw, Robin Cook, the noble Baroness, Lady Scotland, the police, the security services, various intelligence agencies and, inevitably, the lawyers. Why should they all conspire to construct this extraordinary facade, which they knew would be highly controversial? (*HL Hansard*, 27 March 2001, col 172)

There is, however, considerable reason for caution in presuming elected representatives to be either above reproach or guardians of the national interest. As John Anderson argued seventy years ago, in relation to those agitating for the banning of the Communist Party in Australia:

> To forbid by law the propagation of a particular political view is to treat the people at large as incapable of determining for themselves the merits of different positions, and to permit a privileged section to decide what positions are to be ruled out without public discussion. (1948, 7)

Normative issues

Moving now to normative issues, proscription powers are often seen to suffer from an inability to differentiate between groups engaged in violence. The challenge of safeguarding a legitimate right to self-determination is a familiar one within the crafting of terrorism legislation (McSherry 2004, 358), despite the right to resist oppressive or alien rule constituting a well-recognised international norm. As a UN High Panel 2004 report stated explicitly, 'people under foreign occupation have a right to resistance and a definition of terrorism should not override this right' (cited in Richmond and Franks 2005, 33–34). Yet, the expansiveness and ambiguity of many statutory definitions of terrorism mean proscription powers are frequently incapable of making any such distinction (Cram 2006, 344). This, in turn, may have deleterious impact on efforts at peace-building (Gross 2011), on conflict resolution (Haspeslagh 2013) and for resistance struggles (Muller 2008). This lack of nuance poses ramifications for the fundamentals of democracy, too, not least where organisations designated terrorist by the United States have achieved electoral success, whether Hezbollah in Lebanon, Hamas in Palestine and the Unified Communist Party of Nepal (Gross 2011). In short, while the right to rebel might be desirable at times, even via violence, movements attempting to invoke principles such as self-determination are often 'routinely criminalised through proscription' (Muller 2008, 120).

A similar challenge emerges for refugees fleeing state violence, where proscription lists increase the risk of their asylum claim being rejected. In 2008, the Council of Europe issued a rebuke of states that cynically used blacklists to deny otherwise legitimate claims of asylum:[34]

> The Assembly finds that the procedural and substantive standards currently applied by the UNSC and by the Council of the European Union, despite some recent improvements, in no way fulfil the minimum standards laid down above and violate the fundamental principles of human rights and the rule of law. 6.1. Concerning procedure, it must be noted and strongly deplored that even the members of the committee deciding on the blacklisting of an individual are not fully informed of the reasons for a request put forward by one member. The person or group concerned is usually neither informed of the request, nor given the possibility to be heard, nor even necessarily informed about the decision taken – until he or she first attempts to cross a border or use a bank account. There are no procedures for an independent review of decisions taken or for compensation for infringements of rights. Such a procedure is totally arbitrary and has no credibility whatsoever.[35]

A further concern relates to the transgression of domestic common law norms, and the fear that proscription legislation criminalises individuals for who they are, rather than for what they have done. McSherry's (2004; also Allen 1996) critique of proscription in Australia, for example, argues that an important premise behind the rule of law is that governments should punish criminal conduct, not criminal types (McSherry 2004). In the scrutiny of the Terrorism Bill, the UK MP Simon Hughes expressed similar apprehension:

> I hope that the amendments will give us the chance to address the principled argument that it is actions that should give rise to criminal offences, not indications of support for political organisations or involvement in them. To include being involved in something or expressing support for something takes the criminal law much further than is traditional. The criminal law normally requires both intention and action. (Simon Hughes, Standing Committee D, 20 January 2000)

The concern here is that proscription creates a crime from an individual's 'status' – i.e. as a member of a proscribed organisation – rather than any act, or *actus reas*: 'the outer physical, behavioural, objective ingredient of crime' (Husak 1991, see also Bronitt 2003).

As this suggests, there exist very real concerns over the way proscription laws transgress rights to self-determination as well as domestic legal protections. Security concerns have frequently been used to legitimate such developments. Yet, the circumvention or erosion of parliamentary scrutiny explored above – including via the laying of orders containing multiple organisations for wholesale approval in the UK – renders the detection and mitigation of proscription abuses far more difficult. As Lord McNally put it during one proscription debate:

> I am not content to allow Ministers simply to pat us on the head, give us a knowing look to the effect that they are in receipt of secret information which, if only we could see it, would make our toes curl and, therefore, we should nod through every piece of new legislation that they want. (*HL Hansard*, 27 March 2001, col 152–153)

Efficacy and unintended consequences

It might be possible – depending on one's political commitments – to dismiss all the above were there sufficient evidence that proscription worked as a counter-terrorism strategy. One might, for example, approach the lack of parliamentary safeguards as a necessary precaution subsumable to concerns of national security. Alternatively, the problems of identifying and labelling organisations might be viewed either as incidental to the broader task of prevention, or as resolvable via a deliberate and strategic essentialism that involved acting *as if* terrorist organisations exist as such. The difficulty, however, is that evidence-based assessments of the effectiveness of proscription are, in the first instance, scarce. And, in the second instance, generally sceptical of the value proscription poses.

In the context of Northern Ireland, for example, Walker argues that proscription powers were of 'marginal utility' in reducing political violence (2000, 15). Despite its proscription, the IRA managed to maintain widespread publicity of, and support for, its cause. Others go further and advance convincing arguments that proscription regimes actually enhance the legitimacy and profile of terrorist organisations. Nadarajah and Sriskandarajah (2005, 97), for instance, suggest that 'proscriptions may even have consolidated the resolve of the Tamil diaspora organisations to support the Tamil nationalist project and the LTTE'. Mary Baber, in a House of Commons Library research paper, likewise argues that groups waging violent campaigns often seek to provoke government into the use of heavy-handed measures and 'hope the use of these measures will alienate the general public and possibly lead to greater public sympathy for the bombers' cause' (1999, 11). This perspective was expressed by former IRA commander Jim McVeigh who claimed that the UK government's internment policy in Northern Ireland was 'among the best recruiting tools the IRA ever had' (cited in Blackbourn 2008, 69). Proscription may play a similar role, enhancing the profile of 'crackpot groups' who 'would be delighted with the publicity if a Secretary of State were foolish enough to dignify them with proscription in the first place' (Walker 2000, 15).

A related concern is the resentment and alienation proscription may cause within diaspora communities sympathetic to opposition groups proscribed in their host country (Pantazis and Pemberton 2009; Sentas 2010, 16). For Muller, 'The illegitimate or legally botched use of these proscription procedures is dangerous as it breeds long-term resentment among many exiled dissident groups and communities' (Muller 2008, 129). His assessment of the banning of the Kurdistan Workers' Party (PKK) goes further still, arguing, 'If anything the manner by which the proscription regime was deployed merely fuelled the PKK's eventual return to violence as all avenues for dialogue were closed' (Muller 2008, 128). On this view, proscription 'can undermine peace efforts, exacerbate violence and further entrench and broaden conflict' (Hocking 2003; also Shapiro 2007; Hogg 2008, 312). Indeed, the stigmatising effect of proscription can spill-over onto domestic, often minority, constituencies that might subsequently be seen as 'guilty by association' with newly proscribed groups: 'anyone or any activities associated with [proscribed] organizations can now be criminalized. It is at this point that the [Terrorism] Act serves to create a "suspect community"' (Pantazis and Pemberton 2009, 652; also Sentas 2010, 16).

Within this scholarship, we have seen the recent emergence of a small number of studies focusing specifically on the US FTO list. Chou (2015, 1131), for instance, offers an empirical analysis of US designations to argue there is a disproportionate designation of weak and non-representative groups, of 'Islamist' groups, and of groups in countries with greater state capacity. Phillips (2015), in a more conceptual vein, argues that the non-representativeness of the FTO list may have broader implications in encouraging inaccurate generalisations about terrorist groups amongst researchers. Audrey Cronin's (2003) earlier analysis for Congress traces a series of the US FTO list's advantages and disadvantages, noting its provision of legal clarity for counter-terrorism purposes (an advantage) to its inflexibility and risk of inconsistency (as disadvantages).

Because the empirical evidence underpinning this work remains limited, we might approach some of its assumptions and inferences with some caution. Such analyses do, however, offer an important warning to policy officials who, in the absence of evidence to the contrary, continue to outlaw organisations on the understanding that proscription contributes to a reduction in terrorist activity. If the opposite is in fact true, then the sacrifice of political safeguards and social freedoms for the sake of security is even more questionable. For, as the UK's former Independent Reviewer of Terrorist Legislation argued, 'the utility of proscription must always be balanced against the freedoms of speech and association' (Lord Carlile 2010, 14).

Cross-national differences

It is also, finally, important to mention a small number of broadly comparative studies on the various differences of process, outcomes and consequences that accompany terrorist designation across time and space. Beck and Miner, for example, compare lists maintained by the United States, the United Kingdom and the European Union to argue that 'the organizational profile of a militant group, including its strategies and ideological basis, will affect the likelihood of designation net of all other factors' (2013, 839). Haspeslagh (2013) adds the United Nations' list to those studied by Beck and Milner in her exploration of the global proscription regime's impact upon engagement with armed groups in the context of peace processes. Freedman (2010) offers a wider if shallower analysis, identifying significant discrepancies in the lists of six 'major' countries and those of the European Union and the United Nations. These discrepancies are attributed, in part, to regional security concerns such as the Indian listing of groups based in Pakistan. A more recent illustrative example of such concerns might be found from June 2017, when Bahrain, Saudi Arabia, Egypt and UAE blacklisted three Qatari organisations as supporters of terrorism: the Qatar Charity, the Sheikh Eid Al Thani Charitable Foundation and the Sheikh Thani bin Abdullah Foundation for Humanitarian Services. This blacklisting was notable not only for its overtones of inter-state rivalry, but also because one of the groups, the Qatar Charity, is closely linked into UN-funded programmes. Perhaps unsurprisingly, the UN rejected the blacklisting.

Conclusion

As the above suggests, proscription powers cause some consternation amongst scholars, policymakers, journalists and activists for a number of reasons. These include, on the one hand, fears that proscription: (1) is ill-suited or inappropriate for its nebulous targets; (2) may intrude upon other security or political goals; (3) is unlikely to deter or prevent terrorism; (4) may increase the resolve of or support for listed organisations; and (5) is used inconsistently – perhaps antagonistically – between states. A second set of – rather different – concerns focus on proscription's implications for fairness, rights and justice. These include fears that the power: (1) might be employed for reasons other than its stated purpose (countering terrorism); (2) is employed with a lack of political, judicial or public oversight; (3) may have unequal outcomes – being more easily resisted by well-resourced or well-positioned organisations; (4) may intrude upon rights to resistance and/or self-determination movements; (5) may complicate asylum applications; and (6) likely impacts upon common law norms.

This is, clearly, a significant list, about which three broad points might be made. First, as argued already above, although this power is much criticised, it remains rather less researched and debated than many alternatives within the contemporary counter-terrorism experience. There is, for instance, far less scholarship on proscription than, say, extraordinary rendition or drone strikes which have far more successfully captured the attention of academics, activists, publics and journalists alike. Second, the fact that this list *is* much criticised is, itself, distinctive within research on counter-terrorism which has – historically, at least – tended to be fairly sympathetic towards national security ambitions and projects. Third, and most importantly for our purposes, the above list of criticisms effectively boil down to two primary concerns, characterised here as efficacy and ethics. Where the former asks 'does proscription work' in inhibiting the actions and ambitions of terrorist organisations; the latter asks 'is proscription legitimate' given its implications for rights, justice, peace processes and so forth. These concerns are clearly significant, but our argument in the next chapter is that we might also ask rather different questions of this power.

Notes

1 According to Bourne and Bértoa (2014), since the end of the Second World War several countries have not banned political parties, including Cyprus, Denmark, Estonia, Finland, Hungary, Ireland, Malta, Luxembourg, Portugal, Slovenia, Serbia, Sweden and Macedonia.

2 *Legal vs. Illegal Status: Some Considerations Relevant to Banning a Communist Party*, Senior Research Staff on International Communism, Central Intelligence Agency, 4 January 1957, pp. 25–26, NARA, CREST CIA-RDP80.

3 Despite the strong language employed by its Congressional drafters, the Act was broadly held to be imprecise in its clauses and definitions; a shortcoming most clearly determined in its specification of the Communist Party of America, which left untouched the legal status of other communist organisations in the United States (see Franz 1982, 71).

4 Amongst communist states, of course, the liberalising ideals of democracy (and the even higher authority of religion) were prohibited. For such states, the Communist Party was the only possible political organisation, thus any opposing political entities were precluded from participating in the political process; and, more often than not, were ruthlessly pursued and crushed by government security forces.

5 Available at: www.un.org/sc/suborg/en/sanctions/un-sc-consolidated-list#entities (accessed 20 March 2018).

6 The text of *The Immigration and Nationality Act* is available at: www.uscis.gov/ilink/docView/SLB/HTML/SLB/0–0–0–1/0–0–0–29/0–0–0–5017.html (accessed 18 February 2018).

7 Mackintosh and Macdonald (2013).

8 See: www.nia.gov.in/banned-terrorist-organisations.htm (accessed 18 February 2018).

9 See: https://nacta.gov.pk/proscribed-organizations/ (accessed 18 February 2018).

10 See: www.justice.gov.il/En/Units/FBPS/DNFBPDuties/Pages/List-of-Terrorist-Organizations-and-Individuals.aspx (accessed 18 December 2019).

11 See: http://en.nac.gov.ru/unified-federal-list-organizations-including-foreign-and-international-designated-terrorist-courts.html (accessed 18 February 2018).

12 www.egm.gov.tr/en/pages/terrorist_organizations.aspx (accessed 18 February 2018).

13 Unlike other states, these states have jointly designated individuals and entities as terrorist, and released this list through the media and not on state-run websites. See: https://english.alarabiya.net/en/News/gulf/2017/06/09/Arab-countries-release-list-of-terrorist-financiers-supported-by-Qatar.html (accessed 18 December 2019).

14 Available at: www.un.org/sc/ctc/resources/databases/recommended-international-practices-codes-and-standards/united-nations-security-council-resolution-1373–2001/ (accessed 18 February 2018).

15 2(d) Prevent those who finance, plan, facilitate or commit terrorist acts from using their respective territories for those purposes against other States or their citizens.

16 Commonwealth Secretariat. *Model Legislative Provisions on Measures to Combat Terrorism*. September 2002. Criminal Law Section, Legal and Constitutional Affairs Division. Available at: http://thecommonwealth.org/sites/default/files/key_reform_pdfs/P153470_21_ROL_Model_Terrorism_Provisions.pdf (accessed 15 March 2018).

17 We refer to this methodology to trace policy or legal antecedents as Lexical Transfer Analysis. The methodology uses search engines' Boolean function to determine if and where specific phrases or words are copied in different jurisdictions or institutional contexts. The methodology highlights links between documents – such as legislation – but does not indicate the direction of lexical transfer. Simple chronology usually provides a clue to the direction of transfer: here the UK legislation was published in 1999, the UN best practice in 2001, indicating the UN as the borrowing agent.
18 Anti-Terrorism Ordinance (ATO), 2008.
19 Unlawful Activities (Prevention) Act, 1967. Central Government Act. Section 21 in the Prevention of Terrorism Act 2002.
20 The Prevention of Terrorism Act 2002.
21 Terrorism (Prevention) Act 2011.
22 Prevention of Terrorism Act 2002.
23 Anti-Terrorism Order 2011.
24 Anti-Terrorism Act 2008.
25 The Suppression of Terrorism Act 2008.
26 Prevention of Terrorism Act 2004.
27 Prevention of Terrorism 2012.
28 For example, the total number of groups on the US list of designated foreign terrorist organisations currently stands at sixty-one, the UK's list at eight-eight, fifty-two in Canada, and in Australia twenty-one. Only sixteen groups are proscribed across all four of these countries listed above.
29 The designation of the Qatar Charity by Gulf states is a case in point (see below), but perhaps the most prominent example is the People's Mojahedin Organization of Iran (PMOI). The Iranian opposition group, which is also known as the Mojahedin-e Khalq (or MeK), has long been described as a terrorist organisation by the Iranian government and was designated as such by the United States in 1997, the UK in 2001 and the EU in 2002. Yet its 'terrorist' designation has since been subject to intense lobbying by US Congressmen and UK MPs. It was deproscribed by the UK in 2008, the EU in 2009 and removed from the US FTO list in 2012.
30 A. Koppel and E. Labott, 'U.S. puts 3 Chechen groups on terrorist list', *CNN*, 28 February 2003. Available at: http://edition.cnn.com/2003/US/02/28/chechens.terror/ (accessed 18 December 2019).

31 The EU's offer to Iran is cited by an Australian Senator in a parliamentary debate, 29 November 2004, p. 126. Available at: http://parlinfo.aph.gov.au/parlInfo/search/display/display.w3p;query=Id%3A%22chamber%2Fhansards%2F2004-11-29%2F0139%22 (accessed 18 February 2018).

32 Boko Haram was formally banned in the UK in July 2013.

33 Andrew Marr Show, BBC, 28 May 2017. Available at: http://news.bbc.co.uk/2/shared/bsp/hi/pdfs/28051703.pdf (accessed 18 February 2018).

34 The following year, the UNHCR issued a similar warning: 'It should be noted that lists established by the international community should not generally be treated as reversing the burden of proof, in view of the fact that the evidentiary threshold for inclusion in at least some cases may not meet the standard of proof required for exclusion cases.' UNHCR Statement on Article 1F of the 1951 Convention, 2009, p. 30.

35 Parliamentary Assembly of the Council of Europe, Res. 1597 (2008): United Nations Security Council and European Union blacklists. Available at: http://eur-lex.europa.eu/legal-content/en/TXT/PDF/?uri=CELEX:32017D1426&from=EN (accessed 18 December 2019)

3 Theorising proscription: discourse, argumentation and ritual

The preceding chapters highlighted the longevity and reach of contemporary proscription regimes, as well as the surprising lack of concerted scholarly reflection on the place of these powers in relation to the modern state, and indeed liberal democracy. As we saw, the UK's own history of proscription is one that we can trace back to the earliest days of the criminal code, although the mechanism is no less significant an expression of political authority today. We argued, therefore, that proscription is reflective of embedded structures of power and authority that have contributed to the emergence of the modern sovereign state. Its significance for how we narrate the state's adherence to the rule of law, for free political expression and association, for transparent decision-making, for security, and for political rights and participation can barely be overstated.

The concluding discussion of the previous chapter then highlighted how scholarship on proscription remains relatively unusual in the context of counter-terrorism politics. In the first instance, this literature is unusual because of its sparseness. A remarkable, and frequently discussed, feature of academic debate in the post-9/11 period, in particular, has been the dramatic increase of scholarship on terrorism and counter-terrorism. Young and Findlay (2011, 1), for example, begin their review article by noting that 'the amount of research on terrorism being published in political science journals has doubled several times over what it was pre-9/11'. A long-standing expert in this field, Martha Crenshaw (2014,

556–557), similarly suggests, 'it is extraordinary to see that what was once a marginal subject for social science has developed into a full-fledged program of "terrorism studies"' (see also Silke 2004). As she (Crenshaw 2014, 564) continues:

> Before the 9/11 attacks, almost none of the academics working in the fields of international relations and foreign policy thought of terrorism as a threat to national or international security. Their focus was primarily on the interests and power of states, not shadowy underground conspiracies or the weak states that might assist them. After 9/11 it became imperative to understand the phenomenon of terrorism.

Marc Sageman (2014, 566) makes a similar argument in a more immediately critical vein as part of a provocative polemic on the 'stagnation' of terrorism research: 'the post-9–11 money surge into terrorism studies and the rush of new-comers into the field had a deleterious effect on research'. Proscription, then, is distinctive within (counter-)terrorism studies, in part, because it is yet to generate such a 'rush' of analysts and researchers.

A second distinctive feature of work on proscription, however, is its largely – although not entirely – critical emphasis. As outlined in Chapter 2, much scholarship on this power has tended either to deploy a sceptical stance on proscription's utility for enhancing national security. Or, to express significant concerns about the implications of proscription for normative, legal or political rights and protections. In a particularly critical admonition, Jenny Hocking asserts:

> Proscription is the end product of a fear of democracy itself, a desire to limit the realm of legitimate political debate, to exclude political voices and to structure politics in a manner which is, by its very design, anti-democratic. Whilst this may usher in a system which is outwardly secure, reassuring, predictable, it cannot any longer be considered democratic. Proscription is perhaps the classic example of the interests of security superseding the interests of individuals; effectively executive government will, on the grounds of security, determine who can and who cannot participate in the political sphere. (2003, 369)

This broadly critical stance contrasts with much other terrorism literature, which has – at least until very recently – been dominated by a discernibly problem-solving orientation aimed at facilitating or improving counter-terrorism activities (Gunning 2007; Jarvis 2009a; Jackson *et al* 2011; Jarvis 2019a). The critical orientation within scholarship on proscription, we argue, boils down to two overarching concerns, which we characterise as concerns of efficacy and ethics. Under the former are discussions about whether proscription orders impact on the provision of (national) security from terrorism: does the listing of a specific organisation significantly reduce its ability or ambition to commit future acts of terrorism at home or abroad? Under the latter may be found primarily normative discussions about the extent to which proscription powers destabilise citizenship protections, erode democratic processes or reduce the scope for political dissent.

Such questions of efficacy and ethics are clearly significant given the importance of legitimacy and utility to any serious assessment of security policy. The broadly sceptical stance within these discussions, moreover, is at once refreshing vis-à-vis much work within terrorism studies, and one that we share in the chapters that follow. At the same time, the prominence of these two foci within the (again, relatively restricted) literature on proscription has important implications for the types of question that have been asked of this power. Put otherwise, a concern with issues of ethics and effectiveness in relation to proscription has significantly shaped how this power is approached and evaluated. There are at least three examples of this worth mentioning here.

First, is a tendency towards – or, more generously, a risk of – reification in existing work on proscription in which the characters in proscription's dramas (not least 'the national self' and various 'terrorist others') tend to be essentialised and treated as already-existing entities who are engaged in a dynamic interplay of banner and banned. So – to take two examples from the discussion that follows – the UK state and al Qaeda tend to be approached as fully formed, coherent entities within this research, which leads to an emphasis on how the former should respond to the threat posed by the latter. This tendency, we argue, risks overlooking the extent to which proscription (as well as other counter-terrorism powers) functions as part of the process through which such identities are themselves (re-)produced. Proscription debates, as argued in Chapter 6, are saturated by attempts to story or perform the British identity as a liberal, democratic, tolerant, moderate and responsible actor. This is done, of course, by juxtaposing this identity to various antagonistic, 'terrorist' others who are characterised as illiberal, undemocratic, immoderate and irresponsible. In this sense, these debates contribute to the making of these identities, and proscription should be seen as a process which helps bring these actors into being, rather than a tool or an instrument employed by a pre-existing actor against another.

A second limitation is that much existing literature tends to focus on the outcomes or consequences of proscription, rather than the processes through which groups become added to specific lists. This focus, in part, reflects a recognition – and a concern – with the *politics* of proscription, precisely because it encourages us to reflect on the fact that the listing of organisations is, ultimately, a decision or choice. Such choices might be contingent upon specific national contexts, or entirely unrelated (geo)political concerns, or transnational alliances, but they are precisely that: contingent, not automatic. While clearly significant, this emphasis on outcomes also – in our view unfortunately – militates against a questioning of the politics that takes place *before* those decisions are made. Yet this politics matters, we will argue in the following chapters, not only for deepening our analysis of this particular policy process, but, in addition, because it sheds light on broader dynamics around the exercise of state power, and the relations between branches of government.

A third limitation – really an extension of the second – is that literature on proscription tends to focus on causal rather than constitutive questions. Drawing, here, on Alexander Wendt's (1998) distinction, causal questions refer to 'why' or 'how' questions of the sort enquiring into some form of change that has taken place between a before and an after. Thus, questions of efficacy – such as 'how does proscribing ISIS make us safer?' – *and* questions of ethics – 'how does proscription deleteriously impact upon freedom of speech?' – *both* represent causal questions akin to the examples given by Wendt (1998, 105) 'how are babies made?' or 'how does the AIDS virus spread?'. As he summarises: 'In providing answers to causal questions, in saying that "X causes Y", we assume three things: 1) that X and Y exist independent of each other, 2) that X precedes Y in time, and 3) that but for X, Y would not have occurred' (Wendt 1998, 105). Constitutive questions, in contrast, tend to ask 'how possible' or 'what' questions, in order to unpack the structural contexts within which things emerge, and to provide insight into 'what it is that instantiates some phenomenon, not why that phenomenon comes about' (Wendt 1998, 105). Such questions – Wendt's (1998, 106) examples include 'how is it possible for a gas to have a temperature?' and 'how is it possible for the Earth to keep the moon in its orbit?' – encourage enquiry into the conditions of possibility behind that which is under scrutiny. And, as Roxanne Doty notes, such questions allow for exploration of far more of the process through which political outcomes emerge by calling into question the field of possible outcomes against which decisions were made:

> What is explained is not why a particular outcome obtained, but rather how the subjects, objects, and interpretive dispositions were socially constructed such that certain practices were made possible. (Doty 1993, 298)

Our approach in this book shares such an emphasis on constitutive questions. Fundamentally, we have set out to ask how it is that proscription emerges as an appropriate, legitimate and perhaps necessary response to terrorism within the contemporary British state? Answering this question, however, involves engaging also with prior questions such as: how is that particular organisations become added to the United Kingdom's list of proscribed groups at specific times; and, how do parliamentary debates around proscription allow for certain types of political intervention or argument (while militating against others)? Engaging with such questions in turn requires investigation of the symbolic, discursive and rhetorical components of proscription, as well as the productivity of power relations within Parliament itself (Doty 1993, 299). Such an approach therefore takes us beyond the three limitations mentioned above – (1) a risk of reification; (2) an emphasis on proscription's outcomes; and (3) a search for causality in the politics of proscription – because, as Doty (1993, 299) continues, it facilitates inquiry into the production 'of meanings, subject identities, their interrelationships, and a range of imaginable conduct … [interrogating the] practices that enable social actors to act, to frame policy as they do, and to wield the capabilities they do'.

In the remainder of this chapter, we now briefly situate our efforts to do this within relevant theoretical work on critical security studies, critical terrorism studies, discourse theory and political ritual. This, we show, sets up our analysis of statements, questions, identity claims and parliamentary ritual in the empirical chapters that follow. We end this discussion with a brief discussion of our methodological framework, outlining as explicitly as possible some of the assumptions of, and limitations to, our approach.

Conceptualising and constructing proscription in Parliament

Our effort to shift focus towards constitutive questions around proscription of the sort discussed above builds, most immediately, on a contemporary critical scholarship around terrorism and counter-terrorism. This work – a lot of which self-identifies as 'critical terrorism studies' – has sought to take seriously the performative and discursive movements through which counter-terrorism powers are produced, framed and subsequently 'sold' to various audiences. Although it is possible to identify a number of important antecedents to this literature (see, especially, Zulaika and Douglass 1996), much of this contemporary work may be read as a product of the post-9/11 war on terror, and its dramatically Manichean, exceptionalist framing by the George W. Bush administration (see Neal 2010), memorably referred to by Peter Singer (2004) as 'The President of Good and Evil'.

Richard Jackson's (2005) book *Writing the War on Terrorism* offered one of the first – and certainly one of the most influential – explorations of this paradigm's discursive parameters. In his book, Jackson provides a detailed tracing of the moments that went into framing this war's parameters, justifications, characters and stakes (political, strategic, moral) within the language of the Bush administration and other influential actors. Subsequent work in similar vein has helped to extend Jackson's account, including by offering further analysis of the workings of political language within the US context (e.g. Jarvis 2009b), and by exploring additional, related, case studies including – amongst others – that of the United Kingdom (Holland 2012; Heath-Kelly 2013; Fisher 2015), the European Union (Baker-Beall 2016), Central Asia (Horsman

2005) and Morocco (Bartolucci 2010). While these contributions have taken as their primary focus the discourse of professional politicians (spoken and written), research with a related ethos has also explored constructions of terrorism (as a specific security threat) and terrorists (as a form of identity) in other discursive sites, including – amongst many others – in the print media (Spencer 2010), popular culture (Croft 2006), video games (Robinson 2012, 2015) and academia (Stampnitzky 2013).

This sketch, of course, does scant justice to the volume and quality of contemporary work in this area (see Jackson 2016 for a fuller exploration of critical terrorism studies research). That notwithstanding, if we approach this research collectively (see Jarvis 2016) it can be seen as amounting to a sustained effort to identify, interpret and deconstruct terrorism discourse and the implications this has for social and political life (e.g. Jackson 2005; Jarvis 2009b; Holland 2012). Amongst other things, this research demonstrates: first, that 'terrorism' can be thought about, represented and produced in different ways: there is no objectivity in constructions of this threat. And, second, that an intimate connection exists between conceptions and constructions of terrorism, on the one hand, and responses to this threat, on the other, with the former helping make possible the latter. Thus:

> it is the act of producing, constructing or labelling something 'terrorist' – be it a bombing or a hijacking – that transforms any particular bombing or hijacking into an act of terrorism … In our efforts to make sense of the world around us, we create the world. And our creations are neither inevitable, nor are they neutral. They involve choices and exclusions, such that understanding violence in one way involves refusing, forgetting, or failing to understand violence otherwise. (Jarvis 2019a, 341)

The importance of this work, for the arguments developed in this book, is that it encourages us to take seriously the ways in which (counter-)terrorism is spoken, represented, performed or justified. Although scholarship such as this – like similar work in other areas of Political Science, International Relations and beyond – has faced predictable accusations of discursive reductionism (e.g. Stokes 2009; Joseph 2011) as well as (related) criticisms of epistemological or moral relativism (e.g. Jones and Smith 2009), it has unquestionably contributed to an opening up of terrorism research to the legitimacy of new types of question, methodology and research agenda (Jarvis 2009a, 2019a). Notable within this – and speaking directly to our argument in this book – is a highlighting of the mechanisms through which knowledge of terrorism is fabricated, packaged and disseminated, and the importance thereof.

This broad emphasis means that much of this critical terrorism research may be characterised as sharing a broadly constructivist orientation towards security politics. Constructivism, as approached here, refers not to a specific theoretical framework from which the world may be known, understood or explained. Rather, we use the term to describe an orientation or commitment to viewing the world and its constituents as something which is produced or 'made' in the efforts of situated actors to render it meaningful. Steffano Guzzini's (2000, 174) summary, in which he argues that 'constructivism is epistemologically about the social construction of knowledge and ontologically about the (social) construction of the social world', remains a useful one in its foregrounding the need to take seriously the ways in which reality *and* our ideas about reality are made, and made meaningful. This, as Guzzini (2000, 174) notes, involves working with an intersubjective analytical framework, in that these meaning-making practices are to be found in the interactions of subjects, not inside the heads of isolated, atomised agents. Analysing such practices in turn requires engagement with 'the role of ideas, norms, knowledge, culture, and argument in politics' (Finnemore and Sikkink 2001, 392), in order 'to "denaturalize" the social world, that is, to empirically discover and reveal how the institutions and practices and identities that people take as natural, given, or matter of fact, are, in fact, the product of human agency, of social construct' (Hopf 1998, 182).

Our analysis in the chapters that follow begins from such a constructivist stance, in which we emphasise the importance of meaning and constitutivity within proscription outcomes (Epstein 2011, 329). Approached thus, threats and their referents (those identities or phenomena that are deemed to be threatened) are understood as entities which are manufactured or constructed within the 'games' or 'dramas' of security politics, rather than objective, pre-existing or natural phenomena. Such actors and their identities – prominent amongst which, in our case, are 'states', 'parliaments' and 'terrorists' – are not given, but 'made' through a constant, never-ending process of (re)production which takes place 'by stepping into a particular subject-position carved out by a discourse' (Epstein 2011, 344). Discourses, here, therefore play a performative role in the creation of social reality in a manner that is neither predetermined nor fixed.

Our discursive approach to proscription, then, seeks to build on, and extend, related constructivist work around security and terrorism. It does so, in part, by attempting to resist the – very understandable – temptation within much of this work to focus attention upon the most structurally privileged of (socio-)political actors: political executives (see also Bubandt 2005; Jarvis and Lister 2013; Jarvis 2019b). US presidential discourse on terrorism, in particular, has been the subject of sustained – and important – analysis (e.g. Jackson 2005; Winkler 2012), which is, perhaps, unsurprising given the US' position in the global order and its centrality to the post-9/11 'war on terror'. Similarly top-down approaches, however, are evident in associated, if equally important, analyses of the language and rhetoric of the prime ministers of states such as the UK (e.g. Kettell 2013) and Australia (e.g.; De Castella *et al.* 2009; Holland 2010).

Although this emphasis on executives is, as noted above, understandable, it also risks reproducing a rather specific image of political topography in which world-making power is construed as being concentrated in the hands of a few decision-makers. As the Critical Security Studies scholar Ken Booth (2007, 149) has argued – in a point whose legitimacy resonates beyond his immediate focus on the 'Copenhagen School' model of securitization:

> Securitization studies therefore suffer from being elitist. What matters above all for the school is 'top leaders', 'states', 'threatened elites' and 'audiences' with agenda-making power. Those without discourse-making power are disenfranchised, unable to join the securitization game.

One problem with the emphasis on executives in approaches such as securitization studies is that knowledge of terrorism today – and indeed subsequent responses to the threat posed by terrorism – is formulated and enacted by a far more complex set of dynamics than narrowly top-down models of political agency suggest. 'Terrorism' is constructed in a complex discursive field in which numerous subjects play multiple, varying and, at times, unpredictable roles. These subjects include – amongst others in an extremely wide cast – journalists, academics, writers of popular culture, police forces, border guards, speech-writers, think-tanks, civil servants, armed forces, non-governmental organisations and, indeed, 'ordinary' members of the public. They also include one category of actor – the focus of this book – that has, to date, remained largely neglected within critical work on security and terrorism (although, see Huysmans 2006; Huysmans and Buonfino 2008; Neal 2012; Fisher 2015; Neal 2019): legislators or parliamentarians.

This lack of engagement with the role of legislators as co-producers of terrorism discourse is a little surprising for two reasons. First, and most simply, legislators are obviously and explicitly political actors whose responsibilities include the formulation, consideration and (depending upon where one, quite literally, sits in the UK context, at least) opposition to national security policy and law. Since the passage of the already-extensive TA 2000 in the United Kingdom, for instance, Parliament has passed multiple major pieces of counter-terrorism legislation including: the Anti-terrorism, Crime and Security Act 2001; the Prevention of Terrorism Act 2005; the Terrorism Act 2006; the Counter-Terrorism Act 2008; and the Counter-terrorism and Security Act 2015. Although the extent of parliamentary scrutiny around any of these Acts is difficult formally to measure (see Bright 2015, for one effort to do so), each of these efforts to refashion the UK's counter-terrorism machinery was fundamentally shaped by the work of parliamentarians in the House of Commons Chamber, and, of course, beyond.

A second reason we might have expected more work on the role of legislators is their engagement in a direct relationship with the political executives upon whom much of the relevant literature has, to date, focused. This relationship is brought clearly into focus in recent work on security and the executive/legislative dynamic; a common argument being that the former has managed to wrestle power from the latter in the context of the war on terror, with potential costs for public legitimacy, amongst other things (Shephard 2009). The relationship between these two branches of government is, of course, a complicated one in the United Kingdom. First, because the executive is itself drawn from Parliament (Neal 2012, 362), and, second, because the latter is frequently capable of securing procedural or policy concessions from the former (Shephard 2009). As such, parliamentary *debates*, specifically, offer a potentially rather promising case through which to explore and unpack the dynamics of security politics (see also Neal 2019). This is, not least, because – in the case of proscription – the extension of these powers to hitherto unlisted organisations takes place within discrete and identifiable contexts with immediately traceable consequences. And, crucially, the nature of such consequences – including the banning of identified groups from a designated territory and the criminalisation of membership of those groups – speak to precisely the kinds of security logic and outcome – boundary drawing, the exclusion of enemies, exceptional powers, interruptions to the normal workings of liberal democracies – that are presupposed by much critical work around security.

Discourse, argument, question, identity

Having situated our research, it will be useful now to offer a more detailed account of our analytical and methodological framework and its constituents. Beginning with the former, the book proceeds in two stages. We begin with a tripartite discourse analysis of *arguments*, *questions* and *identity formation* as these emerge within parliamentary proscription debates. Then follows a second stage in which we conceptualise these debates – as a whole – as an important example of political *ritual*. Figure 3.1 provides a summary of our framework.

Our specific analytical starting point comes from contemporary theories of discourse (e.g. Foucault 1986, 2002; Laclau 1990; Laclau and Mouffe 2001). Discourses, here, are seen to constitute relatively consistent systems of meaning that serve – temporarily and sometimes precariously – to stabilise social reality. As such, there is no automatic correspondence between the world 'as it is' and the efforts of social actors – in our case parliamentarians – to make sense of the world. Understandings of the world and the components of that world – which include, in this example, proscription, terrorists, parliament and liberal democracy – are both made possible *and* delimited by the availability of particular discourses which impose coherence and intelligibility upon that which is possible. This does not mean, however, that discourses are immaterial

Figure 3.1 Analytical framework

	Chapter 4	Chapter 5	Chapter 6
Stage 1	In Chapter 4 we consider the *arguments*, assertions, rationales and justifications that are made by parliamentarians about the principle, function or purpose of proscription (e.g. as a strategy of deterrence; or an infringement on human rights). Our analysis explores how these arguments are made rhetorically, and how they function performatively as a shared rehearsal of proscription's importance.	Chapter 5 turns to the ways parliamentarians ask *questions* of the executive within these debates. Our emphasis here is on the significance of the very visible presentation of scrutiny or contestation, arguing this is both heavily circumscribed, and productive for the (re)production of the UK' s liberal democratic self-identity.	Chapter 6 focuses on identity constructions relating to self and other within these debates, including via specific metaphors and tropes. We trace the emergence of a consistent, yet contestable antagonism between: (1) the liberal, democratic UK self which is moderate, cautious, and respectful of difference; and (2) a set of apolitical, sometimes evil, immoderate and intractable, terrorist others bent on waging and celebrating violence against states such as the UK.
Stage 2: Chapter 7	*Political ritual* concerns the confluence of symbolism, authority and beliefs, performed by privileged actors within established procedures of political institutions. Chapter 7 approaches proscription debates as contributors to a ritual that is located within an acknowledgement of Parliament as highly bounded institution steeped in tradition, history and symbolism. We adduce that actors – both executive and non-executive parliamentarians – occupy roles that are conferred upon them, along with political, social and procedural expectations thereof. The framework is empirically derived from the earlier exploration of arguments, questions and subject positionings in Chapters 4, 5 and 6. From this, we identify four key aspects of this ritual, relating to *orchestration*; *constitutivity*; *performativity*; and *sedimentation*.		

or purely ideational. Rather, that the material world becomes relevant and meaningful to social actors via discourse. In an example offered by Laclau and Mouffe (1987, 82) 'If I kick a spherical object in the street or if I kick a ball in a football match, the *physical* fact is the same, but its meaning is different'.

As Laclau, Foucault and others have shown us, assuming that meaning is produced – or imposed upon the world – discursively does not entail any commitment to structural determinism. No attempt to stabilise the meaning of anything will ever be complete or completely successful – precisely because there is no fixed foundation or horizon 'beneath' our efforts to make sense of the world. However stable or coherent a discursive framework appears at any particular moment in time, it will always be possible to contest, transform or re-articulate existing rules, practices, institutions, identities, norms and so forth. In Laclau's (1990, 29; see also Torfing 1999, 62–66) illustration drawing on Wittgenstein's account of rule-following:

> If I begin counting the numerical series, 1, 2, 3, 4, and ask someone to continue, the spontaneous answer would be 5, 6, 7, etc. But I can adduce that this is wrong, since the series I have in mind is 1, 2, 3, 4; 9, 10, 11, 12; 17, 18, 19, 20; etc. But if my interlocutor believes that s/he has now understood the rule and tries to follow it by continuing the series in the stated way, I can still adduce that s/he is wrong since my initial enunciation was merely a fragment of a different series – for example, one comprising the numbers 1 to 20, 40 to 60, and 80 to 100 etc. And obviously, I can always change the rule by continuing the series in a different way … the rule itself is undecidable and can be transformed by each new addition.

As this suggests, any ostensibly stable understanding or practice contains within it the possibility of future transformation: and efforts to deny this possibility of change are, in Laclau's (1990, 89–92; 1997) terminology, 'ideological'. Ultimately, then, it is the political that determines which understandings, arguments, identities become dominant or hegemonic at particular moments (Laclau 2004, 3). And, paying attention to this involves rethinking the operation of power in concrete socio-political contexts, such that:

> Power is not analysed in terms of a resource or capacity one can possess, store, or retrieve, or as a relation of domination. Power is

> conceived in terms of the political acts of inclusion and exclusion that shape social meanings and identities and condition the construction of social antagonisms and political frontiers. The construction of discourse always involves both inclusion and exclusion of identity and this means that discourse and power are intrinsically linked with each other. (Torfing 2005, 23)

This broad set of theoretical commitments means that the analysis which follows focuses, in large part, on what can and cannot be said, by whom, about what, and where. All of this, we argue, is contingent: a product of, and a way of reproducing, a particular discourse around the functions of parliament, sovereign authority, national security, and – most narrowly – proscription as a form of counter-terrorism policy. Each of these phenomena (or discursive 'moments' to use Laclauian terminology) are brought into being, transformed and contested in spaces beyond parliamentary debates on proscription. But proscription is both shaped by and a major contributor to these, we suggest, in the pages that follow.

We therefore begin our analysis, in Chapter 4, by exploring the various ways in which proscription itself – as a political power – and specific proscription decisions, are described, defended and contested within parliamentary debates. These descriptions and arguments, we argue, work to imbue meaning and significance upon this power. They produce it – rather than reflect it – as something to be taken seriously, because (as the debates appear to demonstrate), it *is* being taken seriously. Proscription, we show, becomes discursively fixed (for advocates of this power) as significant for its contribution to British national security efforts. At the same time, it becomes discursively fixed as significant (for critics of proscription) because of its implications for rights, citizenship and so forth. This disagreement is important for two reasons. In the first instance, although advocates and sceptics of proscription mobilise competing political, normative and empirical arguments, they work together to reproduce the significance or relevance of proscription as the object of those arguments. (They do a great deal more than this, too, of course, to which we return below.) This is not atypical: discourses tend to be characterised by contradiction, dissension and other forms of opposition (Foucault 2002, 166–173). But the key point here is that this disagreement helps to create rather than demonstrate proscription's importance. In the second instance, these competing arguments already point to the centrality of contestation within the parliamentary politics of proscription. And this matters, we argue, because it highlights a very particular type of performance upon which the legitimacy of proscription rests: one of agonistic liberal democracy. This apparent consensus that it is, at once, important to debate proscription (because it matters) and appropriate to debate proscription (because 'we' are a parliament in a liberal democracy) helps us to witness the relative consistency within these debates over time.

Our exploration of these diverse claims and arguments also involves charting some of the discursive strategies that are brought to bear by contributors to these debates. We suggest two things in doing this. First, that there exists a basic semantic strategy running through these debates which works to valorise the self and condemn its terrorist others (see Van der Valk 2003) – a feature to which we return in our discussion of identity in Chapter 6. And, second, that specific rhetorical figures do considerable discursive work in these debates: metaphors of balance and burden, for instance, are frequently invoked to characterise parliamentary efforts and the challenges facing parliamentarians seeking to do their work with diligence.

The next stage of our analysis – in Chapter 5 – focuses specifically on the role of parliamentary *questions* which form a particular and recurrent feature within these debates. These questions, we argue, are an important part of these debates for a number of reasons. First, they matter because of their sheer prominence therein: attempting to make sense of these debates without paying attention to them would provide for an unnecessarily and peculiarly partial analysis. Indeed, many of the statements and identity claims we discuss in Chapters 4 and 6 respectively come out of responses to, or reflections on, questions posed by other parliamentarians. Second, such questions are of interest because of their heterogeneity. As we argue in Chapter 5, proscription debates are characterised by questions on everything from bureaucratic procedure to matters of fundamental principle. They include, *inter alia*, requests for additional information on the activities of, or threat posed by, particular organisations, as well as appeals for clarification on why specific organisations have been brought 'to the table' for debate (and, indeed, why others have not). In an effort to make sense of this heterogeneity we offer a typology of security questions that is drawn inductively from these debates. A third reason for taking them seriously is that they encourage us to pay attention to the diversity of roles performed by participants within this particular (and recurrent) security drama, many of which fall between straightforward acquiesce or resistance to executive efforts in this context. Parliamentary discourse, in other words, is considerably more nuanced than any straightforward binary between government and opposition, at least in the case of proscription.

Where Chapters 5 and 6 focus primarily on the construction of discursive objects – whether counter-terrorism policy or human rights – Chapter 7 moves our analysis to the ways in which proscription debates also produce their own subjects. Here, we look at the identification and negotiation of distinct subject positions which span, on the one hand, those claimed by speakers for themselves either individually or collectively such as politician, member of the opposition, citizen, Parliament and/or Great Britain. And, on the other hand, those identities carved out for various others, primarily either terrorists in general, or specific terrorist organisations. In doing this, we show, as David Campbell argued, that: 'Security and subjectivity are intrinsically linked … security (of which foreign policy/Foreign Policy is a part) is first and foremost a performative discourse constitutive of political order' (Campbell 1992, 199).

Our discussion of identity constructions within these debates emphasises the relational (and often oppositional) character of this dynamic, arguing that there can be no self without its 'others', for: 'the relationship to the other is the condition of possibility for the self' (Campbell 1998, ix). In so doing we build on related work in this area, including Mark Salter's (2002) *Barbarians and Civilization*, which demonstrated how 'the identity of a group claiming the status of "civilized" – in this case Europe – requires a group that can be represented as barbarians against which to define themselves – in this case the colonial subjects'. Developing Roxanne Doty's (1993) seminal article, Jack Holland (2013) more recently similarly showed how the war on terrorism connects foundational claims around national identity to the importance of conceivable and communicable foreign policy frameworks. Work such as this has 'enormously broadened the theoretical scope and concerns of IR as a discipline' (Solomon 2012, 909), not least by demonstrating 'the significance for how constructions of "us" depend upon, and are mutually constituted by, "our" encounters with "them"' (Solomon

2012, 909). Whilst this literature spans thinner and thicker versions of constructivism, it shares with our analysis a focus on the generative capacities of discourse.

The power of proscription, approached thus, is not, therefore, a tool by which a pre-existing actor mitigates or responds to an external threat. Rather, it is a mechanism through which the identities of actor and threat are themselves constituted and brought into a relationship with one another. So, on the one hand, debating whether a particular organisation merits proscription involves representing that organisation in particular ways (frequently as terrorist, but often, also, in other ways too, including as evil, dangerous, intransigent, irrational or Islamist). And, at the same time, participating in such a debate also involves a representation or performance of one's own self-identity, frequently – in our context – as a member of a democratic, liberal or responsible political community (see Jarvis and Legrand 2016).

Political ritual

If we approach the above together, we begin to see that the 'debate' label within proscription debates may be insufficient or even a misnomer – not least because, as argued in Chapter 1, the outcome of these debates is always identical. Because of this, Parliament emerges as an important constitutive site in which security dramas play out, we will argue, according to a familiar and relatively consistent framework of speakers and script. This sense of predictable familiarity brings our analysis into contact with an increasing scholarship on the ritualistic aspects of political life and decision-making. Amongst political scientists, Steven Lukes (1975) was an early exponent of this approach, identifying rituals as a cognitive mode of exercising power through shaping participants' thoughts and feeling. As Kertzer puts it, through rituals beliefs are 'acquired, reinforced and eventually changed' (1989, 9). More recent work on political institutions (see, in particular, Rai and Johnson 2014) recognises ritual as a locus of change, power and conflict (Waylen 2010), operating often as a gendered means of control (Lovenduski 2012). For these scholars, attention to ritual practices can reveal 'the sedimentation of power' (Rai 2010, 284), as well as their role in the (re-)production of national cultures and political orders (de Lomnitz *et al.* 2010; Atkins and Finlayson 2016; Finlayson 2017). It is a role, indeed, that is not unfamiliar to participants in such rituals – as illustrated by Du Cann's characterisation of Prime Minister's Question Time in an intervention on a 1978 debate on parliamentary control of the executive:

> This is an ancient place. Not one of us who is here is not deeply sensible of its traditions and the way in which we have evolved our systems – many of which are ancient – over a period of time in the light of practical experience. (Du Cann 1978)

The confluence of belief, symbolism and repetition/invariance is the *sine qua non* for security ritual. Indeed, Oren and Solomon (2015, 313) argue that rituals can be central to securitisation; in their work they suggest that the 'ritualised chanting' of 'weapons of mass destruction' in the lead-up to the Iraq War was pivotal to its acceptance as a real threat. In political settings where security questions are at stake, rituals can therefore be extremely powerful: through ritual we produce – and reinforce – beliefs about the world and our place in it: they are therefore heavily constitutive of identity(ies), intertextuality(ies), epistemology(ies) and ontology(ies). Ritual becomes ritual by regular repetition, over long periods of time, and through a common subscription to the meaning it is intended outwardly to symbolise. Rituals also, however, implicate a legitimacy: their incumbent symbols, meanings and beliefs confer an unchallenged authority on the process and outcomes. Thus, rituals are highly resistant to challenge and change, representing a reliable institutional continuity.

So Chapter 7 borrows from anthropological, sociological and political literatures to assemble a heuristic of political ritual. This heuristic collects and builds upon the emphasis on symbolic language, regular themes and established subject positions set out in Chapters 4, 5 and 6, while attending in more detail to broader features of proscription debates. Here, we emphasise the importance of such characteristics as: understood and rehearsed roles performed by a narrow and authorised cast of participants – some as advocates, some as dissenters; a process conforming to a template timetable; the meaning-laden setting of Parliament; and conformity to an expected and relatively unvarying script. Crucial within this is the expression of contestation and argument, which – although they effect no material change – contribute to the authority of government decisions, and without which the democratic legitimacy of Parliament is lost. Again, though, it is unlikely that dissent's performativity and symbolic significance is lost on participants, as illustrated in an unrelated discussion from 1999 in which the procedural issue of 'guillotine debates' was the focus.

> Paul Tyler (North Cornwall): Such debates have become something of a ritual, and the House does not perform well when we go through the motions ritualistically. (Tyler 2000)
>
> [...]
>
> Tony Wright: We have hour upon hour of debate, or of the depressing spectacle that passes for debate, going through the ritual whose words we all know by heart, to prevent us from discussing matters that we are supposed to discuss. (Wright 2000)

Understood thus, the performed dissent in parliamentary debate – in our case on proscription – becomes *part of the ritual*, holding symbolic value for the conferring of a perceived legitimacy on the decision-making process itself.

Methodological considerations

To explore these issues further, the following chapters draw on material taken from each of the debates on proscription that took place within the UK's Houses of Parliament between October 2002 and the spring of 2018. These debates incorporate every effort to increase the list of proscribed groups within the UK between the passage of the TA 2000 and the time of writing. Each transcript was accessed online via the UK Parliament's Hansard service, with the total corpus constituting some 193,000 words.

Having completed the collection of our data, each debate was subject to a discursive analysis structured around five primary themes derived iteratively via a detailed immersive reading of this material using a 'framework' approach to qualitative discourse analysis (Ritchie and Spencer 2002). This involves a systematic process of sifting, charting and sorting research material for the purposes of summarising and classifying large volumes of data in a manner grounded in the text's own categories (Jones 2000, 560). The five themes, identified by one of the book's co-authors, referred, first, to general reflections on the UK's proscription powers, with sub-themes including descriptions of proscription; positive evaluations of proscription; potential limitations of proscription; and, questions and criticisms regarding the implementation of proscription in specific circumstances. The second theme referred to constructions of self-identity, including of individual politicians, of Parliament, of government, and of the United Kingdom. Sub-themes in this category included expressions of cross-party consensus or unity; references to the UK's liberal heritage; accounts of the legislative process, including the importance of checks and balances; and, representations of the United Kingdom's role and importance within global politics. The third theme concerned generalised reflection on the UK's counter-terrorism framework, including expressions of vigilance, toughness or resilience; descriptions of, and praise for, the UK's security and intelligence services; accounts of the challenges of counter-terrorism; claims of the need for international engagement; and, discussion of the importance of 'balancing' core political values such as security and liberty. A fourth theme focused on constructions of otherness, including general descriptions of terrorism; articulations of the terrorist threat; and, references to specific groups under consideration for proscription. The final theme was miscellaneous, under which was located additional material that did not fit neatly into any of the previous categories. This included information on the naming of specific events; the drawing of analogies and comparisons with other areas of political life; and the discussion of matters entirely unrelated to proscription within these debates.

Conclusion

This chapter concludes the book's scene-setting. Having sketched our broad conceptual approach and methodological framework we are now in a position to begin unpacking the specifics of this particular political ritual. We begin this, as noted above, in Chapter 4, by turning our attention to the ritual's production of proscription itself, through diverse statements and arguments.

4 Debating proscription: sources of parliamentary support and opposition

This chapter begins our analysis of parliamentary debate around proscription by asking how parliamentarians – as contributors to these debates – make sense of this power. We begin by exploring the primary ways in which parliamentarians introduce or situate this power vis-à-vis the range of alternative counter-terrorism mechanisms available to government, and in relation to the role and responsibilities of government more broadly. As demonstrated below, especial emphasis is placed, in these discussions, on the seriousness and significance of proscription as a political tool, as well as its specific advantages for combating terrorism. A second section then elaborates on the diverse ways in which parliamentarians describe proscription's value, including the multiple functions of deterrence, disruption and communication claimed for this power. A third section explores four recurrent types of criticism or limitation identified within these debates. These relate to: questions of effectiveness; fears around proscription's counter-productivity; worries around intrusions upon civil liberties; and broader concerns for democracy, especially in relation to external interference within British affairs. Having traced these discussions, we conclude the chapter by arguing that proscription debates are characterised by a particular discursive framing, which includes the recurrence of particular topics, semantic strategies and rhetorical figures. This is complemented, we argue, by a shared performance of proscription's significance in which this power is reproduced by its advocates and critics alike as something that matters – and something that matters a great deal. Given this, it might seem surprising that parliamentarians also use these debates instrumentally as an opportunity to discuss other events, issues or priorities beyond the very narrow question of whether or not to add organisations to the UK's list.

'An important part of the government's strategy' (Wallace 2017)

Every parliamentary debate on a proscription order made by the executive – almost without exception – either begins with or includes a brief summary of the act of proscription itself. Given the nature of the legislative process within the British bicameral system, these summaries are offered first in the House of Commons and then repeated, frequently near-verbatim, in the House of Lords. Indeed, as argued in Chapter 7, these opening summaries – which include descriptions of this power, a brief indication of the criteria for its employment, and a specification of the consequences for listed groups – typically vary little within debates on different organisations that take place over extended periods of time. Thus, in the first post-2000 increase of the UK's list from October 2002, for instance, Home Secretary David Blunkett (2002) of the Labour Party offered the following rationale for adding four additional organisations to the spectrum of banned groups: Jemaah Islamiyah, 'involved with and are part of the broader federal network of al-Qaeda'; Abu Sayyaf, 'a group based in the Philippines; the Islamic Movement of Uzbekistan, which has links with those whom we believe were involved in the hostage taking in Moscow; and Asbat Al-Ansar, which is based in Lebanon':

> The proscribed organisations fall within criteria of which it will be useful to remind hon. Members. They are specified in the definition of terrorism provided in the Terrorism Act 2000, which refers to those who commit or participate in acts of terrorism, prepare for terrorism, promote or encourage it or are otherwise concerned with it. The factors spelt out alongside the original decision a year last February were as follows: consideration by the Home Secretary of the nature and scale of the organisations; the specific threat to the UK or British nationals overseas; and the presence and support of the international community. It is the support of the international community and the threat to our citizens overseas that we have weighed

> very carefully indeed, along with other factors, in proscribing the four groups. (Blunkett 2002)

In June 2014, James Brokenshire, Minister for Security and Immigration, provided a similar account in setting out the Conservative/Liberal Democrat Coalition government's case for the proposed banning of five additional groups, including most prominently, the Islamic State in Iraq and the Levant (ISIL). The one significant difference from Blunkett's opening comments of twelve years prior is the addition of the 'glorification of terrorism' offence, which was introduced within the Terrorism Act 2006:

> Proscribing the groups that we are discussing today will send a strong signal to terrorists operating on both sides of the conflict in Syria and those who may be thinking of joining them. Under section 3 of the Terrorism Act 2000, the Home Secretary has the power to proscribe an organisation if she believes that it is currently concerned in terrorism. Under the 2000 Act, an organisation is concerned in terrorism if it commits or participates in acts of terrorism, prepares for terrorism, promotes or encourages terrorism—including the unlawful glorification of terrorism—or is otherwise concerned in terrorism. If the test is met, the Home Secretary may exercise her discretion to proscribe the organisation. (Brokenshire 2014a)

A far more recent – the twenty-second – proscription order under the TA 2000 was introduced by the Conservative government's Minister for Security, Ben Wallace, in December 2017. Although Wallace begins his remarks with a brief summary of the UK's terrorism threat level ('severe'), he again moves quickly to an overview of the power's operation, criteria and consequences for the four latest additions to the list: 'al-Ashtar Brigades, including its aliases Saraya al-Ashtar, Wa'ad Allah Brigades, Islamic Allah Brigades, Imam al-Mahdi Brigades and al-Haydariyah Brigades; al-Mukhtar Brigades, including Saraya al-Mukhtar; Hasam, including Harakat Sawa'd Misr and Harakat Hasm; and Liwa al-Thawra' (Wallace 2017). In so doing, Wallace sets out the significance of proscription, arguing the power constitutes 'an important part of the Government's strategy to disrupt the activities of terrorist groups and those who provide support to them ... [sending] a strong message that terrorist activity is not tolerated wherever it happens' (Wallace 2017).

Wallace's comments are entirely typical of proscription debates, which are replete with reference to the significance of decisions to list additional groups. Parliamentarians work hard, in these debates, to underscore their understanding of the task at hand, framing proscription as 'a heavy power' (Filkin 2002), 'an important power' (Blears 2005), 'a tough power, which has the effect of outlawing previously lawful activity' (Bassam 2005), a 'very serious matter' (McNulty 2006) and 'an important tool' (Hayes 2016). More poetic, but similarly explicit, was a framing of proscription by then Minister for Security, John Hayes (2016) in a debate on the twentieth order under the TA 2000:

> Proscription matters, and our determination to counter the malevolence that I have described matters too. In thwarting terror, we must act – as a people, a House and a Government – with an iron will and strong determination. The American poet Robert Frost wrote: 'Don't ever take a fence down until you know why it was put up.' In these dangerous times, we must – and will – do all we can to protect ourselves and others from attack. I believe it is right that these four groups should be proscribed in the way that I have set out.

Proscription, then, matters, and it matters, in part, because of this power's appropriateness for countering terrorism. A necessary, if not sufficient tool – 'proscription is a useful power, but it will certainly not resolve the [terrorist] situation overnight' (Blears 2005) – proscription emerges as a significant weapon in the Home Secretary's arsenal, such that: 'there is not much doubt that it has great value in disrupting the activities of terrorist organisations' (Bassam 2005).

Part of this worth is the speediness of its deployment: 'We have sought a shortened timetable to ensure that the power is as effective as possible' (Bassam 2005), with proscription orders being 'clinical and immediate' (Vaz 2014b), and giving 'the services extra power to their elbow' (Wallace 2017) to deal with proscribed organisations. Important, too, however, is the latitude it offers to those working within the criminal justice system, whereby 'proscription opens up a whole new level of offences for which people can be prosecuted … [giving] law enforcement agencies more powers with which to prosecute a campaign against them' (Wallace 2017). Of similar value, of course, is the latitude this power provides to the political executive: 'The Home Secretary may proscribe an organisation only if she believes it is concerned in terrorism. If that test is met, she may then exercise her discretion to proscribe the organisation' (McNulty 2008). As the Minister for Policing, Crime and Counter-Terrorism put it in a 2010 debate on the banning of al-Shabaab:

> The decision to proscribe an organisation is not taken lightly. It entails building a case that meets the legal test under the 2000 Act, and which is examined by officials in the Home Office and other Government Departments. That case is assembled over many weeks and months as the evidence is brought forward and collated. (Hanson 2010)

Lest critics fear the scope for error or abuse opened by this combination of alacrity and discretion, proscription is also widely depicted in these debates as impartial – 'We take action irrespective of the creed or nationality of those involved' (Blunkett 2002); evidence-based – 'this approach is the result of very careful intelligence gleaned from international sources' (Bridgeman 2002); rigorous – 'Decisions to proscribe are taken with great care by the Home Secretary, and it is right that the case for proscribing organisations must be approved by both Houses' (Brokenshire 2013); transparent – 'the criteria are clear, as are the offences that follow on from them' (McNulty 2008); and, open to appeal – 'if groups feel that they have been wrongly proscribed they have recourse to a review' (Blears 2005). At the same time, and as discussed further below, even proscription's advocates acknowledge its limitations, which include procedural complexity – 'I do not know or understand the procedure that puts the organisations together in one order' (McNulty 2007); possible (geo)political influences impacting its employment – 'there are tactical considerations as well, regarding the optimum time to intervene. We also need to work in collaboration with our international partners; there may be a reason why they do not want us to take action at a particular point' (Attlee 2013); and material costs – 'failure to proscribe an organisation that turns out to be violent and to have terrorist intent could threaten British citizens on our soil, but equally, proscribing an organisation mistakenly or inappropriately could tie up significant resources' (Ruffley 2008). As McNulty (2008) summarises: 'A proscription order is not a magic wand that makes things any easier.'

'Proscription rightly sends out a strong signal' (Hermon 2002)

As discussed in Chapter 2, a peculiarity of the (vast) academic literature on counter-terrorism is the lack of sustained analysis of the effectiveness of specific powers. As one large review article put it: 'From over 20,000 studies we located on terrorism, we found only seven which contained moderately rigorous evaluations of counter-terrorism programs' (Lum *et al.* 2006, 2). Part of the reason for this lacuna is the absence of counter-factuals; there is no *ceteris paribus* ground against which to assess the impact of a any counter-terrorism initiative such as – in our case – listing (see also van Um and Pisiou 2015, 239–240). And, in a policy domain which is, by its nature, clandestine, secretive and ill-disposed to information sharing (Sageman 2014) such counterfactuals are perhaps less reliable still. Another reason, however, is that the purposes of counter-terrorism mechanisms are multiple, and perhaps also ambiguous, serving symbolic, strategic and political functions at once (Jarvis and Lister 2015, 18).

Parliamentary debates on proscription illustrate this ambiguity well, with multiple functions frequently claimed for this power. In a 2002 House of Lords debate, for instance, Lord Filkin (2002) argued that proscription not only works to prevent, disrupt and deter acts of terrorism, but that it also serves to pull attention to the immorality of its targets:

> The impact of proscription is to make it more difficult for international terrorist organisations to operate in the United Kingdom and seeks to deter them from coming here in the first place. The proscription offences are a means of tackling some of the more low-level support activities for terrorist organisations. Finally, the Act is a powerful signal of the government's and society's rejection of those organisations' claims to legitimacy. (Filkin 2002)

This framing of proscription's contribution to diverse counter-terrorism ambitions has become embedded in contemporary parliamentary discourse. Illustrative, here – again from the upper chamber – is Lord West of Spithead's contribution in a discussion of Hezbollah's military wing:

> The proscription of Hezbollah's military wing will contribute to making the United Kingdom a hostile environment for terrorists and their supporters. It will signal our condemnation of the support that Hezbollah provides to those who attack British and other coalition forces in Iraq, as well as Iraqi civilians. It will support our international partners in disrupting terrorist activity in the occupied Palestinian territories, and it will also send a strong message that the United Kingdom is not willing to tolerate terrorism either here or anywhere else in the world. (West 2008)

Similar arguments are in evidence, too, in the Home Office's (2017) policy paper on 'Proscribed Terrorist Groups or Organizations', and more recently, in the House of Commons July 2016 debate:

> Proscription can support other disruptive activity including the use of immigration powers such as exclusion or prosecution for other offences. It also acts to support strong messaging to deter fundraising and recruitment. Additionally, the assets of a proscribed organisation are subject to seizure as terrorist assets. (Hayes 2016)

Proscription, then, reduces the likelihood of planned terrorist attacks ('proscription can be an important mechanism to disrupt activity' (Brokenshire 2013)); complicates the preconditions required for terrorism ('proscribing such organisations in the UK is a practical step to stop funding that supports them in other countries' (Mahmood 2007)); has a deterrent function for future attacks ('it also deters international terrorist organisations from coming to this country in the first place' (Blears 2005)); and has significant, and multiple, communicative roles from taking 'the drastic step of telling those who belong to, work for, and associate themselves with certain organisations that such activities are unacceptable in this country' (Hughes 2002), through to sending out 'a clear message that the United Kingdom takes seriously its role in fighting terrorism' (Scotland 2006). Moreover, as Ben Wallace, Minister for Security, put it in a July 2016 House of Commons debate, which remains significant as the first time a proscription order had been laid for a far-right group – National Action – the power also has implications for preventing radicalisation:

> Proscribing this neo-Nazi group will prevent its membership from growing and prevent it from spreading propaganda, which allows a culture of hatred and division to thrive. It will also help to prevent National Action from radicalising people who may be vulnerable to extreme ideologies and at risk of emulating the terrorist acts it glorifies.

Proscription, then, occupies 'a vital part of our national security powers' (Brown 2016). For its advocates, moreover, 'proscription works' (Wallace 2017) for, as Ben Wallace (2017), then Minister for Security, continued:

> 51 people have been charged with membership of proscribed groups and 32 have been convicted. There are currently 71 proscribed international groups and 14 Northern Ireland groups. The law enforcement agencies often tell us how useful proscription is, and we will always listen to any changes they request.

Even more than this, however, proscription is seen to have value beyond its immediate counter-terrorism function. On the one hand, it may contribute to the policing of other terrorism offences –'arrests are being made in relation to alleged proscription offences. That may lead to other charges relating to terrorism' (Brokenshire 2015) – or, indeed other issue areas: 'Proscription can support other disruptive activity including the use of immigration powers such as exclusion or prosecution for other offences' (Hayes 2016). At the same time, it may facilitate international cooperation with allied countries, whereby the power 'provides a coherent approach involving the UN and other international partners in seeking to attack and undermine terrorism' (Blunkett 2002). As Baroness Smith (2015) noted in a March 2015 debate, 'when we proscribe organisations we support the international community'. Such cooperative benefits are visible domestically, too, in the context of inter-party consensus, with proscription being 'part of the mutuality and solidarity that we have expressed in the House on a number of occasions' (Blunkett 2002).

This value is further evidenced, finally, in the (likely) popular support for the banning of specific organisations amongst sections of the British public at home: 'I believe – if I reflect on these matters carefully, as I have done – that the UK Somali community will welcome this action because it shows that we are concerned to tackle terrorism in their home country and the impact of such terrorism on the interests of citizens in their adopted country' (Hanson 2010). Here, the existence of sufficient 'safeguards ... [and] checks and balances' (Bates 2015) within the proscription regime may help assuage the concerns of this power's critics. As, perhaps, might the power's unbiased construction – 'Proscription is not targeted at any particular faith, social group or ideological motivation. It is based on clear evidence that an organisation is involved in terrorism' (Wallace 2016) – and proportionate application: 'The Government continue to exercise the proscription power in a proportionate manner, in accordance with the law' (Wallace 2017).

'Banning and proscription do not necessarily work' (Corbyn 2011)

Despite the above claims to importance, British parliamentary debate on proscription is also run through with significant criticism of this power. Although it is possible to identify regular contributors to this – linked, at times, to specific parliamentary roles[1] – such critiques are not party political in nature, nor are they specific to particular organisations seen as potential targets for banning.

Uppermost amongst these concerns are fears around the effectiveness of proscription, not least given the tendency of terrorist groups to splinter, discussed in Chapter 2. In a 2005 debate, for example, Mercer suggested, metaphorically: 'an aphorism, I know, but we are not considering concrete organisations. We are considering ideologies and organisations that have more in common with a piece of mercury, which, when hit with a hammer, will split into various different parts and spring up enormously dangerously' (Mercer 2005). Andrew Dismore, the following year, offered a similar argument, drawing historical parallel between contemporary 'Islamist' groups and, 'the Trotskyists in the 1970s [whereby] whenever one looked at them, they were a different organisation' (Dismore 2006). Although the UK's proscription regime accounts for the possibility of organisations changing their name,[2] the ability of groups to evade censure through use of an alias constitutes a common concern around the power's effectiveness (as we see further in Chapter 5). The Minister for Immigration, Damian Green, in response to a 2011 question, for instance noted, on this issue: '[name changing] is one of the activities that concerns Ministers and it is one of the things that has happened in the past. Organisations have sought to reappear under different names and have been re-proscribed. We are extremely aware of the very serious problem' (Green 2011). For Freer (2014), too, more recently:

> As soon as Muslims Against Crusades was proscribed, the web page came down, but the group reinvented itself within hours, and a simple name change got round the proscription. My worry is that we can list the names of the five organisations in the order, but within hours of their names being listed, they reinvent themselves as a fringe group under another name and seem to get round proscription.

Labour MP Andrew Dismore raised similar concerns in consecutive years arguing, 'the serious issue is how we keep up with the continual name changes of organisations that are effectively the same organisations as those that were proscribed' (Dismore 2006); and subsequently, 'When a group is proscribed, it suddenly reinvents itself as something else – it changes its name' (Dismore 2007). Keith Vaz – a regular critic of these powers – expressed his own 'worry about proscription orders, especially in respect of new groups, [where] the heads of those groups can be chopped off, and, amoeba-like, they can form themselves into different organisations with different names' (Vaz 2013). Jim Shannon, of the Democratic Unionist Party, more recently still, posed a similar concern in the context of ISIS's potential future fragmentation following successful military action against that organisation. Did this possibility, Shannon (2016a) asked, bring into question the value of the proscription regime more broadly:

> The Prime Minister, in today's Prime Minister's questions, said that Daesh has had 20,000 of its terrorists killed in battle and has lost some 40% of its territory. As that has happened, and as Daesh is becoming more fragmented and is not the overall body that it was in the past, there will be more organisations to proscribe, as small splinter groups and organisations spring up from across the whole of the middle east. The shadow Minister also touched on this, but let me ask the Minister: is there a better way for us to proscribe organisations than by coming to this House every time?

Concerns around proscription's effectiveness extend, importantly, beyond these issues of name and structural change. For some contributors to these debates, it is the bluntness of this tool which causes unease, given that this reduces proscription's capacity to successfully differentiate between very different groups that have been, or may be, similarly designated 'terrorist':

> we need to be conscious that what are being proscribed are terrorist organisations. Terrorism is defined broadly in section 1 of the Act ... [It] catches, for example, people who want to supplant Saddam Hussein. Distinctions exist between sheep and goats in relation to terrorism. Some terrorists are goats, and some are sheep. The interesting question is who makes that decision ... we need to know more definitely how the distinction between one set of terrorism, which we regard as good because it does not threaten us, and another set of terrorism, which we regard as bad because it does, is made. (Hogg 2002)

Others, such as David Winnick (2006), point to the global nature of contemporary terrorism, and the limited purchase of domestic jurisdictions and mechanisms for dealing with a transnational threat of this sort: 'what about the people behind these organisations: the racists and hate-mongers who are not UK citizens?'. Proscription's questionable effectiveness as a deterrent concerns other critics – 'I have yet to see a suicide bomber who would have been deterred by a law' (Mercer 2005); with some (echoing arguments from other contexts such as around anti-social behaviour orders) fearing that listed status may even become coveted by illicit groups: 'When it was added to the American list of banned organisations, a senior operative is reported to have told the BBC that the organisation felt honoured to be included on the list and that it was on the right path – a usual characteristic of martyrdom' (Hamwee 2010); and, 'we do not have huge confidence in the effectiveness of banning orders. They may have negative practical effects, such as becoming a badge of honour and driving a group underground' (Hamwee 2010).

Problems of attribution are mentioned on occasion, especially in contexts comprising multiple violent organisations – 'Given the Taliban practice of claiming attacks on behalf of the insurgency as a whole, it can be difficult to identify the Haqqani network's specific responsibility for attacks' (Brokenshire 2015). More serious concerns, though, focus on whether proscription potentially substitutes for 'real' or more meaningful forms of counter-terrorism activity – 'I ask the Minister why all we see from the government is lists of names and suggested legislation' (Mercer 2005) – asking about its translation into identifiable outcomes: 'why are so few prosecutions brought?' (Heath 2006), and, 'if we proscribe organisations, it is all very well talking and generating hot air, but what is done about asset seizure? There must be delivery, not just talk' (Mercer 2006).

The very need for proscription vis-à-vis other (often wide-ranging) counter-terrorism powers is questioned by some critics: 'I have never quite understood the purpose of proscribing organisations in this way ... what additional and valuable powers does the order actually give over the individuals who may be covered by such proscription?' (Harris 2014). Such concerns become, perhaps, more pressing with the increasing use of this power, as Diana Johnson (2015) noted:

> as we come to the end of a Parliament during which there has been an exceptional number of proscription orders, we need to consider whether the proscription powers we currently use are having the results we require ... it seems that proscription orders are not having the effect of reducing a group's presence on social media.

Others point to the questionable relevance of proscribing an organisation with no demonstrable presence, or interest in, the UK. The Conservative MP Dominic Grieve, for instance, noted in a July 2007 debate on Jammat-ul Mujahideen Bangladesh and Tehrik Nefaz-e Shari'at Muhammadi – organisations then primarily active in Bangladesh and Afghanistan – that: 'proscribing something that does not really exist in this country serves little purpose in reality' (Grieve 2007).

A final set of concerns around proscription's effectiveness focus on its potentially counter-productive nature. Some, such as Sylvia Hermon, an Ulster Unionist MP, draw on the earlier experience of the Northern Ireland 'Troubles' to identify proscription as a potential *cause* of new intelligence challenges, noting that 'proscription often leads to fragmentation and splinter groups, which go underground and change their names' (Hermon 2002). As Patrick Mercer (2013) more recently argued:

> There are also good intelligence reasons why it is sometimes necessary – or advised – to be less robust with such organisations than

> might otherwise be the temptation. Simply put, if Hizb ut-Tahrir were to be banned, as appears likely at the moment, it would soon spring up as 'son of' or 'bride of' or 'ghost of' Hizb ut-Tahrir, under a different name with a different faction and a different flag.

More troublesome, however, are concerns that proscription may inhibit opportunities for de-radicalisation, restricting a potential route out of terrorism in the very act of criminalising certain groups and their members. As Labour MP Jeremy Corbyn, for instance, argued – again with reference to Northern Ireland:

> Banning and proscription do not necessarily work. What works is political dialogue. Let us consider what happened in Northern Ireland. Gerry Adams and John Hume came to an agreement and we eventually brought about a whole peace process there. It is important to look for positive solutions, rather than instant banning and the use of the state apparatus to suppress legitimate political activity. (Corbyn 2011)

'It is very easy to be unjust in the context of a crisis, an emergency, or terrorism' (Hogg 2002)

Jeremy Corbyn's concerns around banning, and his advocacy of political dialogue as a route to end terrorism, speak to a second set of criticisms within these debates. These focus not (only) on questions of effectiveness, as above, but (also) on the normative implications of this power for rights and civil liberties. As Corbyn (2011) argued in the same debate on Tehrik-e Taliban Pakistan – but with reference not to its focus, but 'Kongra Gele Kurdistan [which] is listed, together with a number of Somali organisations': 'proscribing organisations that probably do not exist, and in some cases naming people or suggesting naming people who are alleged to be representatives of those organisations, in turn limits their opportunity for legitimate political activity and political dialogue' (Corbyn 2011).

Normative concerns such as these – as with those issues of efficacy above – point to a striking parallel here between parliamentary debate and the academic literatures on proscription considered in Chapter 3. Douglas Hogg (2002), in a House of Commons debate, for example, argued 'we are curtailing civil and political rights and … extending the criminal law to British citizens who may or may not be our constituents'. Indeed, even the Minister of State for Countering Extremism, Baroness Williams (2017), recognised this risk when introducing the December 2017 proscription order to the House of Lords, noting: 'We recognise that proscription potentially interferes with an individual's rights, in particular the rights protected by Articles 10 and 11 of the European Convention on Human Rights, and should be exercised only when absolutely necessary.'

The risk of particular (often diaspora) communities being stigmatised, even criminalised, through guilt by association constitutes a more specific concern across these debates. Crispin Blunt, for instance, asked in 2010: 'Does the Minister agree that when we proscribe organisations, we must be emphatic in saying that we are not labelling entire communities or nationalities?' (Blunt 2010). And, as the following indicates, Keith Vaz returned to this point a number of times, frequently with reference to the UK's Tamil community, arguing of Hezbollah's military wing in 2008: 'no matter how bad this organisation is, others who support general, charitable causes will be caught within the overall net of what is proposed' (Vaz 2008), and in subsequent debates:

> The Government need to pay heed to the effect of that proscription on the wider Tamil community, and to the effect that the proscription of al-Shabaab will have on the 45,000 Somalis who live in the United Kingdom. (Vaz 2010)

> Although this is, of course, a narrow order and the proscription applies to those who support the Pakistan Taliban, it is possible that other members of the community who are completely unassociated with this terrible organisation will in some way be caught up in the problem. (Vaz 2011)

The danger of proscription attenuating significant rights to resist unjust, illegitimate or downright tyrannical regimes emerges as a further civil liberty concern, given this instrument's bluntness noted above. John McDonnell, for example, argued, 'whenever it is argued that the organisations that we are proscribing seek to overthrow a legitimate government, we should have a thorough discussion about the legitimacy of that government' (McDonnell 2005). As he continued, 'We must be sure that not all those who are engaged in armed struggle are defined as terrorists' (McDonnell 2005). Lord Archer, more recently, praising the impending deproscription of the Iranian opposition group, the PMOI, highlighted the problematic state/non-state dichotomy that still organises much political and academic debate around the (il)legitimacy of various campaigns of violence, noting:

> It is perverse that those who so courageously opposed a regime, which is the very centre and source of a web of terrorism and has been condemned by United Nations' human rights bodies on more than 54 occasions, and whose families in Iran are suffering persecution for their resistance to terrorism, should ever have been labelled as terrorists. (Archer 2008)

Adam Price, of Plaid Cymru, called into question the stability of state/non-state binaries in the outlawing of enemies, comparing the Islamic Jihad Union (IJU) with the Uzbekistan state, and asking: 'should we not tread very carefully before proscribing an organisation that has less blood on its hands than a government with whom we still maintain diplomatic relations?' (2005). As these comments suggest, proscription, then, not only risks inconsistencies, but poses potential civil liberty implications in which, 'There is a difficult balance to strike. We must not become [a haven for terrorists], but on the other hand we must be a haven for free speech and liberty for those who, within the law, want to be critical of – in spoken word and in writing – regimes, faiths and practices that they consider unacceptable' (Hughes 2002).

The impact of proscription on freedoms of speech, association and resistance, in particular, is more troubling still, for some, because of the lack of parliamentary, judicial or other oversight of this process. Douglas Hogg (2002), for instance, expressed his disquiet that:

> In reality, the criminal law is being extended and civil rights curtailed without anybody outside the Home Office having the opportunity to review the evidence. I view that, as a matter of principle, with great anxiety; that is not to say that it is not right in this case, but we should be very cautious.

A similar point was made by Labour MP Alan Simpson in a 2005 debate, in which he argued: 'it seems reasonable to ask what evidence we have of the involvement of any of them [organisations] in current actions that have threatened the security of the United Kingdom. To be unable to get an answer to that is deeply worrying in the democratic process' (Simpson 2005). One implication of this secrecy – the need for which constitutes a recurrent feature of these debates – is, of course, that many parliamentarians (especially non-members of the privy council), 'have to rely a great deal on trust, which is often well placed in ministers and the advice that they receive' (Heath 2006). Less trusting readings of this expectation, however, see it as potentially indicative of 'a very serious democratic deficit' (Grieve 2005), in which 'It is difficult for those of us who are out of the loop, so to speak, to make meaningful comment about the individual organisations' (Harris 2006). Such concerns become particularly pronounced given the tendency for proscription orders to list multiple organisations for simultaneous banning. Lord Goodhart, for instance, argued that 'there should be separate orders for each organisation' (Goodhart 2002); the absence of which, for Simpson (2005), casts 'a shadow of doubt over the fairness, the even-handedness and the wisdom with which parliament deals with this process'. Lord Russell-Johnston made a similar argument, noting: 'because we are dealing with a list of 21 proscribed organisations you have a wholly unfocused debate. That is not sensible' (Russell-Johnston 2006). As did Jeremy Corbyn more recently still, complaining: 'We add to the list of banned organisations during a Parliament, but the additions cannot be amended and the subject of the proscribed list is not open to general debate' (Corbyn 2011).

The democratic deficit and wider normative problems associated with proscription are augmented by some participants in these debates by fears of lobbying from external governments seeking addition of their own enemies to the United Kingdom's list. This concern – shared by many academics, as noted in Chapter 3 – brings with it a further, concomitant, risk that proscription decisions become instrumentalised for purposes other than counter-terrorism. Mike Weir (2006), for example, noted that 'many Kurdish organisations are accused of terrorism by the Turkish government, and their members are imprisoned, when in fact they are democratic organisations fighting for the rights of the Kurdish people' (Weir 2006), while Jeremy Corbyn drew historical parallel with the UK's previous tolerance of dissident movements from across the world:

> it is important that this country does not just automatically proscribe an organisation because Government X, Y or Z has said so. If we did that, our history would be very different. Apartheid South Africa banned the African National Congress, yet the ANC had offices in this country, organised in this country, was completely open in this country, and eventually apartheid fell and the ANC became the Government of South Africa. I think we have to be a little careful about making instant responses all the time to banning requests made by particular regimes. (Corbyn 2011)

Liberal Democrat MP David Heath (2006) was amongst those fearing the dragging of proscription into wider geopolitical games – 'that the government are in danger of putting themselves in a difficult diplomatic position whereby they accede to requests for proscription from some countries but not from others'. Others, such as Keith Vaz, pointed to the executive's reliance on unelected officials, worrying that: 'Decisions are based on civil service rather than elected officials … and Home Office Ministers have to accept the advice presented to them by their civil servants' (Vaz 2010). McDonnell (2005) worried that the hastiness of proscription decisions circumscribed meaningful scrutiny of the executive, arguing: 'I would welcome a longer time scale in terms of the indication of organisations that may be listed for proscription so that we can be more engaged in the debate, if only through informal discussions'; a point made more strongly still by Hogg (2002) for whom: 'we can commit serious acts of injustice in the context of a national emergency, and the House must be slow in becoming party to such a process'.

As the above suggests, parliamentary critiques and concerns relating to proscription powers are extremely wide-ranging and often strongly held. At the strongest, such powers are deemed 'draconian', 'heavyhanded' (Goodhart 2002) and unnecessary, given the availability of normal criminal law with which to deal with such threats: 'We should not always reach out to anti-terror laws to deal with our problems in security; we should instead use the criminal law that we have' (Corbyn 2012). Less frequently aired, finally, but perhaps no less significant concerns include: worries around the integrity of the UK's intelligence services upon whose information such decisions inevitably draw: 'There is deep scepticism about some of that information, certainly since the Iraq invasion and the basis on which intelligence decisions were made at that time' (McDonnell 2005); fears that proscription (in the context, here, of glorification offences) might contravene international law: 'there is a concern that those powers may, at some point, be struck down and therefore need to ensure that we use them in the right way' (Harris 2006); the cost of implementing proscription decisions, which put 'a requirement – not just a pressure – on the police to do those things. Therefore, there is the potential for an enormous waste of resources, not to mention damage to community relations' (Corbyn 2011); and a fear that proscription decisions might serve to amplify or create unwarranted fears around terrorism:

> If there is no evidence that this organisation, al-Shabaab, exists or is behaving in a way that is causing serious concern, some in our community – with some justice – will be concerned that the Government are exaggerating the existence of terrorist threat in this country. That is the last thing that we should ever wish to countenance. (Taylor 2010)

Making sense of proscription

The above indicates the ways in which parliamentary debate around proscription serves to position this power politically and normatively. In the first instance, proscription consistently emerges, in these debates, as a political power of significance and import: as something which matters and should be taken seriously. More supportive stances toward this power clarify this significance by depicting proscription as an important mechanism for countering terrorism. This is a power which ostensibly contributes, no less, to the prevention, deterrence and disruption of terrorist ambitions, as well as having symbolic value in communicating British or parliamentary resolve to would-be terrorists. At the same time, as we have seen, critics of proscription pose numerous concerns, including around its effectiveness; counter-productive implications; civil liberty consequences; and impact upon democratic processes. Within such criticisms – which, as we have seen, recur across the period of our analysis (from the passage of the TA 2000 onwards) – proscription emerges once more as vitally important, if for different reasons to those trumpeted by its advocates.

Leaving aside, for the moment, some of the differences between contributors to these debates, this discussion of proscription is characterised by four basic principles often identified as cohering a discourse's basic semantic strategy: emphasising positive things about us; emphasising negative things about them; de-emphasising negative things about us; and de-emphasising positive things about them (Van der Valk 2003: 317, drawing on Van Dijk 2000). Repeatedly emphasised, in these debates, are the responsibilities of parliamentarians; responsibilities: to their constituents – especially to minority communities at risk of suspicion; to Parliament itself as a site of democratic scrutiny; to parliamentary protocols and standards which must be understood and, for some, questioned; and, to national security. Indeed, even those contributions which emphasise the limitations of proscription typically reference a commitment to the legislature's role as a check on executive power, or to long-standing liberties at risk from hasty or ill-conceived action. That such responsibilities are taken so seriously by legislators – even in the context of banning organisations so anathema to the UK – points already to the work done by Parliament in the ritualistic reproduction of a democratic, liberal self and an anti-democratic, illiberal other (Jarvis and Legrand 2016, 2017): themes to which we return in Chapters 6 and 7.

It is also worth noting that these debates are characterised by specific rhetorical strategies that clearly contribute to the meaning-making process around proscription itself. In the first instance, advocates of this power – or those arguing for its extension in a particular case – draw regularly upon figures implying precision, responsibility and reasonableness, employing metaphors of *balance* – 'It is the support of the international community and the threat to our citizens overseas that we have weighed very carefully' (Blunkett 2002); *burden* – 'a heavy power' (Filkin 2002); and *medicine* – such as in the presentation of proscription as 'clinical and immediate' (Vaz 2014b). Those less straightforwardly enthusiastic about the prospect of proscription's extension are no less likely to invoke figurative language. This includes through questioning this power's effectiveness via specific depictions of terrorist groups employing *physical metaphors* where they might 'have more in common with a piece of mercury' (Mercer 2005); *biological ones*: 'amoeba-like they can form themselves into different organisations' (Vaz 2013), 'a web of terrorism' (Archer 2008), and 'some terrorists are goats, and some are sheep' (Hogg 2002); or by drawing upon the *supernatural*: 'if Hizb ut-Tahrir were to be banned ... it would soon spring up as "son of" or "bride of" or "ghost of" Hizb ut-Tahrir' (Mercer 2013) to further demonise the threat. Others employ *journey* metaphors to describe some of the ways in which proscription might be circumvented by its targets: 'Muslims against crusades ... got round the proscription' (Gapes 2014), or how these targets might otherwise navigate this apparent obstacle to terrorism: 'a senior operative ... felt honoured to be included on the list and that it was on the right path' (Hamwee 2010). Others still repeat the *balance* metaphor to describe not a careful consideration of evidence, but rather – and in the context of counter-terrorism – a much more commonly invoked trade-off between security and liberty, describing such decisions as 'a difficult balance to strike' (Hughes 2002). Historical analogies, moreover, also offer a useful discursive resource for contesting decision-making in the present: 'the ANC had offices in this country ... and eventually apartheid fell' (Corbyn 2011).

Finally, although proscription is widely positioned in these debates as a power which matters – whether for national or public security, *or* for matters of justice, liberty, rights or multiculturalism – debating this power clearly also allows for discussion of other political values or policies. In other words, although these debates evidence the airing of competing perspectives on proscription, they also function as an opportunity for parliamentarians to explore a wide range of concerns with only transversal connection to the power of proscription itself. Within the above discussion, for instance, we see proscription debates housing discussion of, *inter alia*: the effectiveness of Britain's security services; the fundamental characteristics of a terrorist group; ostensible British values of fairness and democracy; the value of the law to ameliorate violence; the violences of other regimes around the world including Iran and Uzbekistan; and much more besides. Proscription debates, then, function as a platform either to air or to create related objects of concern; allowing parliamentarians to exercise their political imaginations, and to perform their perceived responsibilities to historical legacies (e.g. the African National Congress in South Africa) or contemporary concerns (e.g. minority communities within the United Kingdom). It is interesting, then, that parliamentary debates – here, at least – seem to function similarly to public discourse around counter-terrorism which often blurs into reflection on related or unrelated matters (Jarvis and Lister 2016); shedding considerable light, in the process, on social imaginaries and:

> the ways in which people imagine their social existence, how they fit together with others, how things go on between them and their fellows, the expectations that are normally met, and the deeper normative notions and images that underlie these expectations. (Taylor 2002, 106)

Viewed thus, we might therefore ask under what conditions a debate ceases to be a debate. As outlined in Chapter 3, one of the most striking features of this particular power is that executive efforts to add groups to the list of proscribed organisations are – without exception – successful. Indeed, since the power's introduction under the TA 2000, every government effort to expand this list – often through the naming of multiple groups at once – has been accepted by the opposition; irrespective of the particular party in office at the time. One might, therefore, ask what, if anything, is at stake in these debates if their ostensible and immediate purpose – to consider expanding the list of designated groups – appears a foregone conclusion (and a conclusion which is often described as foregone in these debates). These are the questions to which we now turn.

Notes

1 Keith Vaz MP – as Chairman of the Home Affairs Select Committee – for instance, has been a regular contributor to parliamentary debates on proscription, often speaking on behalf of specific communities within his constituency.

2 As the Home Office guidance states: Section 3(6) of the Terrorism Act 2000 allows the Home Secretary to specify by order that an alternative name or alias is to be treated as another name for a proscribed organisation listed in Schedule 2 to the Act. The Secretary of State can make an order where she believes the proscribed organisation is operating under that alternative name or that an organisation operating under a name not included in Schedule 2 is for all practical purposes the same as the

proscribed organisation. The use of an alternative name which has not been formally recognised in an order does not prevent the police and Crown Prosecution Service from taking action against an individual for proscription offences. For a successful prosecution, it is necessary to demonstrate that: (1) the organisation in question, whatever name it professes to be operating under, is for all practical purposes the same as the proscribed organisation listed in Schedule 2; and (2) that the person in question has committed one of the proscription offences in relation to that organisation.

5 Questioning proscription: holding government to account?

We saw, in Chapter 4, that parliamentary debate around proscription positions this power as a matter of some significance. For those advocating extending the UK's list of banned groups, this significance relates to proscription's (multiple) contributions to national counter-terrorism efforts, and its capacity simultaneously to disrupt, deter, prevent and communicate with those individuals and groups plotting acts of terrorism at home or elsewhere. More cautious or sceptical voices on the other hand have tended to pose proscription's significance in relation to issues around citizenship or democratic politics: the kinds of concern, as we saw in Chapter 3, raised within much of the academic literature in this area. Importantly, and in spite of often-significant political and normative differences between the staunchest and most cautious contributions to these debates, we encounter a recurring and shared articulation of the importance of parliamentary responsibility to *something*; whether national security, human security, multiculturalism, executive accountability, civil rights, or beyond.

This depiction of UK parliamentary debate on proscription as the trading of competing claims, perspectives and concerns, however, tells only part of this story. For, as we argue in this chapter, such debates are characterised not only by statements and assertions, but also, and importantly, by the asking of *questions*. That this is so is, in a sense, perhaps unsurprising given that the role of parliamentarians is not only a legislative one, but one that stretches to include tasks often well-served by question-asking, including representing the interests of constituents, criticising the executive, enacting political opposition and implementing party programmes (van Dijk 2004, 356). Such responsibilities, of course, vary between political systems – with the United Kingdom's 'talking parliament' perhaps better suited to public scrutiny of the executive than the 'working parliaments' of comparable liberal democracies, at least in relation to matters of defence (Rozenberg *et al.* 2011). Here, as Cole (1999, 83) argues, 'Parliamentary questions have traditionally been held in high esteem by scholars', although, as Martin (2011, 259) more recently notes, 'the content and nature of questions posed by parliamentarians in most legislatures remains relatively obscure, leaving the specifics of the questions parliamentarians ask and their reasons for asking open to conjecture'.

Our interest in this chapter is less in attempting to assess the contribution of parliamentary questions to effective oversight or accountability (for an overview, see Martin 2011, 261). Rather, our argument is that such questions contribute to the construction of proscription, and – as we go on to argue in Chapters 6 and 7 – to performances of identity and political sovereignty, in the process. Parliamentary questions, put otherwise, are an important part of the dynamic through which proscription becomes meaningful: offering attempts and appeals for greater clarification of this power's working and consequences. And, as such, paying attention to such questions offers insight into the politics of security, which emerges, in this context at least, as more complex and nuanced than assumed in prominent constructivist models thereof. To this end, this chapter not only provides a detailed empirical description of this particular security problematic, it also offers a typology of five types of security question asked within these debates. These questions – of timing, criteria, mechanics, consequences and exclusion – function, we argue, as demands on the government to variously justify, explain, clarify, elaborate and defend the decision to proscribe one or more terrorist organisations. This has implications, we suggest, for thinking through issues of audience and agency within security politics, as well as the temporalities therein.

'I am somewhat puzzled' (Alderdice 2008): questioning proscription decisions

The following discussion is organised thematically around five different types of question that emerge in parliamentary debates on the extension of the UK's list of banned organisations. These questions refer to: (1) the timing and (2) criteria behind proscription decisions; (3) the mechanics of proscription; (4) the consequences of proscription decisions for designated groups and other populations; and (5) other organisations not under consideration within a particular debate. This typology is intended as a heuristic – rather than definitive – and rooted in our reading of these debates.

Questions of timing

Although the control of time – within and beyond Parliament – is a deeply political and frequently useful resource (Jarvis 2009b), temporality is a prominent feature within counter-terrorism (and, more widely, security) discourse (Fisher 2013). Proscription debates are no exception here, with parliamentarians repeatedly questioning the executive on such issues. Such questions are, at times, framed neutrally, for instance in Keith Vaz's (2014b) intervention in a November 2014 debate: 'How many months or years have those particular organisations been on the radar of the Government or the security services?' Typically, though, they focus on perceived delays in the exercise of this power, and the lack of greater alacrity in responding to emergent threats.[1] Oliver Letwin, in a 2002 House of Commons debate, for example, noted: 'I want to probe the question of the timetable that led to the proscription of Jemmah Islamiyah today rather than at an earlier date', noting that, 'the question arises as to why this has taken so long' (Letwin 2002). Fellow Conservative MP Patrick Mercer, in 2005 – in the case of Ansar Al-Islam, Ansar Al Sunna and Al Qaeda in the Country of Two Rivers – wondered why the government had 'taken so long to ban one, two, or possibly three organisations, that, so far as I can see, probably represent the same thing' (Mercer 2005). Future leader of the Liberal Democrats, Nick Clegg, asked in 2007 of Jammat-ul Mujahideen Bangladesh and Tehrik Nefaz-e Shari'at Muhammadi, 'why is the move to proscribe those two organisations only taking place now?' (Clegg 2007). Meanwhile Lord Dholokia, in the upper house, asked similarly in the same context:

> Why, when we knew months ago of the bombings in at least 500 places in Bangladesh, are we only now being told about the proscription of the [Jammat-ul Mujahideen Bangladesh]? Why are we considering the proscription of the [Tehrik Nefaz-e Shari'at Muhammadi] now,

> when its role, attacking coalition forces in Afghanistan and Pakistan has been pretty clear? (Dholokia 2007)

Related, but at times more pointed, questions around the timing of proscription focus on whether particular political or conjunctural factors have intervened to force a decision at a specific moment. Liberal Democrat MP Tom Brake, for example, asked in relation to Tehrik-e Taliban Pakistan (TTP): 'was it prompted by the attempted car bombing in Times square in May 2010? … has there been any evidence of any activity in the UK, or any expectation that any assets may be seized?' (Brake 2011). Keith Vaz, in 2010, enquired of al-Shabaab: 'Have the Government received evidence that that particular organisation … has been involved in any of those activities? Has he seen that evidence? Is that, therefore, why he [The Minister for Policing, Crime and Counter-Terrorism] has come before the House with this order?' (Vaz 2010). Meanwhile, a March 2015 debate in the House of Lords saw Baroness Smith (2015) dress a similar question in more internationalist clothing:

> We are now at the end of March 2015, which seems quite a time lag. If Canada, the USA and the UN had information, was that not shared with us or did we not think before now that there was a case for proscription? I note that the attack on the British embassy vehicle was carried out in November 2014, and I hope that is not the case – I am sure that the Minister can reassure me on this – that we wait for British interests to be attacked before we act, because these are international issues.

The decision to proscribe the Lebanese organisation Hezbollah at a moment of its apparent openness to dialogue was questioned in the House of Lords: 'I am somewhat puzzled by the timing of the order … [given] the moves by Hezbollah towards the democratic process' (Alderdice 2008). Elsewhere, it is the significance of public opinion that captures attention, as with Crispin Blunt's asking whether the timing of Islam4UK's proscription was related to that group's 'proposals for a demonstration and [therefore] in response to public pressure' (Blunt 2010). Perhaps most pointed of all, however, are questions about the potential intervention of outside influence. As Lord Harris of Haringey asked of TTP (with an emphasis on Hizb ut-Tahrir's continued escape of proscription): 'was there a specific request from the Government of Pakistan or perhaps the Government of the United States in support of such a ban?' (Harris 2011). Where such questions are answered, responses, of course, vary, but include assertions of serendipity – 'I can give the hon. Gentleman a firm assurance that the decision on Islam4UK was coincidental, not subsequent, to the march in Wootton Bassett' (Hanson 2010) – and, indeed, governmental diligence:

> That is why the timing might seem a little strange. I am afraid that it takes a long time for these things to flow through and to do all the checks. We have arrived at that stage now. There is no nefarious plan. It has not been done as a clever move to send a particular message. I agree that it might not be the best moment, but it is important to make it absolutely clear that we are unwilling to let terrorists act in the way that they do, particularly when they injure and kill our people who are operating in Iraq. (West 2008)

Responses such as these notwithstanding, concerns regarding the timing of particular banning decisions remain pivotal to debates on this power. And, as Liberal Democrat MP Jo Swinson (2008) makes clear in an intervention worth citing at length, as do concerns over the broader political contexts in which such debates are situated:

> I would like to pose a few questions to probe their [the government's] motivation in doing this and get a little more information so that the House can come to a clear decision. It would be helpful to have more of an outline of why this change in legislation has come about now. What specific activities undertaken by Hezbollah have prompted it? I appreciate the sensitive nature of the issue, but it would be advisable for the House to have the maximum information possible. I think that the Minister said – I hope that he will confirm and clarify this – that some of the intelligence had been confirmed following the apprehension of a senior individual on 20 March 2007. If so, why has it taken more than a year for the Government to get to the stage of bringing this order before the House? Is it just because the information was gleaned from the individual only recently, or have there been delays for some other reason? On the same day that the order was announced, The Daily Telegraph reported that some Iraqi MPs had accused Hezbollah of planning and supervising the kidnapping of five British citizens from the Iraqi Finance Ministry in Baghdad in May 2007. Does the Minister have any reflections on the coincidence of those two events and whether they were related? While

> the activities of terrorist organisations must of course be condemned, the Government cannot entirely escape criticism for their role in creating conditions in which terrorism can thrive. Is it not the case that Hezbollah's activities in Iraq stem partly from a fatal lack of planning for the post-Saddam Hussein situation? Iraq has become a magnet for fundamentalists, and the implications of that failure of planning are still unfolding across the entire region.

Questions of criteria

A second, related, set of questions focuses on the criteria that are brought to bear upon specific proposed proscriptions. Simon Hughes, in 2002, for example, asked of Jemaah Islamiyah: 'What triggered the Government's view that the organisation should be proscribed? I understand the delicacy of the intelligence issues, but that organisation clearly has a reputation in the areas in which it is based' (Hughes 2002). A common theme underpinning these questions – and evident within some of those relating to timing above – is whether the decision to ban was connected to any indication of a direct threat to the UK or its interests. Lord Ahmed, for example, in 2002, asked: 'What evidence is there that a group operating in Uzbekistan or Lebanon is also a danger to British citizens in the United Kingdom?' (Ahmed 2002). Conservative MP David Ruffley asked of Hezbollah: 'Will the Minister share with us the evidence in his possession about Hezbollah's fundraising activities in the United Kingdom?' (Ruffley 2008). Keith Vaz asked a similar question of al-Shabaab two years later: 'does the minister have any evidence that it is operating in the United Kingdom – where he is a minister and we are the Parliament?' (Vaz 2010). As did Diana Johnson, more recently, of the Indian Mujahadeen (IM):

> May I also ask whether there is any evidence linking that group to forces attacking UK troops operating in Afghanistan? ... [Also] there is the issue of the extent of the organisation's presence in the United Kingdom, and the question of whether any specific threat is posed to the UK. Is there any evidence that the IM is active in the UK, or receives direct support from it? Have the Government any estimate of the number of people in the UK who might be affected by the proscription of the group? (Johnson 2012)

Fear of external interference again colour many of these questions of criteria. Alan Simpson, for instance, fearing that the UK's list of proscribed groups served American interests – 'We [the UK] have a proscription list that is friendly for the current US Administration' – noted 'a dreadful lop-sidedness to that sort of approach … [such that] we must ask what has changed to require their addition to our list of known risks or threats to the UK' (Simpson 2005). John McDonnell, in the same debate, wanted to know: 'how much [information] comes directly from British intelligence services and how much is provided by the CIA and others?' (McDonnell 2005). Baroness Harris of Richmond asked whether proposed targets for proscription appear on the lists of other organisations: 'Have other European Union member states, for example, imposed proscriptions on them? For that matter, have any other Government asked us to proscribe them?' (Harris 2006). Labour Peer, Lord Rosser (2017), sought further information on the Home Secretary's decision-making process in the proscription of four additional organisations in December 2017: 'In the case of the four groups or organisations covered by the order, which of those five [discretionary] factors … were key to the Home Secretary deciding to exercise her discretion to proscribe?' Lord Dholokia (2005), finally, combined an appeal for greater specificity on the criteria for inclusion upon the UK's list of banned organisations, with a concern about the hastiness of proscription:

> We are unhappy for the Government to rush terrorism-related legislation in the manner in which we seem to be dealing with it at present. In future, it would be helpful to know what criteria are used for proscribing international terrorist organisations, and whether they are different from those for national organisations. Could the Minister spell out the criteria by which we judge their particular threats? As I say, do these organisations know they are being proscribed? What sort of assets do they hold in this country? Do they have contacts with organisations in the United Kingdom? Why has no nationally based organisation been proscribed, when some of them have already been identified in speeches made by the Home Secretary and Prime Minister? What provision is being made in the Terrorism Bill – soon to reach this House – for the future proscription of organisations?

Questions of procedure

A third set of questions focuses on the mechanics of proscription, with numerous parliamentarians asking how the outlawing of enemies works in practice. Simon Hughes, for example, enquired in 2002 whether a domestic threat was required for a group to be proscribed by the UK: 'Is it sufficient for the purposes of the legislation for the Home Secretary to be of the view that a threat exists abroad?' (Hughes 2002). Douglas Hogg, the same year, asked of ministerial responsibility: 'which minister decides on proscription? I refer to the substance and not the form' (Hogg 2002). Others enquire into this power's flexibility and ability to counter terrorist groups which fragment or re-brand: 'As soon as organisations are banned, they change their name' (Mercer 2006). This concern – a recurrent one as we have already seen – resurfaced recently, with the emergence of ISIS from al Qaeda in Iraq. As Diana Johnson noted in the relevant 2014 debate, this development raised important (and interesting) questions around the origins of ISIS's proscription:

> The proscription of ISIS is unusual, because it is rare for an organisation to get so large and well funded before a proscription order is imposed. The US State Department proscribed ISIS in 2004, when ISIS was known as al-Qaeda in Iraq. Will the Minister confirm whether it was regarded as a proscribed group at that time because it was an affiliate of al-Qaeda? In 2013, ISIS attempted to merge with the al-Nusra Front, another affiliate of al-Qaeda. That merger seemed to prompt the United Kingdom Government to list the al-Nusra Front as an affiliate of al-Qaeda, and therefore as a proscribed organisation. Will the Minister be clear about the status of ISIS at that time and why it was not specifically listed? (Johnson 2014b)

Baroness Smith, in the House of Lords debate on the same order, similarly asked: 'I am trying to understand how such proscription orders work in practice. Was there a gap during which ISIL was neither proscribed as being part of al-Qaeda nor, until Friday, proscribed in its own right?' (Smith 2014). And the question emerged again, too, in the December 2016 debate on the far-right organisation, National Action: 'how easy or otherwise will it be for this organisation to get round the order? Can it do that simply by renaming itself or setting up another organisation, which may not be all that difficult?' (Lord Rosser 2016).

Less common, but related, are questions relating to membership of proscribed organisations. As one intervention had it – in relation to: 'the wearing of clothing, the distribution of materials, the use of flags and so on' - 'Several organisations are attempting to subvert proscription through slight alterations in those materials. How robust are the measures to ensure that people are not attempting to evade the system of proscription?' (Doughty 2014). Similarly unusual – because of the rarity of this practice – are questions around the UK's ability to differentiate between internal branches of organisations in cases where proscription is to be applied only to a part of the whole. As Lord Kingsland (2008) asked of Hezbollah: 'the Government have emphasised that this order will not affect Hezbollah's political, social and humanitarian activities ... can the minister explain how this distinction will work in practice? Can the group be simultaneously legitimate and a terrorist organisation?' This issue of conceptualising terrorism was addressed head on in a 2014 intervention by Diane Johnson (2014c), in which she asked: 'does the Minister think that the way of defining terror for the purpose of proscription is sufficient to allow a terror group to be clearly identified?'

Parliamentary discussion on the mechanics of proscription also includes much comparative questioning. Some, such as Keith Vaz (2014c), seek to put the British experience in broader context: 'Will he tell the House whether the organisation responsible has already been proscribed in the United States of America, and whether it has been proscribed in any other European country?' Others focus instead on the politics of international cooperation, such as Shabana Mahmood who asked of TTP in 2011: 'What co-operation has there been between the government and our allies engaged in operations in Afghanistan and other parts of the world in terms of proscribing it?' (Mahmood 2011). Conservative MP Tobias Ellwood, similarly, asked of the Indian Mujahideen: 'What international coordination is there to ensure that if such an organisation is proscribed in one country, it is proscribed in other countries that we see as our allies?' (Ellwood 2012). Keith Vaz (2014a) asked, more specifically, about international consultation within proscription decisions:

> When we proscribe an organisation that has links to other countries—the first two the Minister mentioned have links to Egypt; the second

> two have links to Tunisia—do we consult those countries before placing an order before the House? I support what the Minister is doing today, but I just want to be clear about the process. Did we tell those countries that the orders were on their way?

Lord Rosser wanted to know whether the UK was encouraging other governments to follow its lead: 'are we pressing other countries to take similar action in respect of this organisation?' (Rosser 2011). Meanwhile, Shabana Mahmood – in the Commons debate on the same order – sought further detail on the exercise of ministerial discretion in the case of TTP: '[the] criteria seem to be perfectly sensible in providing the basic test against which a Secretary of State may decide to exercise his or her discretion, but will the Minister shed some light on how, in this particular case, they have been applied?' (Mahmood 2011).

A particularly prominent source of procedural questioning in this context are the mechanics of *de*proscription and the processes by which organisations are removed from the Home Office's list. Shabana Mahmood – again in the debate discussed above – asked: 'will the Minister give the House some details about the procedure by which the government intend to keep the list of proscribed organisations under review?' (Mahmood 2011). Jeremy Corbyn, the following year, asked in a debate on the Indian Mujahideen: 'what reviews have been conducted of all the other organisations on the list? Every time these orders come up, we seem to add to the list, rather than subtract from it' (Corbyn 2012). Diana Johnson, in 2014, sought justification for the continuing failure to remove groups from the UK's list:

> According to the independent reviewer's website last summer, the Home Office had compiled a list of up to 14 groups that no longer met the criteria for proscription. Will the Minister confirm that that is correct? (Johnson 2014a)

In the same debate, she asked for elaboration on how individuals affected by proscription might appeal that decision:

> does the Minister consider it appropriate to set out in detail how that [deproscription] procedure takes place, so that hon. Members can fully understand how an individual, who might put themselves

> in difficulty by coming forward, might access it and take it forward? (Johnson 2014a)

MP for the Democratic Unionist Party Nigel Dodds, in a debate on Ansar Bayt al-Maqdi (ABM), sought similar clarification on the description of deproscription contained within an accompanying explanatory memorandum:

> Paragraph 12 of the explanatory memorandum states: 'If a proscribed organization ... applies to the Secretary of State for deproscription, the proscription of the organisation will be reviewed'. How does that work in practice? If an organisation and its members are illegal – proscribed – how do they have the locus to apply to have the proscription reviewed? (Dodds 2014)

Labour MP Rudi Vis wondered whether the (common) practice of multiple proscriptions would have implications for deproscription decisions, whereby: 'in 2001 we had one vote on the proscription of 21 organisations. If any of those organisations were to be de-proscribed ... would there have to be a review of all 21 proscribed organisations, because there was just one vote?' (Vis 2006). Meanwhile, Keith Vaz wanted to know where responsibility lay for bringing forward a case for deproscription: 'How do we de-proscribe an organisation that does not exist? Who makes the application when no members of the LTTE are operating in the United Kingdom? Who will write a letter to the Home Secretary to say, "Dear Home Secretary, please de-proscribe us" when the group no longer exists?' (Vaz 2012a).

Questions of consequence

A fourth set of questions focuses on the outcomes of proscription. Although some of these concentrate on artefacts of terrorism – 'what becomes the status of such websites in British law once proscription has taken place?' (Grieve 2005) – most of these emphasise the consequences of this power for individuals or organisations. More critical interventions concentrate their attention on the implications for the rights and human security of those accused of association with proscribed organisations. The use of this power to smooth deportation, for instance, and the impact of this upon protections afforded by the European Convention on Human Rights, concerned Lady Hermon:

> If a non-British national who is within the jurisdiction of the UK is a member of, or associated with, any of the four proscribed organisations listed in the order, can he be deported to a country where he will almost certainly be put to death or at least subjected to inhumane and degrading treatment or torture? I am greatly worried about the powers that we are taking to ourselves because the rights, privileges and the guarantees of the convention apply to everyone in the jurisdiction, irrespective of nationality. (Hermon 2002)[2]

Others focus more closely on the utility of proscription within the criminal justice system, asking 'how can we be sure that adding organisations to the list in any way makes our authorities effective in combating them?' (Gapes 2017). Such questions often involve requests for case study or statistical evidence. They include Mike Hancock's request for greater information on the power's application: 'Can the Minister give us details of any charges that have been brought against individuals who have been involved with organisations since they have been proscribed? Have any of those charges led to successful convictions?' (Hancock 2006). Baroness Anelay, similarly, wanted to know: 'Can the Minister … tell the House what direct action is taken by the police to deal with organisations after they are proscribed?' (Anelay 2006). Each of these questions returned to a more wide-ranging query of proscription's evidence base raised by Lord Kingsland the previous year:

> The Government have already proscribed 39 organisations. Have they engaged in an assessment of the effectiveness of proscription as a means of protecting the citizens of this country against the terrorist threat? In other words, how successful has been the effect of putting organisations on the proscribed list? Have any of the proscribed organisations put on the list been closed down as a result? Is there any evidence to demonstrate that listing leads to increased terrorist arrests, or assists in seizing terrorist assets – or that listing simply drives these organisations underground and makes them harder to monitor? I use these questions as illustrative of a general request to understand exactly how the Government are assessing the effect of the policy they set out under the Act. (Kingsland 2005)

David Heath wondered about the worth of proscription, given the availability of alternative, less dramatic, charges: 'Why are so few prosecutions brought? Prosecuting for incitement could be more effective than the heavy-handed approach of proscription' (Heath 2006). Lord Rosser (2014), more pointedly still, asked: 'it appears that there have been very few such successful prosecutions [relating to proscription]. Why is this the case?' As he continued:

> It would be helpful if the Minister could say why successful prosecutions appear to be the case very infrequently. Can he also provide, now or subsequently, information on the number of people who have been, first, prosecuted, and, secondly, successfully prosecuted under each of the 15 [proscription] orders that have previously been laid under the terms of the Terrorism Act 2000 for supporting, belonging to, inviting support for or arranging a meeting to support a proscribed organisation?

Conservative MP David Ruffley returned to the existence of exploitable loopholes noted above, with especial focus on Hezbollah: 'What consideration has been given to the possibility of people getting around the proscription order?' (Ruffley 2008). A concern shared by Lord Davies (2016), but with emphasis here on terrorist financing: 'has it been possible in this case, and would it normally be the Government's practice, to freeze these funds in some way before the announcement of the proscription?' In a subsequent debate on al-Shabaab, Baroness Neville-Jones – later appointed Minister of State for Security and Counter-Terrorism – asked about the consequences of proscription for diaspora communities, in light of the UK's counter-radicalisation framework, Prevent:

> What, if anything, are the Government able to do to encourage UK diaspora communities here to exercise their responsibilities regarding that group? Obviously, we need to encourage people not to support it. As noble Lords, know, we take the view that it is very important for the Government to promote the notion of shared values. Is anything being done to surround the proscription order in the area of what we might call 'Prevent'? (Neville-Jones 2010)

Questions such as these, as demonstrated by the Liberal Democrat Tom Brake, frequently return to those questions of effectiveness discussed in the context of relevant academic literature in Chapter 2:

> At the risk of being criticised by the Government for asking some questions, let me say that it is legitimate for us to use this opportunity to examine the effectiveness of such bans. I would like the Minister to confirm whether there has been any analysis of the effectiveness of bans. We know that organisations such as Islam4UK have had a number of name changes and may have sought to get round bans in that way. It would be interesting to know how often that has happened, how many organisations, having been banned, have simply changed their names to escape that ban, and how many people have been prosecuted and found guilty of belonging to a proscribed organisation that has been banned in that way. It is incumbent on us to ensure that the legislation we pass is as effective as possible in tackling terrorism, but there is still a fundamental question about banning and whether it is productive in any shape or form. (Brake 2010)

Questions of exclusion

A final category of questions that returns repeatedly across these debates is on the status of groups not presently under consideration for proscription. Conservative MP John Redwood framed this question broadly during a 2006 debate on al-Ghurabaa, the Saved Sect, the Baluchistan Liberation Army and Teyrebaz Azadiye Kurdistan, asking: 'How many organisations that are as bad as the ones that we are proscribing today should be proscribed?' (Redwood 2006). Far more frequent than this, however, are enquiries about specific organisations which are deemed similarly – or more – worthy of banning than those being considered. Numerous organisations have been put forward as candidates for the UK's list including, *inter alia*: the Al Aqsa Martyrs Brigade – 'I ask her what the situation is with groups such as the Al Aqsa Martyrs Brigades, which, for all I know, may be on a previous list' (Lewis 2005); other parts of Hezbollah – 'Will the government explain why the external security organisation of Hezbollah is proscribed, whereas Hezbollah's political arm and its guerrilla forces in south Lebanon are not?' (Mercer 2006)[3]; the Supporters of Sharia – 'Why is Abu Hamza's old group, the Supporters of Sharia, not proscribed?' (Mercer 2006); and the Students' Islamic Movement in India – 'Will the Minister explain why the SIMI has not been included in the order?' (Johnson 2012).

Questions such as these often make reference to the banning of specific organisations in other countries. Michael Gove, in 2006, for instance, asked of the Muslim Brotherhood – 'Why is the Muslim Brotherhood – a proscribed organisation in other countries … not being adequately dealt with here?' (Gove 2006). Labour MP Chris Bryant, in the same debate, asked Tony McNulty, then Minister for Policing, Community, Security and Community Safety: 'Will my hon. Friend explain why we have not got on today's list the organisation Hizb ut-Tahrir, whose activities are proscribed in Germany and many other countries and are of deep concern to many people in this country?' (Bryant 2006). Patrick Mercer, in the same debate, asked similarly of Hizb-ut-Tahrir (HuT): 'HUT is banned from many Arab countries, the former Soviet Union and Germany, yet London appears to be its headquarters. Its UK branch was founded by Omar Bakri Muhammad, who founded al-Muhajiroun, and it talks endlessly about anti-Muslim integration. On 5 August 2005, the Prime Minister said that HUT would be proscribed. Why has it not been?' (Mercer 2006).

Less common, but equally important, are questions on the deproscription of specific groups already on the UK's list. In a 2002 House of Commons debate, for example, Simon Hughes asked: 'will the Home Secretary say whether de-proscription of the LTTE is under active consideration? Which organisations currently on the list have appealed to the Home Secretary and, beyond him, to the commission?' (Hughes 2002). Jeremy Corbyn asked a similar question in a critique of proscription's stymieing impact on conflict resolution: 'Can the Minister tell us whether he has any plans to review any other organisations that are on the list, such as those representing the Kurdish and Tamil communities, as a way of promoting political dialogue and discourse to bring about peaceful resolutions to conflict?' (Corbyn 2011). Particularly pronounced, however, were those around the Peoples' Mujahedeen of Iran (PMOI) in debates that took place before this organisation was successfully delisted in June 2008 following judgements of the Proscribed Organisations Appeals Commission and the Court of Appeal. Baroness Harris, for example, asked: 'Do the government feel that it is time to look again at the proscription of the PMOI?' (Harris 2006). For, as Conservative peer Lord Waddington put it, the PMOI 'always looked very different from the other bodies listed in the schedule … proscription was at Iran's behest and borne of an understandable wish that we should be seen to be playing a full part in the international community's fight against terrorism' (Waddington 2006).

Questions, audiences and temporalities in proscription debates

It is frequently argued that matters of national security see increased deference to political executives, even amongst elites such as those parliamentarians whose words are considered above (on this, see Neal 2012, 359). Indeed, proscription powers would appear an initially appealing candidate through which to make such an analysis for at least two reasons. In the first instance, very explicit arguments about the need for parliamentary acquiescence constitute a recurrent feature of these debates. Such arguments include statements of ignorance about the proposed targets for proscription – 'At the time of our last debate, I think that few members of the public had heard of Boko Haram' (Smith 2014); professions of trust in the executive – 'We must, of course, give the Home Secretary the benefit of the doubt. I am sure she has looked at this case very carefully indeed' (Vaz 2012b); and, regular, repeated assertions of the need for cross-party consensus on national security – 'we will work with the Government to protect our national security, and in that spirit we will support the order' (Mahmood 2011).

The second reason is that – in the UK at least – Parliament *always* acquiesces to the addition of new organisations to the list of proscribed groups, even when the targets or consequences of this designation are themselves ill-understood. In the UK to date, every organisation brought forward by the executive for proscription has been accepted by Parliament; a feature which becomes, perhaps, more telling given that relevant orders frequently list multiple organisations for simultaneous proscription which must be accepted or rejected in their entirety (Legrand and Jarvis 2014, 453). Thus, although three organisations have successfully achieved deproscription and therefore no longer find themselves on the UK's list (Home Office 2017) – the Peoples' Mujaheddin of Iraq (PMOI, also known as the Mujaheddin e Khalq) in June 2008; the International Sikh Youth Federation (ISYF) in March 2016; and Hezb-e Islami Gulbuddin (HIG) in December 2017 – there does, at least at first glance, seem to be considerable evidence of legislative deference in this context.

Yet, as the above discussion demonstrates, there also exists substantial indication of parliamentary deliberation and even scrutiny around proscription decisions, much of which takes the form of legislative questioning in relation to the executive's efforts (see

Neal 2012; Roe 2012). The asking of questions such as those considered above, clearly, falls frequently short of the sort of contestation implied in existing frameworks of audience engagement in security politics, such as, for example, discussion of desecuritisation, reverse securitisation and counter-securitisation (Vuori 2011: 192; also Aradau 2004; Roe 2004). Yet, there is more taking place here than straightforward or immediate acceptance of an attempted securitising act. For, as the above shows, these questions include quite significant appeals to the executive that it explain or justify a chosen course of action, and that it clarify the process and consequences thereof. In the above case of exclusion, moreover, we also see questions functioning as demands that the executive defend its decision *not* to take alternative courses of action.

How parliamentary audiences participate in the security politics associated with proscription is, therefore, both important and diverse. Figure 5.1 offers a typology of these, highlighting five logics of enquiry constituted by the above questions.

Figure 5.1 clearly imposes artificial parsimony on the range of questions uncovered in our research. Its aim, however, is to illuminate the diversity of roles that one particular 'audience' – here parliamentarians – might play within a very specific dramatisation of security; and the importance of this for that drama's unfolding. These questions are, importantly, asked in a bounded context, which includes, amongst other things, general agreement on the government's mandate to designate proscribed groups; respect for parliamentary institutions; a UK party system which circumscribes space for dissent; and – indeed – a set of codified rules around the appropriate form and content of questions.[4] As the House of Commons Information Office (2010) clarifies: 'A parliamentary question must: either (a) seek information ("what, how many, when…") or (b) press for action ("if he will…")'.

Some of these questions may function simultaneously as demands for justification and clarification. Others asked in this or other contexts may not fit any of our five types. This, in a sense, is less significant than the typology's primary purpose, which is to demonstrate a diversity of ways in which parliamentarians engage in the politics of proscription that fall short of outright advocacy or contestation of specific decisions to extend the UK's list of banned groups. A parliamentarian asking the executive who made a particular (proscription) decision, or why such a decision was made,

Figure 5.1 Towards a typology of security questions

Security question	Illustration from parliamentary debate	Description	Example
Justification	Questions of timing	Why is this decision being taken [at this moment]?	'Why is the move to proscribe those two organisations only taking place now?'
Explanation	Questions of criteria	How was this decision arrived at?	'What triggered the Government's view that the organisation should be proscribed?'
Elaboration	Questions of procedure	What does this decision entail?	'Which minister decides on proscription?'
Clarification	Questions of consequence	What are the effects of this decision?	'What becomes the status of such websites in British law once proscription has taken place?'
Scope	Questions of exclusion	Why were other potential decisions not taken?	'Why is Abu Hamza's old group, the Supporters of Shariah not proscribed?'

for instance, does not necessarily imply, evidence or lead to the acceptance or rejection of such a decision. Yet, at least in this context, such questions are an integral part of the discursive and performative politics in which security dramas play out, incorporating but extending beyond matters of legality and legitimacy that are vital to the efficacy of security practices (Balzacq 2015b).

Taking such questions seriously also generates a more nuanced understanding of the workings of security discourse than that offered by some of the most prominent and influential theories thereof. Where Buzan *et al.*'s (1998, 33) original framing of securitisation, for instance, suggested that security's grammar consisted of 'a plot that includes existential threat, point of no return, and a possible way out', the above analysis illustrates some of the ways in which a specific form of audience – parliamentarians – participate in the elaboration, refinement and even critique of such plots, in this specific scenario. This includes by asking questions around: the nature of the existential threat (questions of criteria and exclusion); when the point of no return was reached (questions of timing); and, indeed, the nature of the proposed way out (questions of procedure and consequence).

In light of this, these questions therefore pose considerable analytical potential for extending and nuancing existing theorisations of securitisation in at least three directions (see Balzacq 2005, 2011, 2015a; McDonald 2008). In the first instance, engaging with them in debate on proscription contributes to the rethinking of securitisation's various temporalities that has become more prominent within sociological critiques of the so-called 'Copenhagen School' approach. Just as multiple unexceptional, unspectacular 'little security nothings' do much of the work in producing contemporary insecurities (Huysmans 2011), the above shows that the role of a specific audience – parliamentarians – in securitisation's drama, too, extends back in time – prior to the 'moment' of decision – to include any number of earlier, smaller, interactions with (in this case) the political executive. Exploring the operation of these interactions therefore not only sheds light on the shaping of a drama's denouement: clarifying how the 'urgency of emergency' (Salter 2011, 116) is produced within and across a period of time characterised by its own interruptions and pauses. It also – more obviously – expands understanding of the mechanism of justification often considered vital for successful securitisation. Thus, where

Balzacq (2015b, 6), drawing on Vuori (2008), argues: 'justification is the mechanism that creates and sustains security practices … Leaders make security practices essentially by arguing their case that X counts as a threat', the above demonstrates that 'leaders' may be called upon to do far more than this, including having to clarify why other security practices and other threats were *not* pursued.

Second, the above analysis also problematises the strict actor/audience separation which was integral to the initial formulation of securitisation theory. In one sense, the above acts of questioning situate legislators as an independent audience scrutinising the executive through demands for justification, clarification, explanation and elaboration. At the same time, this scrutiny occurs within an intersubjective framework that entails non-questioning, or *a priori* consensus around: the normative probity of proscription; government's democratic mandate; the power's general appropriateness to the problem; and procedural rigour. Approached thus, and as we argue further in Chapter 7, the asking – and answering – of such questions works alongside the instances of critique explored in Chapter 3 to offer a significant contribution to the reproduction of executive credibility through a performance of democratic scrutiny: positioning these parliamentarians as partners in the production and selling of a particular security discourse to wider (public) audiences, rather than – only – as potential 'customers' of such a discourse. This, clearly, blurs any neat distinction between actor and audience in this context – highlighting the scope for movement between, or multiple occupancy of, these roles in security politics.

Third, our elaboration of the types of discursive manoeuvre evident within parliamentary security politics around proscription also poses methodological insight for exploring heterogeneities within seemingly undifferentiated audiences. By centring the content of questions within our analysis, the above points to considerable opportunity for future work on the constitution of cleavages, fractures or subsidiary audiences within singular settings populated by ostensibly identifiable (here, elite) communities (see Salter 2008). Such work could draw upon tools within (critical) discourse analysis and related fields such as critical communication studies to map potentially pertinent relationships between topics, speakers and attributes (perhaps, in our case, including party affiliation, House membership, or constituency). And, in the process, to explore how members of internally differentiated audiences position themselves as critics of, or contributors to, securitising moves over a period of time.

From questions to identity and ritual

It is not self-evident whether proscription necessarily constitutes the type of security politics Buzan *et al.* (1998) had in mind when they initially introduced the notion of securitisation to capture the construction of security threats by politically powerful actors. In the first instance, as demonstrated in this and the preceding chapter, efforts to add particular organisations to the UK's list of banned groups often lack the language of emergency associated with the Copenhagen School framework. Indeed, several parliamentarians discussed above are explicit in calling for a deceleration of decision-making in this context. On top of this, an argument might also be made that the proscription regime becomes increasingly normalised with each successive stretching of its scope to additional organisations. Engaging with audience questions, then, might perhaps be further justification for – as much as a consequence of – recent attempts to move beyond the strictures of the Copenhagen School approach to securitisation, its importance in establishing this research agenda notwithstanding.

Regardless, our aim in this chapter has been to show how parliamentary debate around proscription incorporates a wide range of questions that help to situate this power discursively. In this context, at least, the legislature seems to play an important discursive role in shaping proscription's meaning; a role, moreover, that involves appealing for – perhaps even demanding – justification, explanation, elaboration, clarification, and, no doubt, more besides, from the executive. And, as demonstrated above, this analysis has additional significance for thinking through the temporalities and fixedness of roles within security dramas, as well as for future investigation of audience heterogeneities. In this sense, as outlined in the chapter's introduction, we are more interested here in the constitutive role of such questions than their causal impact on the outcome of any particular debate, any parliamentarian's vote, political accountability, or, indeed, any wider audience.

As we go on to argue in Chapter 6, these debates, which are characterised by the questions explored above, as well as by statements such as those investigated in Chapter 4, are integral to the politics of identity made apparent through the proscription process. This is, not least, because of their contribution to a performance of democratic accountability within the British political system.

Notes

1 These debates very occasionally include appeals for a slower decision-making process, as, for instance, in John McDonnell's (2005) contribution to a House of Commons debate in which he argued: 'I would welcome a longer time scale in terms of the indication of organisations that may be listed for proscription so that we can be more engaged in the debate, if only through informal discussions.'
2 A distinct, if related, concern around torture in proscription decisions was raised by Helen Goodman in a 2005 House of Commons debate, in which she asked about the reliability of efforts to identify members of proscribed organisations: 'I am sure that what the Minister said about the IJU is correct, but after the uprising in Andijan people were massacred by the Government, and others were tortured into saying that they belonged to radical Islamist groups. How will the Minister make a judgment in practice about whether people truly belong to the IJU, which is to be proscribed, or have simply been tortured into claiming that they do?' (Goodman 2005).
3 Hezbollah's military apparatus was subsequently proscribed by the United Kingdom in 2008. Other states, including the US and Canada, have gone further and listed the entire organisation.
4 In several debates on this power's extension, a relevant spokesperson *begins* the discussion by expressing the opposition's decision to support the proposal.

6 Proscription and identity: constructions of self and other in parliamentary debate

In Chapters 4 and 5 we saw how parliamentarians debate orders from the executive to extend the UK's list of proscribed organisations. As argued there, these debates include, amongst other things, diverse perspectives on proscription's significance, as well as a range of questions regarding proscription's mechanics, consequences and beyond. These perspectives and questions, we argued, help to make proscription meaningful (for national security, citizenship and so forth), shedding light on a more complex politics of security than we might expect, and than is assumed within prominent understandings and theorisations of the workings of security discourse.

Our argument in this chapter is that these proscription debates perform a further constitutive function – and one that remains largely overlooked within the existing academic literature on this power considered in Chapter 2. That is, the language, tropes, arguments and other rhetorical devices employed by parliamentarians are (also) an important part of a process of identity formation in which the UK self – or components thereof such as Parliament or parliamentarians – is distinguished from its (here) terrorist others. Proscription debates – and the banning of terrorist groups – are, we suggest, therefore performative in that they confer illegitimacy on their target(s): producing particular organisations and their members as 'unacceptable in this country' (Hughes 2002). In so doing, moreover, they (re-)produce the United Kingdom as a particular type of political entity with specific – and, very explicitly, liberal, democratic – attributes and characteristics.

We begin our analysis by exploring some of the ways in which terrorism, in general, is constructed within these debates. As we shall see, there are clear intertextualities with other forms of political (and other) discourse here, including, for instance, the recurrence of familiar metaphors and characterisations of this threat. A second section explores how specific groups being considered for proscription are represented, and the ways in which specific identity claims contribute to, and dovetail with, constructions of threat. A third section then investigates explicit and implicit constructions of the United Kingdom and its constituents (especially Parliament and politicians). Taking these themes together, we contend that these debates help to (re)produce a relatively straightforward antagonistic relationship between, on the one hand, a liberal, open and responsible UK self which is mindful of cultural and religious difference, and both cautious and moderate in its actions. And, on the other, a series of illiberal, irrational and extremist terrorist others steadfast in their determination to wage immoral violences. Importantly, although there are examples of genuine dissent in these debates, critics of proscription or its application tend to *reproduce* rather than contest this binary relationship, by appealing for the UK to be truer to its own self-identity.

Important to note here is that the content and tenor of political debate in this context has remained stable and unvarying across the eighteen years or so of our empirical focus despite some notable fluctuations in this period, which has included: five political administrations – the Labour governments of Tony Blair and Gordon Brown, the Coalition government headed by the Conservative Prime Minster David Cameron, and the Conservative governments of Cameron and his successor Theresa May; a number of high-profile incidents (actual and attempted) designated 'terrorist' including the London bombings of 7 July 2005, the attempted attacks of 21 July 2005, also in London, a June 2007 attack at Glasgow International Airport, the May 2013 killing of Lee Rigby in Woolwich and the 2017 attacks at the Manchester Arena, London Bridge and Finsbury Mosque; and, considerable alteration to the UK's military contribution to the 'war on terror'.[1] This sense of discursive continuity, of course, feeds into our discussion of ritual that follows in Chapter 7.

'Like battling a hydra' (Heath 2006): constructing the terrorist threat

Parliamentary debate around proscription is saturated by references to terrorism in general, and the threat posed thereof. Much discursive work is done by familiar metaphors in this discourse, including those associated with animalism – 'Abu Qatada, one of the spiders at the centre of the terrorist web in Europe' (Dismore 2002); disease – 'the awful scourge and threat of terrorism' (Hermon 2002) – the 'plague of our time' (Abbott 2016) in which 'terrorist ideology has become a cancer' (Abbott 2016); and, monstrosity – '[counter-terrorism] is like battling a hydra' (Heath 2006).

There is, to be sure, reflection on terrorism's causes in these debates. This includes attention to macro-level, geopolitical developments – 'instability and violence in Libya has provided an environment for groups such as Ansar al-Sharia-Benghazi to operate. Syria and Iraq have become a crucible of terror and violence' (Brokenshire 2014b); through to internal dynamics within established organisations – 'as Daesh is becoming more fragmented ... there will be more organisations to proscribe as small splinter groups and organisations spring up' (Shannon 2016a); and – in more recent proscriptions – anxiety around the influence of social media and the internet as a 'safe haven for terrorists and extremists' (Brokenshire 2015). There is also, though, metaphysical and moralised condemnation in which terrorism and terrorists are equivalenced to historical threats – 'al-Qaeda, Boko Haram and, above all, ISIS ... form an international fascist movement specialising in spreading terror' (Marllesford 2015) – or contemporary taboos 'people are being radicalised and groomed, perhaps in their bedrooms, on the internet' (Wallace 2016) – or simply reviled as 'dastardly' (Kerr 2017), 'grotesque' (Johnson 2015) and 'evil' (Maclean 2017).

Terrorism, constructed thus, is deceitful and opportunistic: 'there are those, terrorists among them, who crawl on the back of human disasters ... such as earthquakes, and the money directly funds terrorism' (McNulty 2007); craven, 'cowards like to target civilians' (Hopkins 2011); calculating, '[we were] horrified by the death of Drummer Rigby a few weeks ago, in a manner that was not only bestial, but designed to shock and grab national and international headlines' (Mercer 2013); unrepentant, 'they almost boast; they claim responsibility for their activities and they damn themselves by what they say' (Smith 2016); and, immoral, such that 'a small number of contorted and evil individuals can grab international headlines. That, of course, is what terrorism is about' (Mercer 2013).

Presented in this way, terrorism is reduced to an irrational acting out of 'twisted' (Wallace 2016) individuals – 'fundamentalist organisations are, by their nature, barking mad' (Simpson 2005) – and extra-political activity: 'The random slaughter of innocent individuals can play no part in the process of trying to bring about political change' (Grieve 2005). Terrorism's nature means the current threat may be ill-understood by the public – 'We must not just proscribe those organisations, but have a campaign for public information and public training that makes people understand what the threat is and know what to do about it' (Mercer 2005). And, indeed, unforeseeable even for those political elites with privileged access to security knowledge denied to others:

> As we look forward to 2017, the major threats we face are asymmetric – a couple of young men in their bedroom can wreak terror in their community – international and deadly, and they are so rapidly changing that we could not in the House have foreseen them a decade ago. (Abbott 2016)

Contemporary groups – as constructed in these debates – benefit from a decentralised organisation in which, 'the nature of terrorism has changed. The structures used are more fluid and international' (McNulty 2006), and thus 'one core or central organisation may have many different parts' (Smith 2013). This threat has a 'dynamism and intensity' (Hayes 2016) that is global – 'Our borders are not such that terrorism will not cross them ... this sort of contemporary terrorism knows no boundaries' (Smith 2016), whereby:

> In the end, one cannot seriously distinguish between the effect of terrorist activities abroad and the security of the United Kingdom, as if somehow they represent a threat to this country or to our allies only if they are active in this country. One has to take a view that makes it clear that terrorism is a global phenomenon and that it is extremely interactive in its character. (Neville-Jones 2011)

These characterisations of contemporary terrorism work to (re) produce this phenomenon as a 'grave and relentless' (Brokenshire 2015) threat of considerable magnitude: 'This is not an academic debate … on which we can all take a view; it is a real situation … We face a serious threat and these people are concerned in terrorism … people have been murdering other people' (Blears 2005). Indeed, it is commonplace in the opening remarks in these debates to cite the Home Office's current assessment of the threat level, for instance: 'The international terrorist threat to the UK, our interests abroad and our international partners remains severe and sustained' (McNulty 2008). Or, in more elaborate form, more recently:

> By way of context for tonight's debate, the Joint Terrorism Analysis Centre has raised the threat level for international terrorism from substantial to severe, as it assesses a terrorist attack on the United Kingdom to be highly likely. The House will be aware that the Home Secretary stated earlier this week that we believe that more than 500 British nationals have travelled to Syria and Iraq, and that thousands from other European and western countries have joined them. (Brokenshire 2014b)

Terrorism, here, is capricious – 'events in Bali … show how unpredictable terrorism can be' (Bridgeman 2002) – hitherto under-estimated – 'Many of us have ignored the problem of terrorism – writing it off, thinking it would never happen here in this country' (Mercer 2005), and unprecedented – 'The extent to which [the 9/11] terrorists would go in pursuit of their goals was a shock to all the civilised world' (Filkin 2002). It is, more simply, 'a perpetual threat in this country' (Ruffley 2008). Although dramatic events such as the post-2011 conflict in Syria are seen to influence national security – 'we face our gravest threat in the past 13 years' (Vaz 2014b) – future attacks are frequently depicted as simply inevitable: 'We will be attacked again. We must ensure next time that we first make things more difficult for our enemies and that casualties are minimised' (Mercer 2005). If such sentiments speak, at least, to a hope of managing the threat of contemporary terrorism – 'The government are determined to do all we can to minimise the threat, including using proscription' (McNulty 2008), the qualitative distinction between this threat and those confronted in previous conflicts encourages circumspection on the challenge of so doing. As James Brokenshire (2015) put it in a March 2015 debate, 'We have a generational struggle against ISIL and the ideology that underpins it'. For Baroness Smith, similarly, in an earlier debate:

> Each generation faces new and different threats. The horrors of war today are very different from those that our predecessors faced on the beaches of Normandy, and the tools needed today to tackle the threats are very different. From talking to Normandy veterans and others, I gather that to many people today's threats seem less tangible and harder to understand.

'A very nasty group' (Hamwee 2010): constructing proscribed organisations

Proscription debates also, as we would expect, contain considerable discussion of the specific groups being brought forward for consideration. These groups vary markedly, spanning, on the one hand, relatively unheard of organisations such as Ansaru, of which, as Keith Vaz noted in November 2012: 'Many of us, myself included, probably discovered this organisation only when we knew that a proscription order was going to be issued on the Floor of the House today' (Vaz 2012b); through to others such as ISIS, which 'has an extremely high profile. There can be few who have not heard of it and it is known worldwide to be ruthless and very hard-line' (Smith 2014). References to the ruthlessness of particular organisations appear fairly frequently. The Parliamentary Under-Secretary of State at the Home Office, Lord Filkin (2002), for instance, noted of the Abu Sayyaf Group: 'The ASG has killed hostages when ransoms have not been paid and is known to have links to Al Qaeda', while the Conservative MP Patrick Mercer more recently noted that those organisations up for proscription in a 2005 debate 'owe their allegiance to Abu Mussab al-Zarqawi, the gentleman who brings us on the television screen the charming views of Britons' heads being sliced off with bread knives' (Mercer 2005). Baronness Neville-Jones, in 2010, expressed her condemnation of al-Shabaab because:

> Having read what this group does and has done, including its near-daily attacks against aid groups and the African Union peacekeepers, one of the most chilling things was to see that its name is Arabic for 'youth'. Its members are very young and it makes a point of recruiting the young. (Neville-Jones 2010)

These characterisations of ruthlessness dovetail with descriptions of duplicity – 'It has a rather innocent sounding name "the community of the learned students of Pakistan" and sounds entirely inoffensive, but in fact it is armed to the teeth, it has some of the nastiest propaganda at its disposal and it particularly selects people who support human rights to target' (Falkner 2011); resilience – 'Boko Haram is a prolific terrorist organisation, based in Nigeria' (Attlee 2013); more generalised constructions of foulness, as in Grieve's (2005) account of the 'murderous and unpleasant' Hezb-e Islami; as well as specific accusations of various forms of (racially and religiously motivated) extremism, such as:

> the rabid anti-Semitism of those groups is notorious. One need only look at some of the statements made on the demonstration, such as, "Butcher those who mock Islam", or "Kill those who insult Islam", and the people dressed as suicide bombers, to apprehend the nature of Al-Ghurabaa. (Dismore 2006)

Identity-based descriptions constitute another mainstay of these debates. Asbat Al-Ansar, for example, 'is a Sunni Muslim terrorist organisation' (Filkin 2002); Minbar Ansar Deen is a 'Salafist group based in the UK that promotes and encourages terrorism' (Brokenshire 2013); the 'Popular Front for the Liberation of Palestine-General Command is a left-wing nationalist Palestinian militant organisation' (Brokenshire 2014a); 'Kateeba al-Kawthar describes itself as a group of mujaheddin from more than 20 countries that seeks a just—as it perversely says—Islamic nation' (Brokenshire 2014a); and National Action is a 'racist, neo-Nazi group' (Wallace 2016). As, indeed, do brief biographical sketches of the organisations in question, illustrated by chronological listings of their atrocities, often in these debates' opening remarks (see Chapter 7). David Hanson's description of al-Shabaab in a March 2010 debate is representative of this:

> the group has waged a violent campaign against the Somali Transitional Federal Government, and against the African Union peacekeeping troops in Somalia since the beginning of 2007. It has undertaken a range of terrorist tactics, such as suicide operations and roadside bombings, and mounted a range of operations since 2007, including in June 2009 in Beledweyne, one of the largest cities in Somalia, a suicide car bomb attack that killed the transitional

> Government's Security Minister and, as a random act of terrorism, about 30 other people in the process. The organisation has launched terrorist attacks outside areas under its control, most notably in October 2008, when five co-ordinated suicide attacks were mounted against targets in Somaliland and Puntland, including the Ethiopian embassy, the presidential palace and the United Nations Development Programme compound. (Hanson 2010)

As, more recently, is James Brokenshire's description of Turkiye Halk Kurtulus Partisi-Cephesi:

> Turkiye Halk Kurtulus Partisi-Cephesi, also known as the People's Liberation Party/Front of Turkey, is a left-wing organisation. It was formed in 1994. The group grew out of the Turkish extreme-left revolutionary youth movements that formed in the 1960s and 1970s. THKP-C now operates as a pro-Assad militia group fighting in Syria, and it has developed increased capabilities since the Syrian insurgency. It is assessed as having been involved in an attack in Reyhanli in Turkey last May, which killed more than 50 people and injured more than 100 people. Its leader, Mihrac Ural, holds Syrian citizenship and was born in the southern province of Hatay, where the organisation has always been most prominent. Ural has formed several other groups under the THKP-C umbrella, including Mukavamet Suriye, which is reported to have been responsible for the recent Banias massacre, which killed at least 145 people. (Brokenshire 2014)

In common with the more generalised constructions of terrorism considered above, representations of these specific groups typically emphasise the danger they pose. Of the PFLP, for instance, MPs are reminded that 'In the past, it has blown up aircraft and used bombs. After a period of little activity over the past 20 years, the group has resurfaced in the Syrian conflict, supporting Assad, and has been active in refugee camps' (Johnson 2014b). Such activities, as Johnson continues, have significant geopolitical ramifications, demonstrating 'the ability of groups in Syria to destabilise the wider region' (Johnson 2014b). In other instances, the clandestine and immoral nature of fifteen separate organisations listed for proscription in October 2005 is highlighted: 'many of them operate in an underground fashion and obviously want to hide their activities because of the nature of the evil in which they are involved' (Bassam 2005). Al-Shabaab is, for Lord Hamwee, 'clearly a very nasty group' (Hamwee 2010); Tehrik-e-Taliban Pakistan, for Damian Green, a 'murderous organisation' (Green 2011). Violences attributed to Ansaru are 'barbaric and despicable' (Smith 2012); while Richard Fuller MP, speaking in the House of Commons, condemned the 'disgusting attacks by Boko Haram in Nigeria' (Fuller 2013). Indeed, in some instances the case for proscription is deemed simply self-evident, as Lord Bassam argued in a 2005 debate: 'we took the view that none of the names in the current order were sufficiently controversial to be likely to be opposed' (Bassam 2005).

References to the specifically Islamist ambitions or essence of many of these groups are a further recurrent feature of many of these debates. Thus, for example, 'TNSM's [Tehrik Nefaz-e Shari'at Muhammadi's] objective is the militant enforcement of sharia law in Pakistan' (McNulty 2007); the Turkistan Islamic Party is 'an Islamic terrorist and separatist organisation' (Hayes 2016), while 'ISIL is a brutal Sunni Islamist terrorist group active in Iraq and Syria. The group adheres to a global jihadist ideology, following an extreme interpretation of Islam which is anti-Western and promotes sectarian violence' (Taylor 2014). Also common is discussion of the links between the groups being proscribed and more prominent organisations. In older instances, connections to al Qaeda, whether ideological or physical, received particular attention. Four groups listed in October 2002, for example, were deemed to 'have discernible links with al Qaeda' (Blunkett 2002). In al-Shabaab's proscription it was noted that the group had 'pledged its allegiance to Osama bin Laden [and] ... announced its intention to combine the jihad in the horn of Africa with the global jihad led by al Qaeda' (Hanson 2010); and, Jund al Khalifa-Algeria is depicted as 'an Islamist militant group believed to be made up of members of dormant al-Qaeda cells' (Bates 2015). In more recent debates, connections to ISIS or Daesh have also begun to trouble parliamentarians:

> MIT pledged its allegiance to Daesh in July 2014 and is assessed to have links to other Daesh- affiliated terrorist groups in the region ... Jamaah Anshorut Daulah ... was established in March 2015, following the merger of several Indonesian extremist and terrorist groups aligned to Daesh. (Ahmad 2016)

To be clear, parliamentarians work hard in these constructions to differentiate supporters of these groups from 'ordinary' Muslims, and Islam more generally. Propaganda from al-Gurabaa and the Saved Sect, for instance, is deemed to constitute 'insidious attacks on the broad values that the overwhelming majority of communities in this country hold dear' (McNulty 2006), and, as Baroness Neville-Jones said of the Tehrik-e-Taliban Pakistan, for instance, it is 'not representative of Pakistani or Muslim communities in the UK … I know that the vast majority of British Muslims joined us all in condemning those abhorrent acts of violence' (Neville-Jones 2011). Indeed, as Dominic Grieve (2005) noted in a 2005 debate: 'some of these organisations have been murdering fellow Muslims'. The emphasis on Islamist organisations within the UK's list of proscribed groups was linked, however, by Alan Simpson, to an implicit or latent Islamophobia – 'We take a very different view of Christian fundamentalists, including those who advocate armed insurgency and the killing of nationally elected leaders, because they are somehow part of civilisation' (Simpson 2005) – although many contributors to these debates have expressed fears that minority ethnic or religious communities in the UK would suffer from guilt by association following the proscription of targeted groups. As Keith Vaz (2010), a regular critic, put it: 'As soon as an order is passed, it has a draconian effect on communities unconnected with the organisation concerned.'

'This is not China' (Vaz 2014b): constructing the UK self

A third important feature of these debates is their (re)production of the UK self as a specific type of actor within the international system. Although allusions to British stoicism come through in places – 'when these events happen, or when it is reported that they have been averted, the British public's response is to just get up and carry on. That is the full measure of the spirit of the people of these islands' (Kerr 2017) – more common is mention of its liberal and democratic traditions, and the need to strike 'balances' (see Waldron 2003) both between security and liberty, and between individual and collective interests.

This construction serves to position the UK as a bastion of those liberal democratic values which are deemed so anathema to the targets of proscription. Crispin Blunt, for instance, argued in a 2010 debate: 'Decisions to proscribe organisations should not be taken lightly. Free speech is a cornerstone of our democracy' (Blunt 2010). Meanwhile, for James Brokenshire (2013) similarly: 'If we are to uphold our values and traditions, and uphold who we are as a country, we must ensure that we properly respect individual freedoms and liberties while providing collective security for the country as a whole.' Comparisons with seemingly less enlightened countries are offered: 'This is not China. We are a parliamentary democracy and therefore we will have to persuade' (Vaz 2014b). As, indeed, are explicit contrasts with those groups specifically targeted for proscription, whereby the power becomes positioned as a way of perpetuating (rather than, say, undermining) Britain's liberal democratic heritage:

> Proscription is a tool for us to stay within the rule of law. Over the past few weeks and months we have heard a lot about dealing with terrorism. The big thing that we have heard on the difference between us and terrorists is that we believe in the rule of law with the oversight of this House. (Wallace 2017)

As David Blunkett (2002), put it: 'there is always a difficult issue concerning the proportionality and balance between the rights of individuals in a free society and the protection and public interest of that society as a whole. We debated that at length last year, and we will continue to debate it because we are a democracy'. Such protections, of course, extend to all of Britain's citizens, given its multi-cultural heritage:

> It is right that we proscribe an organisation only after a great deal of thought and when there is a lot of evidence. As a central London MP, I want to say how lucky we are that the relations between different cultures and races in this country are so good. We too often take that for granted, particularly given the situation in many other western countries, including in the United States and other European countries. The melting pot in my constituency and throughout London operates very well. (Field 2013)

This construction of the United Kingdom as a liberal democratic defender of inclusiveness and freedom feeds into two further identity claims. The first is the construction of the UK as a responsible global citizen: 'working closely with all those seeking to fight terrorism' (Blunkett 2002) and 'supporting the rest of the international community to tackle terrorism' (Blears 2005). Proscription, as we saw in Chapter 4, is positioned within these debates as having a direct impact on the UK's integration within the international society: 'Proscription will align the UK with the emerging international consensus against this murderous organisation' (Green 2011). This recognition of global duty stretches, within these debates, beyond this power alone, including, for instance, to financial generosity towards those suffering from terrorism elsewhere: 'The Government are greatly concerned to support the nation of Somalia and to tackle some of the wider issues to date. In 2009, the UK Government contributed £15.7million to the African Union mission in Somalia' (Hanson 2010). In other instances, it is the cajoling of less democratic, less responsible states that takes precedence: 'While the UK Government continue to work with Nigeria to fight terrorism, we make it clear that human rights must be respected at all times in our work to defeat terrorism across the globe' (Brokenshire 2007).

The second identity claim is to the UK (and its government) as a responsible legislator. Here, explicit recognition that proscription constitutes a 'tough power ... [with] wide-ranging impact' (McNulty 2008) – a perennial feature in this debate, as we saw in Chapter 4 – is accompanied by repeated affirmation of the diligence with which decisions on proscription are taken. As various speakers make clear, such decisions are 'tackled with the utmost seriousness and care' (Blunkett 2002), 'only after the most thorough scrutiny of all the intelligence put forward by the security and intelligence agencies' (Bassam 2005), and kept, importantly, 'under ongoing review' (Hanson 2010). Those bringing proscription orders forward for consideration do so with as much transparency as possible – 'we always seek to present as much information as we can about groups that we are seeking to proscribe' (Brokenshire 2014b) – although (as opposition parties frequently accept) this is likely limited by national security considerations.

This production of Britain as a responsible legislator is augmented by reference to the informed judgement of an executive able to exercise its discretion for the good of the country:

> the Home Secretary has to decide whether it is right in the light of our national interests, even if it meets the statutory definition of terrorism, to proscribe the organisation. Sometimes it may not be. It is important, for example, that it does not adversely impact on any ongoing investigations and supports other members of the international community. (Ashton 2014)

Indeed, in more recent debates, it has become standard to refer, in the opening remarks, to the range of information underpinning proscription decisions:

> the proscription process is a thorough one. It includes looking at open source material, intelligence material and advice that reflects consultation across Government, including with the intelligence and law enforcement agencies. (Hayes 2016)

Beyond any claim to non-partisan and discretionary judgement, this sense of responsibility is augmented, further, by reference to British independence – 'we must consider the evidence properly, rather than automatically taking on board what other states may say' (Brokenshire 2014b), and a willingness to consult with the expertise of critical voices, where appropriate, such as that of Lord Carlile – then Independent Reviewer of Terrorism Legislation: 'I take his words very seriously because he has a great deal of experience in these matters. He has been an intelligent, critical supporter of the legislation that we have brought forward to parliament over a number of years' (Bassam 2005). This rigorous, careful and reflexive approach to proscription – in which Parliament is further assisted by 'a proscription working group … which continually reviews all the organisations on the list which are entirely movable feasts' (McNulty 2006) – helps to ensure that real threats are distinguished from the attention-seeking behaviour of vexatious, if less dangerous, organisations:

> we take the evidence that is presented, and respond at speed, when people are prepared to provide verifiable evidence … and we check the difference between the loud-mouthed extremists who endeavour to provide diversion but, although undoubted irritants, require evidence to show that they are a threat, and those who do not clearly

> spell out their views or identity precisely because they constitute a greater threat and need to be taken more seriously. (Blunkett 2002)

It is this diligence, indeed, that underpins explicit expressions of support for proscription orders from opposition parties – another perennial feature of these debates – where the trustworthiness of political representatives means that support can be given based 'on the assurances of Ministers' (Smith 2014). Decisions to proscribe, then, render 'party political difference' (Blunkett 2002) irrelevant, contributing to 'a long tradition of cross-party co-operation on issues of national security [such that] … In this case, the Opposition are happy to accept the Minister, and the Home Secretary's assurances on the basis that all three groups seem to have been involved in terrorism at the highest end of seriousness' (Johnson 2014b). As Keith Vaz (2012a) summarised in a 2012 debate: 'I have never known Government and Opposition to disagree on the proscription of an organisation.'

'We make sure we are better than them' (Wallace 2017): (re)producing self and other

As the above suggests, parliamentary debate around proscription works to institute a relatively stable binary opposition between a liberal, responsible and democratic United Kingdom, and its 'nasty' (Hamwee 2010) terrorist enemies with their catalogues of atrocities and determination to shortcut the political process through violent means. Proscription, here, constitutes a 'watch list of the lowest of the low and those who threaten the very democratic process that we are privileged to be part of' (Shannon 2016b).

Within this construction, the former is moderate, cautious and circumspect in its exercise of power; cognisant of the ramifications of proscription decisions for abstract civil liberties, as well as for the lives of those likely caught up in their operation. Its terrorist enemies, in contrast – both in general and specifically – are irrational purveyors of 'terrible acts of violence against innocent civilians' (McNulty 2006). Where the UK takes pride in its multicultural heritage, protecting and celebrating ethnic, religious and cultural differences, its enemies possess a hatred of other faiths and ways of life. Where the UK conducts its (legislative) business with openness and transparency – even in matters of national security – its terrorist others choose to 'operate in an underground fashion and ... hide their activities because of the nature of the evil in which they are involved' (Bassam 2005). And, in contrast to the ideological and unwavering dogmatism of its (irrational) foes, Britain remains humble and cautious in exercising such a significant power, even to the point of re-visiting previous decisions: 'Measures such as proscription are very important in forcing the Government, quite rightly, to mark out why they think something should be proscribed, and in holding those groups to account. But when the evidence changes, we change with it' (Wallace 2017).

The starkness of the constructed opposition between the UK self and various 'terrorist' others both feeds and contributes a sense of 'foreignness' to organisations whose membership and ambitions might be entirely domestic in nature. This sense of foreignness is compounded, in part, by the state's official categorisation of banned organisations and groups which offers only two types, distinguishing between 'international terrorist organisations [which] are proscribed under the Terrorism Act 2000', and '14 organisations in Northern Ireland that were proscribed under previous legislation' (Home Office 2019, 6). This typology positions groups such as 'Islam4UK', then, under the former category despite the organisation's very explicit ambitions relating to the Islamisation of the United Kingdom.[2]

Beyond these geopolitical typological issues (see also Jackson *et al.* 2009, 152–153), the character of this articulated antagonistic relationship also, of course, bears considerable resemblance to that constructed in executive speech, popular culture and many of the other more widely studied sites of discourse in the years since 9/11 (see, amongst others, Croft 2006; Hoskins and O'Loughlin 2009; Jarvis 2009b; Spencer 2010; Holland 2012). As earlier literature has shown, metaphors and tropes around disease, animalism, evil and barbarism have been a staple of counter-terrorism rhetoric in the twenty-first century. As, indeed, is the equivalencing of terrorist groups in a way that flattens their differences such that terrorism becomes a more menacing, singular 'Terrorism'. Such homogenisation is compounded, in this case, by the exercise of multiple proscription orders, and the repeated attempt to discern connections between their targets and more familiar foes, especially al Qaeda and ISIS.

Despite the rather formulaic character of these debates, genuine dissent towards specific proposals for proscription is, on occasion, expressed. In some instances, this takes the form of a questioning of proscription's underpinning logic, which relies upon an understanding of terrorism as an identity rather than a tactic. With reference to the now-deproscribed PMOI, for example, Lord Corbett (2008) notes, 'The Government's argument at both the Proscribed Organisations Appeal Commission and the Court of Appeal can be summed up this way: once a terrorist, always a terrorist. This is a nonsense'. This is problematic for some, such as Lord Wallace (2008), because the designations of such groups are as fluid as their behaviour, such that 'one man's terrorist activity outside Britain is another person's armed resistance'. Others build on the types of argument and question explored in Chapters 4 and 5 to articulate principled objections to the proscription process itself, including advocating a right to resist brutal regimes: 'whenever it is argued that the organisations that we are proscribing seek to overthrow a legitimate government, we should have a thorough discussion about the legitimacy of that government. We must be sure that not all those who are engaged in armed struggle are defined as terrorists' (McDonnell 2005). In other cases, it is effectiveness that comes under scrutiny given that such decisions exclude the possibility of negotiating with one's opponents or enemies. As Lord Wallace (2008), again, argued, with reference to the earlier Northern Ireland Peace Process:

> we all have to deal with movements of which we disapprove. Hamas, similarly, is a very unattractive body in many ways but a necessary partner in negotiating to move away from the Israel/Palestine conflict. Many of us intensely disliked negotiating with Sinn Fein but, again, recognised that it was necessary.

These arguments – that terrorists can be engaged politically, and do change their behaviour – are relatively unusual in these debates. More frequently voiced criticisms are those that rely instead upon an appeal for the UK to more consistently enact its political values and traditions. As we saw in Chapter 4, questions about the process of proscription – such as the lack of effective parliamentary scrutiny, or the absence of adequate opportunities for contesting proscription decisions – are common. What is striking about these types of question, however, is that they constitute, in effect, an appeal for greater attentiveness to precisely the sort of – liberal, democratic, responsible, transparent – identity posited by *advocates* of proscription. Douglas Hogg, in 2002, for instance, questioned the dominance enjoyed by political executives in this area of security politics: 'British citizens are made the subject of the criminal law and their rights to support political organisations are constrained by what is very largely an Executive action' (Hogg 2002). Alan Simpson in 2005, similarly, questioned the executive's need to withhold evidence from the UK's primary legislative body:

> When we put names on a list of proscribed organisations, it seems reasonable to ask what evidence we have of the involvement of any of them in current actions that have threatened the security of the United Kingdom. To be unable to get an answer to that is deeply worrying in the democratic process. (Simpson 2005)

Such criticisms are important for our purposes because they work also to (re)construct Parliament and parliamentarians as of especial importance in the fight against terrorism. As a prominent and regular contributor put it:

> It is right that Parliament should scrutinise such important decisions. Even though this order will quite rightly go through the House unchallenged tonight, it is the scrutiny that Parliament gives to such orders and legislation that is so vital. (Vaz 2008)

From identity to ritual

In this chapter, we have explored one significant constitutive function of parliamentary debates on the proscription of terrorist organisations, arguing that these debates play a key role in constructing the identity of the UK self and its terrorist others. Where the former is positioned as a responsible, liberal agent both conscious of and cautious in the exercise of its powers, the latter emerge as irrational bringers of violence driven by enmity and an identification with al Qaeda rather than any concrete, discernible political agenda. The terrorist threat, in this articulation, is significant and genuine, with proscription representing one 'small weapon in the armoury in the fight against terrorism' (Carmichael 2005).

By exploring this constitutive role, the chapter builds on the discussion of proscription's positioning in Chapters 4 and 5, thus further moving debate away from the focus on ethics and effectiveness that has dominated existing scholarship on this power. Our emphasis, as before, has been not on what the United Kingdom or its parliamentarians (seek to) *do* in the use of this power. Rather, on how the discussion and enactment of this power – almost always a foregone conclusion – works to (re)produce the United Kingdom (and its enemies) as a particular kind of actor in world politics. As David Campbell (1992, 9) put it:

> Whether we are talking of 'the body' or 'the state,' or of particular bodies and states, the identity of each is performatively constituted. Moreover, the constitution of identity is achieved through the inscription of boundaries that serve to demarcate an 'inside' from an 'outside', a 'self' from an 'other', a 'domestic' from a 'foreign'.

Underpinning this effort is an argument that processes of proscribing terrorist organisations not only (help) demarcate the limits of political speech and association. They also – by designating specific organisations as banned or 'unwelcome' from, in our case, the United Kingdom – work to institute and govern the polity's boundaries and the separation of self from others that these boundaries mark. In doing this, the debate and exercise of proscription powers are vital for the reproduction of political imaginaries and identities, 'structuring and sanctioning the terms' in which (counter-)terrorism measures are discussed (Huysmans and Buonfino 2008, 767). As we have seen, these debates are themselves part of the process of storying who 'we' are, as well as of justifying how 'we' intend to respond to 'them'.[3] In Chapter 7, we build on this analysis to explore the ritualisation of these debates and their arguments, questions and identity claims.

Notes

1 Most prominent amongst these were a thirteen-year military campaign in Afghanistan and a six-year campaign in Iraq.

2 Our thanks to one of the reviewers of our original manuscript for bringing this point to our attention.

3 As the above discussion illustrates, the 'we' in this story is not fixed, referring variously to the British state, society or the UK Parliament. We are grateful to an anonymous reviewer for clarifying this point.

7 The ritual of proscription: reproducing liberal democracy

Taken together, the preceding chapters explore three prominent dimensions of parliamentary proscription debates within the United Kingdom. First, Chapter 4 set out competing constructions of proscription's significance, limitations and dangers. Second, in Chapter 5, were a diversity of questions posed (often repeatedly) by contributors to these debates. And, third, in Chapter 6 we turned to the broader contribution of these discussions to identity claims about the national self and various (defined and undefined) terrorist others. In so doing, we argued that these debates both drew upon and helped reproduce a relatively stable antagonistic relationship between, on the one hand, the United Kingdom (and, within this, Parliament and parliamentarians) as a liberal, democratic, cautious and moderate member of the international community. And, on the other, its illiberal, irrational, evil and cowardly terrorist others determined to bring violence upon the United Kingdom, its allies, or innocent citizens therein. Significantly, this constructed antagonism ('us' and 'them') remains relatively stable, and unchanged by any of the dynamics that might bring it under pressure, be they significant events, the specific organisations targeted for proscription, party political allegiances, or even whether contributors to these debates positioned themselves as advocates or critics of the UK's proscription regime.

In this chapter, we bring all of this together by asking, in light of the above: what, exactly, should we make of parliamentary proscription debates and their apparent stability over time? Our answer (hinted at in the chapter title!) involves further reflection on three important characteristics of these debates: their remarkably standardised and repetitive framing; their ability to incorporate – and, indeed, often celebrate – dissent, disagreement and contestation; and, their unfolding toward a predictable, seemingly inevitable, conclusion which results, invariably, in the banning of whichever organisation(s) have been proposed by the Home Secretary or her representative. Foregrounding these characteristics, we argue, indicates that it might be insightful to approach these debates not as a decision-making enterprise in which their outcome is, genuinely, uncertain (to ban, or not to ban). But, rather – and no less importantly – as a form of political ritual that is deeply implicated in the (re)production of political authority and liberal democracy.

Proscription debates offer an excellent opportunity for exploring the workings and implications of parliamentary ritual for two reasons. In the first instance, as noted in Chapter 1, the symbolic importance of this power – and the decisions made in its name – are widely acknowledged by advocates and critics of proscription alike. Hazel Blears, for instance, argued in a 2005 debate, that proscription 'sends out a strong signal … that the UK rejects such organisations and their claims to legitimacy' (Blears 2005). In the same debate, the Conservative MP Patrick Mercer (2005) invoked proscription's symbolic aspect, but – in this case – to appeal for *further* action, arguing: 'I believe that these organisations need to be considered in detail. We need to have time to debate what they stand for. We should not simply take a block of names, philosophies and confused ideologies, give them a convenient tag, and write them off.' Proscription's symbolic dimension, then, is here taken for granted by a supporter and critic of this power, on opposing sides of the British political divide.

Second, as developed below, efforts to extend the UK's list of proscribed groups take place within discrete, self-contained debates which are heavily orchestrated and marked by many of the features associated with any number of more familiar rituals. These include, amongst other things: a core script which is often repeated verbatim, with minor alterations, across parliamentary debates; a set of established and identifiable roles that are taken up by participants within them (participants who, of course, come and go with the passage of time); repeated arguments around the importance of respecting these debates and their outcomes; and – perhaps most significant of all – a predictable, seemingly near-inevitable, outcome which is known in advance to those parliamentarians present at these debates. Approached in this way, the bounded, formulaic nature of these debates renders proscription a conceptually and methodologically promising case through which to explore the operation of contemporary political ritual. So doing, moreover, sheds light upon a number of additional crucial dynamics within contemporary political life, including: the importance – and limitations – of dissent; the performance of cross-party consensus; the preservation and reinforcement of Parliament's sovereign right to delineate the parameters of legitimate political enterprise; and, the importance of ritual for the constitution of political reality, which includes the construction or making real of newly banned 'terrorist' organisations.

In order to do the above, we begin by contextualising our argument within a surprisingly contemporary academic literature on political ritual; one that builds upon a much longer established body of sociological and anthropological work. From there, we offer our own heuristic through which to make sense of rituals, arguing that they: contribute to the orchestration of specific behaviours; are implicated in the constitution of reality; sediment their constructed realities via repetition over time; and, have a significant performative dimension. A third section then re-interprets these proscription debates via this heuristic.

Politics and ritual

Our argument in this chapter builds upon a recent, and arguably belated, burgeoning of interest amongst political analysts in the ritualistic and ceremonial aspects of parliaments. Recent, prominent, contributors to this research have argued it is vital that we take seriously Parliament's 'symbolic dimensions of political action' (Atkins and Finlayson 2016, 15) in order to 'trace the circulation of meanings, the particularity of institutional cultures and the sedimentation of power in political institutions' (Rai 2010, 284). Rituals in parliamentary settings are – for contributors to this literature – vital in sustaining and perpetuating these dynamics, having profound importance in the constitution of political realities within and beyond this rarefied space. As such, attention to them is vital, because:

> In parliaments, rules and norms become in/visible through ceremony and ritual – mirroring dominant social relations on the one hand and, on the other, almost through a sleight of hand, making them disappear from view. (Rai 2010, 287)

This recent interest in parliamentary ritual is a little surprising, given that there has been a long-standing and well-known literature on the socio-political significance of ritual, more generally, stretching back at least to Émile Durkheim's work on religious rituals as mechanisms of social integration (Durkheim 2001). Durkheim framed rituals as vital to the maintenance of social order: approaching these as a means through which to organise sacred symbols and beliefs, reinforce group norms, and cohere social solidarity (Durkheim 2001, 355–365). Subsequent scholarship – often, but not exclusively, located within anthropology and sociology – has built on these insights, albeit with divergence on the specific social significance of ritual. For some, such as Roy Rappaport, rituals matter as a means of constructing human cognition or achieving social solidarity (see Gluckman and Forde 1962; also Bell 2011, 172). Others see ritual as a mechanism for controlling violence (Girard 1977); or for the transmission of culture and identity (Turner 1967). For others still, rituals might be thought of in more sceptical vein, as 'purely activity' with 'no meaning, goal or aim' (Staal 1996, 131).

The role of ritual in space which is explicitly and obviously *political* is, of course, our primary concern in this book, with its focus on the extent to which standardised and repetitive symbolic practices might 'serve certain political interests and undermine others' (Kertzer 1989, 87). Such a concern is represented in a nascent but important scholarship on British politics (e.g. Crewe 2005; Rhodes 2005; Waylen 2010; Lovenduski 2012; Atkins and Finlayson 2016; Rai 2014); securitisation (Oren and Solomon 2015) and public policy (t'Hart 1993). Despite differences therein, many of these authors demonstrate how discursive, rhetorical or performative analysis of various sorts can be employed to reveal the 'symbolic, ritualised aspect of contemporary political and ideological practices' within Parliament (Atkins and Finlayson 2016). Analysing debates from the United Kingdom's House of Lords, for example, Emma Crewe posits a 'theatrical quality' to the 'rituals of debate' that are laden with 'rules and symbols of engagement' (2005, 184). Recognition of these aspects of Parliament, is crucial, argues Shirin Rai (2010, 281), because our understanding of representative institutions is incomplete without consideration of the 'institution-specific culture which socializes members in their participation'.

This scholarship is interesting, in part, because it develops earlier (and often, today, curiously forgotten) observations around the influence of subtle, symbolic and ritualised political behaviours within influential works on power. Peter Bachrach and Morton S. Baratz, for instance, suggest that in reinforcing social and political values, power works via an institutional 'mobilization of bias', understood as 'a set of predominant values, beliefs, *rituals*, and institutional procedures ("rules of the game") that operate systematically and consistently to the benefit of certain persons and groups at the expense of others' (1970, 43; our emphasis). Developing this argument, Steven Lukes (1975) argued that analysis of rituals' 'cognitive role' in society is of fundamental importance, since such activities give meaning to social relations, and organise perceptions of past, present and future. In his words:

> [ritual] helps define as authoritative certain ways of seeing society: it serves to specify what in society is of special significance, it draws people's attention to certain forms of relationships and activity – and at the same time, therefore, it deflects their attention from other forms, since every way of seeing it also a way of not seeing. (Lukes 1975, 301)

In making this argument, Lukes presents rituals as 'rule-governed' symbolic activities that focus participants' attention upon 'objects of thought and feeling' that are held to have special significance (1975, 291). Rule-governed, for Lukes, describes the bringing of patterned and normative pressure on participants (1975, 290) through activities which operate as 'modes of exercising, or seeking to exercise, power along the cognitive dimension'.

Lukes' approach to ritual and the significance thereof has been developed in more recent work. Joni Lovenduski (2012), for example, builds on his analysis in order to shed light upon the gendered dimensions of Prime Minister's Questions in the House of Commons:

> Rituals are a means of control, part of the mechanisms that may privilege certain kinds of masculinity, thereby sending a strong symbolic

> message to women that politicians are men who have repertoires of behaviour that are not available to women (and some men). (2012, 317)

Waylen, similarly, draws on Lukes to locate ritual within institutionalist literature, emphasising the working of rules and norms in formal and informal institutions. Here she frames ritual as key to understanding 'change, power and conflict' as well as for making sense of actors' behaviours in 'legislatures as institutions' (2010, 353). Yet, one of the most prominent scholars on political ritual, Shirin Rai, critiques Lukes' characterisation, arguing that where Lukes reveals the 'cognitive dimension' of ritual in political contexts, he fails to account for the 'sedimented and reflective power of political ritual – of how power is reflected as well as challenged in and through political ritual' (2010, 290). Rituals, for Rai, are a means by which government power is 'constructed and reproduced' and 'new meanings of power are inscribed' (2010, 287). Thus, although this scholarship shares an emphasis on the importance of ritual for political power, there is, clearly, disagreement over how this materialises. As will become clearer in the following section, our emphasis here is, primarily (although not exclusively), on the first of the following four perspectives delineated by Catherine Bell in a recent typology of scholarship in this area: (1) how rituals empower those in charge of rituals; (2) how that power is also constrained; (3) how rituals come to dominate participants; and (4) how that domination involves 'negotiated participation', which in turn may empower participants (Bell 2011, 211).

Understanding ritual

Although the above demonstrates considerable and ongoing contestation over the significance of ritual, it is possible to highlight some of its core characteristics as useful points towards a heuristic for making sense of this type of activity (see Rappaport 1999; Grimes 2014). Consider, to begin with, the following three definitions, separated by twenty years or so:

> Ritual action has a formal quality to it. It follows highly standardized, structured sequences and is often enacted at certain places and times

> that are themselves endowed with a special meaning. Ritual action is repetitive and, therefore, often redundant, but these very factors serve as an important means of channelling emotion, guiding cognition, and organizing social groups. (Kertzer 1989, 9)

> [Ritual includes] performance, formality, invariance, inclusion of both acts and utterances, encoding by other than the performers. (Rappaport 1999, 24)

> [Rituals] may use a delineated and structured space … a special periodicity … restricted codes of communication to heighten the formality of movement and speech; distinct and specialized personnel; objects, texts, and dress designated for use in these activities alone; verbal and gestural combinations that evoke or purport to be the ways things have always been done … particular physical or mental states; and the involvement of a particular constituency not necessarily assembled for any other activities. (Bell 2011, 204–205)

Taking them together, Kertzer, Rappaport and Bell all highlight several characteristics of rituals that move us towards an understanding of their core features. These characteristics include: a sense of formality that separates ritual from more mundane or quotidian social activities; a sense of internal linearity, given the specific sequencing of moments within rituals as they unfold; the idea that rituals tend to be situated within designated and recognisable sites, such that they cannot take place simply anywhere; the participation (and perhaps reproduction) of identifiable social groups and roles; the repetition (and therefore recognisability) of specific rituals over extended periods of time; and the cognitive guidance that they offer to their participants. These characterisations also, importantly, underline that, despite divergent views on ritual's role and significance, there may be scope for some agreement on the identification thereof.

Approached in this way, examples of ritual are not hard to identify. They might include, *inter alia*, rituals that are public – for example, the solemnity of wreath-laying at the Cenotaph and the ubiquity of remembrance poppies in commemoration of those killed in past wars; those that are institutional – such as (in the British political context) the annual Queen's Speech and the dragging of the newly-elected Speaker of the House of Commons to the Chair in order to mark the opening of the British Parliament;

the sectarian – for example, traditional, and controversial, parades in communities within Northern Ireland; the secular – such as university graduations or the singing of Auld Lang Syne during New Year's Eve celebrations; the religious – including, amongst many others, the bar mitzvah, confessionals, periods of fasting, and so on; and the private – such as the spreading of a deceased's ashes upon a symbolically significant place, or the 'toasting' with alcoholic drinks in order to celebrate, remember or wish well. Given that many rituals, of course, fit across and beyond these categories, the point here is the ubiquity and diversity of ritual within contemporary life rather than a formal or exhaustive typology.

The proscription ritual: a heuristic

Our own heuristic for the study of political ritual emerges from our analysis of proscription, as well as our reading of the above scholarship, and is intended to shed light on the unfolding of political rituals, and their significance for generating particular outcomes. It is organised around four prominent qualities, that are simultaneous and interactive, rather than fixed and determined: (1) orchestration: rituals as assemblages of symbolic behaviours; (2) constitutivity: rituals as a means of producing reality; (3) sedimentation: rituals as the reinforcement of constructed realities via repetition; and (4) performativity: rituals as a means of producing new ways of seeing the world. These attributes guide our understanding of the broad contours of a phenomenon which is found across histories, cultures and traditions.[1]

At their base, rituals can be approached as a framework for the *orchestration* of specific behaviours that become laden with symbolic significance through their integration within the ritualistic context. Exchanging rings or throwing one's hat in the air, for instance, provides vital, recognisable moments within many wedding and graduation ceremonies that might be expected by participants and observers alike. They also take on a specific – again, recognisable – significance in these contexts that the same physical behaviours obviously lack in other situations. This orchestration of expected and expectable behaviour is compounded by the fact that rituals typically occur within specific contexts – they are delimited to particular times and places. One is no more likely to get married in an Alabama classroom, for instance, than to pledge allegiance to the US flag in Canterbury Cathedral. It is further compounded by the procedure of rituals through a pre-configured template through which particular actors (interpreting specific roles), draw on established narratives (which may be more or less flexible in their interpretation) in a movement towards a predicted and predictable outcome (Kertzer 1989, 9–12; see also Rappaport 1999, 24; Bell 2011, 204–205).

Second, as well as orchestrating the behaviour of their participants and observers, rituals are also ontologically *constitutive* in that they contribute to the forging of shared understandings or interpretations of the world. This includes shared understandings of the ritual itself and its participants – for instance, that a university does indeed possess the authority to confer degrees – as well as broader understandings of the social and political world – until recently, for instance, a conception of marriage as a desirable goal only for heterosexual couples in love. As Kertzer argues, 'Through ritual, beliefs about the universe come to be acquired, reinforced and eventually changed' (1989, 9). The interplay of beliefs and symbols is central to rituals' constitutive function in which (a version of) reality – as an artifice of values, beliefs, norms – plays out through carefully selected narratives. The form taken by any particular ritual is therefore 'partly attributable to its morphological characteristics. *Its medium is part of its message*' (Moore and Myerhoff 1977, 8; emphasis added).

Third, rituals *sediment* their constituted realities through their 'invariance' (Rappaport 1999, 24) over time. Through 'repeated and simplified cultural communication', observers and participants in such rituals come to acquire and 'share a mutual belief in the descriptive and prescriptive validity of the communication's symbolic contents' (Alexander 2006, 29). In their reiteration over time, rituals *reinforce* and solidify incumbent symbols and ontologies. Rituals maintain links with the past by remaining internally consistent and 'only infrequently depart from the expectations of actors and scripts' (Alexander 2006, 41). Their 'sequestered' (Turner 1967, 183) and 'homeostatic' (Goody 1986, 21) character thereby serves to reinforce constituent symbols, beliefs and values. For Lévi-Strauss (1990, 675), rituals therefore constrict or narrow the critical faculties of their subjects; reinforcing established views and excluding alternatives via a 'bastardization of thought'.

Thus, finally, we draw attention to the *performative* dimension of ritual. Following Jeffrey Alexander's claim that 'all ritual has at its core a performative act' (2006, 38; see also Rappaport 1999), we emphasise the combination of perlocutionary and illocutionary efforts in ritual that together 'produce ontological effects, that is, that work to bring into being certain kinds of realities' (Butler 2010, 147). Illocutionary utterances serve to constitute pre-given ontological realities over time, producing them as necessary and uncontested: 'The point is not simply that such an "effect" is compounded through repetition, but that reiteration is the means through which that effect is established anew, time and again' (Butler 2010, 149). Since the strength of these 'ontological facts' are derived from 'discursive and non-discursive practices and institutions', the emphasis is not on the actor who speaks but the institutional context in which such discourse is licensed and codified. Butler uses the example of a judge to illustrate this point:

> The judge learns what to say, and must speak in codified ways, which means that the codification and ritualization of that discourse precedes and makes possible the subject who speaks. (2010, 148)

The perlocutionary performative represents an attempt by a located actor to persuade, inspire or induce in an audience a particular perception, sentiment or sense of the world. That is, an effort to help others see the world in the way the actor wants them to see it. Unlike an illocutionary act, the ontological effects sought are external to the actor: 'The success of a perlocutionary performative depends on good circumstances, even luck, that is, on an external reality that does not immediately or necessarily yield to the efficacy of sovereign authority' (Butler 2010, 152). Perlocution's corollary then is that all construction is imperfectly aimed, executed and adopted. Thus, where illocutionary capacity to bring into being new ontological realities implies a *sovereign* power to do so in an institutional or authorising environment, the perlocutionary, being dependent on the external felicities of the world, operates on condition of a *non-sovereign* authority.

Operationalising this performative heuristic returns us to the significance of ritual bracketed above. Our argument, in the remainder of this chapter, is that the proscription ritual ontologically 'creates' its targets – 'terrorist organisations' – ascribing those targets specific qualities such as those encountered in the previous chapter. In so doing, the ritual transmits a particular (version of) reality – via an 'interweaving of linguistic repetitions with speakers' and audiences' material performance' (Oren and Solomon 2015, 316) – producing such organisations as representing a threat to 'our' values and beliefs. And, in the process, the ritual also serves to reinforce a wider, but very particular, value system in which Parliament has a sovereign right to make the existence of specific organisations criminal and outlawed (see also Kertzer 1989; Lukes 1975). This reality-making capability, we suggest, is an inter-subjective one that involves shaping the cognition of those involved in, or addressed by, this ritual, even if 'the values and norms of ritual actions may be so axiomatic as to preclude the actor from seeing it in relation to either part or all of society' (Gusfield and Michalowicz 1984, 421). Figure 7.1 summarises this heuristic, with examples taken from the ritual of proscription to which we now turn.

The *orchestration* of the proscription ritual

We begin our elaboration of the proscription ritual by focusing on questions around who speaks, from where, and when, before turning more specifically to what is said.

Fixed authority, place, time and actors

As with other legislation, the proscription debates we have been considering throughout this book occur within Parliament's specific, pre-defined *time* and *place*. This time and place is a rarefied one to which a particular (and in many ways exclusive) cast of *actors* alone have physical access, although the actions therein are 'performed' to wider audiences via dedicated and other media networks, and, after the fact, through Hansard. The process of proscription within this space, as outlined above, is a strictly stylised one that may only be initiated at the fiat of the Home Secretary. Her order is laid before Parliament in accordance with stipulated protocols, and introduced to the House by the Under-Secretary of State for the Home Department, or a deputy. Once the order is put to the House, participation in these debates occurs only via highly stylised language adhering to prefigured types of speech set out in procedural rules, norms and conventions. Further, the format of a proscription debate conforms to a structured inter-personal interaction that is scheduled and policed by institutionally privileged actors – especially the Speaker of the House, assisted by the House's Table Office

Figure 7.1 Analysing political ritual: a framework with examples

Attribute	Ritual precepts	Manifestation	The proscription ritual
ORCHESTRATION	Fixed 'authority figures', time and place	Defined roles, place and time and authority figures administering the ritual	*A structured process; initiated by Minister, closed by Minister in the bounds of Parliament*
	A core script	A lexicon of words, narratives and proclamations that structure and punctuate the ritual	*A configured, unvarying repetition of the powers, their necessity, their lawfulness*
	Respect for ritual	Shared understanding of the norms of behaviour in the ritual	*Admonishment for perceived levity*
	A predetermined outcome	The outcome of the ritual is known by all participants	*All proscription orders have been passed without demur*
	Embedded symbols/ values	A core set of values are enunciated in and through the ritual	*Morally 'good' liberal values threatened by 'bad', illiberal terrorist others*
CONSTITUTIVITY	Intersubjective consensus	Tacit agreement amongst participants of the purpose, process and meanings of the ritual	*Cross-bench a priori assent on the probity and appropriateness of proscription*
	Contingent subject and/ or content	The circumstance and/or subject of the ritual changes	*Variations in organisations; questions of the expected repercussions; ministerial variation in debates*

Figure 7.1 (*cont.*)

Attribute	Ritual precepts	Manifestation	The proscription ritual
SEDIMENTATION	Repetition	Ritual's temporal recurrence reinforces its legitimacy and incumbent meanings	*Thirty-eight debates since 2002, all following the same procedure; each debate reproduces the probity, necessity and lawfulness of proscription*
PERFORMATIVE	Performative *illocution*	The ritual hosts the sovereign 'creation' or reification of subject(s)	*A 'terrorist organisation' is given legal form and cemented into legal texts*
	Performative *perlocution*	The authority of Parliament gives weight to perlocution	*MPs' narratives seek to ostracise/ delegitimise the 'terrorist organisation'*

clerks – who may determine the Order of Business, the posing of supplementary questions, the length of time allowed for any response, and so on. This authority ensures that specific enactments of this ritual adhere to an entrenched structure which is implicitly understood by its participants, and strengthened by frontbench agreement between the main parties. Unlike other debates, no divisions have ever been called in the case of proscription: when a motion is put, it is agreed.

A core script

Proscription debates often seem to forego the turbulence and diversity of many non-security debates. Though individual participants change, for example swapping opposition for government, this ritual's core incantation remains more or less consistent across time. The following example is taken from a July 2012 debate, introduced by James Brokenshire:

> I beg to move,
>
> That the draft Terrorism Act 2000 (Proscribed Organisations) (Amendment) Order 2012, which was laid before this House on 2 July, be approved.
>
> The Government are determined to do all we can to minimise the threat from terrorism to the UK and our interests abroad. Proscription of terrorist organisations is an important part of the Government's strategy to tackle terrorist activities. We would therefore like to add the organisation Indian Mujahideen — the IM — to the list of 47 international terrorist organisations, amending schedule 2 to the Terrorism Act 2000. This is the 10th proscription under the 2000 Act.
>
> Section 3 of the 2000 Act provides a power for the Home Secretary to proscribe an organisation if she believes it is currently concerned in terrorism. The Act specifies that an organisation is concerned in terrorism if it commits or participates in acts of terrorism; prepares for terrorism; promotes or encourages terrorism, including through the unlawful glorification of terrorism; or is otherwise concerned in terrorism. The Home Secretary may proscribe an organisation only if she believes it is concerned in terrorism. If the test is met, she may then exercise her discretion to proscribe the organisation. (Brokenshire 2012)

The following is taken from a December 2017 debate, opened by the Minister for Security Ben Wallace:

> I beg to move,
>
> That the draft Terrorism Act 2000 (Proscribed Organisations) (Amendment) Order 2017, which was laid before this House on 18 December, be approved.
>
> The threat level in the United Kingdom, which is set by the joint terrorism analysis centre, remains at severe. This means that a terrorist attack on our country is highly likely and could occur without warning. We can never entirely eliminate the threat from terrorism, but we are determined to do all we can to minimise the threat to the United Kingdom and our interests abroad, as well as to disrupt those who would engage in it. Recognising that terrorism is a global threat that is best tackled in partnership, it is also important that we demonstrate our support for other members of the international community in their efforts to tackle terrorism wherever it occurs.
>
> Proscription is an important part of the Government's strategy to disrupt the activities of terrorist groups and those who provide support to them. The order before the House today would add four groups to the list of proscribed organisations by amending schedule 2 of the Terrorism Act 2000: al-Ashtar Brigades, including its aliases Saraya al-Ashtar, Wa'ad Allah Brigades, Islamic Allah Brigades, Imam al-Mahdi Brigades and al-Haydariyah Brigades; al-Mukhtar Brigades, including Saraya al-Mukhtar; Hasam, including Harakat Sawa'd Misr and Harakat Hasm; and Liwa al-Thawra. This is the 22nd proscription order under the 2000 Act.
>
> The proscriptions send a strong message that terrorist activity is not tolerated wherever it happens. Under section 3 of the Act, the Home Secretary has the power to proscribe an organisation if she believes it is concerned in terrorism. If the statutory test is met, the Home Secretary may then exercise her discretion to proscribe the organisation. The Home Secretary takes into account a number of factors in considering whether to exercise that discretion. These include: the nature and scale of an organisation's activities; and the need to support other members of the international community in tackling terrorism. (*HC Deb*, 19 December 2017, vol 633, col 1006)

Although we see an extended discussion of the threat level in this second example, the similarity between the two motions is such that the latter would clearly resonate with anyone familiar with the former. Each makes reference to the relevant legislation, each describes the power of proscription and its operational procedure, each names its targets, and each situates the current proposed proscription in context by tallying up the total number of proscription orders since the 2000 Act and (in the former) the total number of proscribed groups. For comparison – and to demonstrate the continuity between the two Houses, here are the near-verbatim remarks from Baroness Williams of Trafford that opened the House of Lords debate that followed the latter example two days later:

> My Lords, the threat level in the UK, which is set by the independent Joint Terrorism Analysis Centre, remains at severe. This means that a terrorist attack in our country is highly likely and could occur without warning. While we can never entirely eliminate the threat from terrorism, we are determined to do all we can to minimise the threat to the UK and our interests abroad, and to disrupt those who would engage in it. Recognising that terrorism is a global threat that is best tackled in partnership, it is also important that we demonstrate our support for other members of the international community in their efforts to tackle terrorism wherever it occurs. Proscription is an important part of the Government's strategy to disrupt terrorist activities.
>
> The four groups we propose to add to the list of terrorist organisations, amending Schedule 2 to the Terrorism Act 2000 are, first, al-Ashtar Brigades. This includes a number of aliases of this group: Saraya al-Ashtar, the Wa'ad Allah Brigades, the Islamic Allah Brigades, Imam al-Mahdi Brigades and al-Haydariyah Brigades; secondly, al-Mukhtar Brigades, including Saraya al-Mukhtar; thirdly, Hasam including Harakat Sawa'd Misr and Harakat Hasm; and Liwa al-Thawra. This is the 22nd order under the Act.
>
> Proscription sends a strong message that terrorist activity is not tolerated wherever it happens. Under Section 3 of the Terrorism Act 2000, the Home Secretary has the power to proscribe an organisation if she believes that it is concerned in terrorism. If the statutory test is met, the Home Secretary may then exercise her discretion to proscribe the organisation. The Home Secretary takes into account a number of factors in considering whether to exercise this discretion. These include the nature and scale of an organisation's activities and the need to support other members of the international community

> in tackling terrorism. The effect of proscription is that a listed organisation is outlawed and is unable to operate in the UK. It is a criminal offence for a person to belong to, invite or provide support for, or arrange a meeting in support of, a proscribed organisation. It is also an offence to wear clothing or carry articles in public, such as flags, which arouse reasonable suspicion that an individual is a member or supporter of a proscribed organization. (*HL Deb*, 21 December 2017, vol 787, col 2293)

The similarities between these comments already indicate the existence of a core script within the ritual of proscription. What is more, the opening remarks of this script have remained remarkably unchanged since the passage of the TA 2000, with only very minor alterations. One such alteration – mentioned originally in Chapter 4 – has been the addition of explicit mention of other, non-counter-terrorism related, offences, such that: 'proscription can support other disruptive activity including the use of immigration powers such as exclusion or prosecution for other offences' (Hayes 2016). Another has been explicit reference to the variety of evidence underpinning a proposed proscription order, which is said to include: 'open source material, intelligence material and advice that reflects consultation across government, including with the intelligence and law enforcement agencies' (Lord Ashton 2014). Although relatively minor, these additions indicate that the core script is not predetermined or unchangeable; there is, of course, scope for interpretation and the intrusion of political concerns, events, discourses therein.

With this in mind, it is important to recognise that this core script extends beyond the introductory remarks within these debates to – as we have seen in the preceding chapters – familiar and repetitive arguments, questions and identity claims relating to proscription and its significance. As we elaborate below, this also includes explicit proclamations of respect for the ritual; assurances of bipartisan support for the proscription order in question; consensus on what proscription is and does; consensus on proscription's necessity, and alignment with liberal values; and, repetition and reaffirmation of the objects of proscription. These themes, in recurrence, form this ritual's scripted elements, namely, those narratives that are both expected and permitted.

Respect for the ritual

A key feature of any ritual is that its participants and observers behave appropriately during its unfolding. This may involve demonstrating a suitable level of decorum – for instance refraining from speech during commemorative periods of silence – or, in other forms of ritual, appropriate demonstrations of joy and joviality, such as joining in with a 'toast'. Chapter 4 revealed how, in the case of proscription, we see the sanctity of this ritual being underlined and preserved by frequent expressions of the seriousness of this debate. Debate on proscription is replete, as we have seen, with reference to its 'importance' and the 'serious' decision at hand, framing it as discussed further in Chapter 4 as 'a heavy power' (Filkin 2002) and a 'very serious matter' (McNulty 2006). Indeed, one further – very recent – addition to the core script was reference, in a December 2017 debate, to the need for bicameral support for proscription *because of* its significance. As Baroness Williams of Trafford (2017) put it in her opening remarks: 'given the impact the power of proscription can have, it is appropriate that proscription must be approved by both Houses'.

We also see examples of criticism within this ritual where parliamentary practice is deemed to have fallen short of the appropriate standards. This includes via the chastising of absent colleagues: 'In previous debates of this kind, the House has been almost empty' (Vaz 2011); reproaches for flippancy: 'these are very serious issues and it is not appropriate to have shouty debates across the Dispatch Box on them' (Smith 2012); or criticism of those accused of self-interested politicking: 'this is not necessarily a moment for any kind of party posturing' (Kerr 2017). For Damian Green, Minister for Immigration at the time of a 2011 debate on Tehrik-e Taliban Pakistan (TTP), for instance: 'I regret that Opposition Front Benchers regard the matter as humorous … There are clearly serious issues about how this country attacks terrorism and defends itself against terrorists, so it is not the time for Opposition Front Benchers to regard something as amusing' (Green 2011). While there are moments of shared levity in these debates – such as Keith Vaz's response to the Deputy Speaker's birthday greetings – 'I can think of no better way to celebrate my birthday than to discuss the proscription of three organisations in Libya, Syria and Egypt.

I am therefore delighted that the Minister has brought this order before the House this evening' (Vaz 2014c) – these are comparatively unusual in a discursive climate more typically characterised by solemnity and earnestness.

A predetermined outcome

Offers of explicit support to the proscription orders brought forth by governments is a further common feature of these debates. Regardless of which party is in power, the Opposition tends to preclude the failure of an order by providing *a priori* support for the government's decision to ban a particular organisation. In a 2005 debate, for instance, MP Dominic Grieve was keen to 'reassure the Minister that the official Opposition will support the order' (Grieve 2005), arguing, 'We have to accept that a great deal of this must be taken on trust … and we must therefore accept the government's word that the security services have told them that they pose a danger' (Grieve 2005). Patrick Mercer MP, the following year, argued in similar terms that the 'opposition are delighted with the four names on the order … we certainly support the government's proscription of those organisations' (Mercer 2006). As did Baroness Smith of Basildon, more recently, in the House of Lords, in her suggestion that 'we base our judgment in support of proscription orders on the assurances of Ministers' (Smith 2014). Indeed, regular contributors to these debates situate their current support against a backdrop of previous unity – 'as far as I can remember, no order of this kind has ever been opposed, because we trust and accept the good faith of the Minister when he tells the House that dreadful organisations are seeking to propagate terrorism, which is indeed true' (Vaz 2015).

Such statements of trust may provoke governmental acknowledgement, in turn, with the guarantee of cross-party support frequently framed as the product of a mature political system guided by a unity of purpose. Hazel Blears, in 2005, for example praised Parliament's responsibility in these matters, noting her gratitude 'to hon. members for the tone and way in which they have responded to the presentation of the order' (Blears 2005). Such consensus is located within 'a long tradition of cross-party co-operation on issues of national security' (Johnson 2014c) and offered, often, in spite of an acknowledged shortfall in access to the relevant information:

> The Opposition do not have access to the same intelligence as the Home Secretary and the Minister. However, on the basis of the assurances that the Minister has given the House and the information that he has set out clearly today, the Opposition are happy to give the motion our full support. (Johnson 2014b)

The proscription ritual, then, is one in which Parliament's deference to the Home Secretary or her replacement reflects an *a priori* and explicit suspension of the Opposition's nominal function (to oppose). This leads to the counter-intuitive claim that 'seriousness' is the basis for relinquishing opposition and becoming complicit in decisions taken, even while acknowledging the imbalance of power in arriving at such a decision:

> Any proscription order should therefore be taken very seriously. For that reason, successive Governments have attempted to ensure that there is cross-party parliamentary support for proscription orders. (Johnson 2014b)

In short, as Keith Vaz noted in a 2012 debate, proscription 'is … almost never opposed by the Opposition … I have never known Government and Opposition to disagree on the proscription of an organization'.

Constitutivity

There are two immediate constitutive moments within the proscription ritual which serve to create intersubjective consensus on proscription's function, as well as its necessity and appropriateness for a liberal democratic state such as the United Kingdom.

Intersubjective consensus on what proscription is/does

First, as we saw in Chapter 4, recognition of the gravity of proscription decisions is accompanied, in these debates, by repeated reflection on the measure's efficacy for counter-terrorism purposes. Portrayed, often, as a necessary though insufficient instrument – 'proscription is a useful power, but it will certainly not resolve the [terrorist] situation overnight' (Blears 2005) – proscription is consistently positioned as a significant weapon in the Home Secretary's arsenal: 'there is not much doubt that it [proscription] has great value in disrupting the activities of terrorist organisations' (Bassam 2005). This positioning is important because it produces, rather than reflects, this power's significance, generating and sustaining intersubjective consensus on its purposes. One argument brought to bear here is its speediness of deployment: 'We have sought a shortened timetable to ensure that the power is as effective as possible' (Bassam 2005) with proscription orders benefiting from their framing as 'clinical and immediate' (Vaz 2014b). Also regularly portrayed as important, however, is the latitude the power affords to well-positioned, and well-informed, decision-makers: 'The Home Secretary may proscribe an organisation only if she believes it is concerned in terrorism. If that test is met, she may then exercise her discretion to proscribe the organisation' (McNulty 2008).

Consensus on proscription's necessity, and alignment with liberal values

If the proscription ritual itself contributes to the constitution of this power as a significant one for counter-terrorism purposes, it also contributes to the lawful and normative probity of the proscription process. In a 2010 debate on al-Shabaab, for instance, the Minister for Policing, Crime and Counter-Terrorism listed in (typical) detailed the conditions which attempted proscriptions must meet before even reaching Parliament for debate, arguing: 'The decision to proscribe an organisation is not taken lightly. It entails building a case that meets the legal test under the 2000 Act, and which is examined by officials in the Home Office and other Government Departments. That case is assembled over many weeks and months' (Hanson 2010). Here, judicial and bureaucratic safeguards combine with an extended timeframe – prior, that is, to the (ostensibly political) moment of decision – to ensure that an appropriate course of action has been pursued.

Sedimentation

Central to the ritual process is the sedimentation both of the ritual itself over time and of its incumbent function, legitimacy and meanings. In recurrence, rituals become familiar and accepted, understood, expected and, crucially, unchallenged. Repetition is inherent to proscription debates in several ways. First, the process – i.e. the debate – itself features frequently in Parliament: between 2002 and the time of writing, there have been 38 parliamentary debates on proscription. In each iteration, the use of proscription becomes less exceptional and increasingly part of a normal process. Indeed, a relatively common feature of these debates is explicit reference to the number of times Parliament has debated a proscription order (see Figure 7.2).

Second, parliamentary debate on the extension of proscription powers follows, almost without exception, the same scene-setting: the order is introduced by the Minister (or her proxy), who offers a brief description of the power, the criteria for its usage and consequences for newly designated groups. As noted above, this description is typically then replicated near-verbatim in the House of Lords, with reference in both Houses often made to previous uses of the power for additional context. Thus, in the first effort to add organisations to the list in October 2002, for instance, Home Secretary David Blunkett offered the following:

> The proscribed organisations fall within criteria of which it will be useful to remind hon. Members. They are specified in the definition of terrorism provided in the Terrorism Act 2000, which refers to those who commit or participate in acts of terrorism, prepare for terrorism, promote or encourage it or are otherwise concerned with it. The factors spelt out alongside the original decision a year last February were as follows: consideration by the Home Secretary of the nature and scale of the organisations; the specific threat to the UK or British nationals overseas; and the presence and support of the international community. It is the support of the international community and the threat to our citizens overseas that we have weighed very carefully indeed, along with other factors, in proscribing the four groups. (Blunkett 2002)

In June 2014, the Conservative MP James Brokenshire, Minister for Security and Immigration, offered a similar account on the Coalition government's case for proscribing five additional groups including the Islamic State in Iraq and the Levant (ISIL). The one significant difference from Blunkett's of twelve years prior is the addition of the 'glorification of terrorism' offence from the Terrorism Act 2006:

Figure 7.2 Sedimentation via repetition in proscription debates

Year	2008	2010	2011	2012
Minister	**The Minister for Security, Counter-Terrorism, Crime and Policing (Mr Tony McNulty)**	**The Minister for Policing, Crime and Counter-Terrorism (Mr David Hanson)**	**The Minister for Immigration (Damian Green)**	**The Parliamentary Under-Secretary of State for the Home Department (James Brokenshire)**
Opening	I beg to move, That the draft Terrorism Act 2000 (Proscribed Organisations) (Amendment) (No. 2) Order 2008, which was laid before this House on 2nd July, be approved	I beg to move, That the draft Terrorism Act 2000 (Proscribed Organisations) (Amendment) Order 2010, which was laid before this House on 1 March, be approved.	I beg to move, That the draft Terrorism Act 2000 (Proscribed Organisations) (Amendment) Order 2011, which was laid before this House on 17 January, be approved.	I beg to move, That the draft Terrorism Act 2000 (Proscribed Organisations) (Amendment) Order 2012, which was laid before this House on 2 July, be approved.

Appeal to higher purpose	The international terrorist threat to the UK, our interests abroad and our international partners remains severe and sustained. The Government are determined to do all we can to minimise the threat	The terrorist threat to the United Kingdom and its interests abroad remains severe and sustained. We as a Government are determined to do all that we can to minimise that threat.	There remains a severe and sustained terrorist threat to the UK and its interests abroad. The Government are determined to do all that they can to minimise this threat.	The Government are determined to do all we can to minimise the threat from terrorism to the UK and our interests abroad.
Reference to recurrence of proscription	This is the seventh proscription order made under the Terrorism Act 2000.	This is the eighth proscription under the 2000 Act	This is the ninth proscription order amending schedule 2 to that Act.	This is the 10th proscription under the 2000 Act.
The authority of the executive	Section 3 of the 2000 Act provides a power for the Home Secretary to proscribe an organisation if she believes it is concerned in terrorism.	Section 3 of the Act provides a power for my right hon. Friend the Home Secretary to proscribe an organisation if he believes that it is concerned with terrorism.	Section 3 of the Terrorism Act 2000 provides a power for the Home Secretary to proscribe an organisation if she believes it is concerned in terrorism.	Section 3 of the 2000 Act provides a power for the Home Secretary to proscribe an organisation if she believes it is currently concerned in terrorism.

Figure 7.2 (*cont.*)

Year	2008	2010	2011	2012
Proscription's strategic alignment	n/a	the proscription of terrorist organisations is an important part of the Government's strategy to tackle terrorist activities at home and abroad	Proscription of terrorist organisations is an important part of the Government's strategy to tackle terrorist activities.	Proscription of terrorist organisations is an important part of the Government's strategy to tackle terrorist activities.
Outward effects of proscription	We believe that this power plays a key role in creating a hostile environment for terrorists and their supporters. It also deters international terrorist organisations from coming to this country in the first place. Equally importantly, it sends out a strong signal throughout the world that the UK rejects such organisations and their claims to legitimacy.	The proscription of those two groups will support our international partners in disrupting terrorist activity by making the UK a hostile environment for terrorists and their supporters. It will also send the strong message to terrorists that the UK is not willing to tolerate terrorism either here or anywhere else in the world	proscription does send out a strong message that we do not tolerate terrorism, and it deters terrorist groups from operating here.	n/a

Recognition of the seriousness and a claim to proscription as essential for security	Proscription is a tough but necessary power and its effect is that the proscribed organisation is outlawed and is unable to operate in the UK.	Proscription is a tough and necessary power, but	Proscription is a tough power, as is clear from the various interventions, but it is necessary. Its effect is that the proscribed organisation is outlawed and is unable to operate in the UK.	We recognise that proscription is a tough but necessary power. Its effect is that the proscribed organisation is outlawed and unable to operate in the United Kingdom.

Figure 7.2 (*cont.*)

Year	**2008**	**2010**	**2011**	**2012**
The a priori *appropriateness and probity of decision-making*	Given the wide-ranging impact of proscription, the Home Secretary exercises her power to proscribe an organisation only after thoroughly reviewing all the available relevant information on the organisation […] Decisions on proscription are taken with great care by the Home Secretary, and it is right that both Houses must consider the case for proscribing new organisations.	The decision to proscribe an organisation is not taken lightly. It entails building a case that meets the legal test under the 2000 Act, and which is examined by officials in the Home Office and other Government Departments. That case is assembled over many weeks and months as the evidence is brought forward and collated. Ultimately, my right hon. Friend the Home Secretary has to take a decision on that case.	Given the wide-ranging impact of proscription, the Home Secretary exercises her power to proscribe an organisation only after thoroughly reviewing all the available relevant information and evidence on the organisation […] Decisions on proscription are taken with great care by the Home Secretary, and it is also right that the case for proscribing new organisations must be approved by both Houses.	Given the wide-ranging impact of proscription, the Home Secretary exercises her power to proscribe an organisation only after thoroughly reviewing all the available relevant information and evidence on that organisation. Having carefully considered all the evidence, she firmly believes that IM is involved in terrorism

International normalisation	There is a wide range of international positions on Hezbollah. As I have said, some countries, including the USA, Canada, and the Netherlands, proscribe the entire organisation. Australia proscribes the External Security Organisation only, while others, such as France, do not proscribe any part of the organisation at all.	Indeed, there is not only a concern in the United Kingdom but an international consensus of condemnation of the organisation's activities. For example-I hope that this further reassures my right hon. Friend-the organisation is already proscribed in the United States, Australia and New Zealand.	It is now right to align the UK with the emerging international consensus condemning this group and its activities. I commend the order to the House.	Yes, the organisation is proscribed in India and in several other countries, including the United States and New Zealand. The proscription here will align the UK with the emerging international consensus.

> Proscribing the groups that we are discussing today will send a strong signal to terrorists operating on both sides of the conflict in Syria and those who may be thinking of joining them. Under section 3 of the Terrorism Act 2000, the Home Secretary has the power to proscribe an organisation if she believes that it is currently concerned in terrorism. Under the 2000 Act, an organisation is concerned in terrorism if it commits or participates in acts of terrorism, prepares for terrorism, promotes or encourages terrorism—including the unlawful glorification of terrorism—or is otherwise concerned in terrorism. If the test is met, the Home Secretary may exercise her discretion to proscribe the organisation. (Brokenshire 2014a)

This incantation which affirms the Home Secretary's competence to make a proscription order characterises the beginning of proscription debates. The debate then proceeds towards a closing consensus which is frequently little more than a facsimile of the opening statement, affirming that the pretext of the proscription has been unaffected by the intervening debate. In between, we see a repetition of elements become manifest especially through the efforts of the nominated Minister or Under Secretary moving the relevant order to proscribe an organisation(s). Figure 7.2 summarises four successive debates taken from 2008, 2009, 2010 and 2010 to illustrate. The order of precepts approximates their general expression, although there is considerable variability within this.

As we see in Figure 7.2, there is close and *repeated* adherence to a cluster of precepts which are deployed, often almost verbatim, in each debate. After a procedural statement – 'I beg to move…' – which is typical to all parliamentary motions, what follows is: (1) *appeal to higher purpose*, in which the government's commitment to combating a threat is affirmed; (2) *reference to proscription's recurrence*, which underlines the normalcy or established precedence of the power enacted; (3) a statement confirming *the authority of the executive* to lawfully enact proscription to combat terrorism; (4) confirmation of *proscription's strategic alignment* with other security initiatives; (5) A claim as to the *outward effects of proscription* as a means of signalling; (6) a statement that underlines *recognition of the proscription's seriousness and necessity for security*; (7) an assurance to the audience of a determination of the *a priori appropriateness and probity of proscription*; and (8) reassurance that the proscription is uncontroversial and expected, i.e. that it forms part of *international normalisation*. Finally, the sedimentation of proscription is completed, of course, in the inevitability of its conclusion.

Performativity and the ritual of proscription

As suggested by the above, the proscription ritual not only hosts a performance of democracy and scrutiny, it constitutes or calls into being proscribed organisations that are made concrete at the moment of their banning. This is the illocutionary power of proscription: the attempt to extirpate an organisation involves its creation and permanence in law. Paradoxically, its existence is brought into being and cemented by the very power that seeks to vanquish it. The proscription ritual also, however, hosts a second perlocutionary power which is to construct – or signal – the UK as a willing partner in the fight against terrorism and a hostile environment for the organisations it condemns.

As the above demonstrates, thinking through proscription debates as a form of political ritual sheds considerable light on aspects of proscription's operation and functions often missed by existing work on this power. Reading these debates through the heuristic introduced in Figure 7.1 demonstrates that whilst this particular ritual has its own specific characteristics – including its core incantation, consensus on its purposes, and the absence of division – it also evidences qualities that are common or even general to other political rituals. The former include its working towards a predetermined outcome which accompanies many, though not all, rituals. The latter include respect for particular rules, and the performative function of ritual in (here) signalling terrorism's unacceptability.

This analysis illustrates how an emphasis on the ritualistic qualities of proscription debate highlights its constitutive functions, predictable outcomes and repetitiveness. This lens, we suggest, brings into focus the symbolic and political strata of proscription, situating debate on this power within Parliament's broader matrix of structures, symbolisms, traditions, norms, hierarchies, procedures, patronages and roles, such that:

> The ritual legitimizes the power and institutionalizes it, but at the same time, the role of power holder itself becomes transferable, no longer the property of any particular individual. (Kertzer 1989, 51)

As we have seen, the contours of proscription debates are highly scripted, conforming to a predetermined structure with little variation in their introduction, core narratives or conclusions. Here we find a process in which identifiable (yet changing) actors are authorised to inhabit specific roles and employ a script that varies little across time or government. This ritual reaffirms 'our' (liberal, democratic) values, and their distance from the 'terrorist' other, and involves the repeated lauding of the parliamentary process at the same time as it militates against deviation and dissent. This is a ritual, moreover – and most important of all – where the predicted outcome is, invariably, achieved. As Edelman noted, some time ago, 'policy-making procedures whose outcomes are known in advance amount to ritual and not to decision-making' (1969, 243).

This ritual of proscription amounts to a performance of democracy in which the probity of process, the lawfulness of decision-making, and the process's alignment with democratic values are regularly affirmed. And, these incantations of democratic values, in turn, cement the legitimacy and licence of Parliament to retain the sovereign power to proscribe. Invoking democratic legitimacy is all the more necessary for parliamentarians in their construction of newly proscribed terrorist organisations because the proscription ritual is seated within Parliament's broader, and rich, matrix of structures, symbolisms, traditions, norms, hierarchies, procedures, patronages and roles. Thus:

> The ritual legitimizes the power and institutionalizes it, but at the same time, the role of power holder itself becomes transferable, no longer the property of any particular individual. (Kertzer 1989, 51)

Note

1 This follows Rappaport, for whom ritual is 'neither substantive nor functional, but gives primacy to the sensible features common to rituals always and everywhere, the features that may, in fact, lead us to recognize events as rituals in the first place' (1999, 26).

Conclusion: securing us?

Proscription, claimed Home Secretary Roy Jenkins in 1974, is 'a wholly exceptional measure and can be justified only by a wholly exceptional situation – a clear and present danger' (Jenkins 1974). However appealing or intuitive such a framing appears, our aim throughout this book has been to show that the United Kingdom's desire to ban specific (listed) foes has been far more widespread and enduring than this claim to exceptionality might suggest. As we saw in the opening chapters, scores of groups have been officially outlawed as enemies of the British state: these include Scottish Jacobites, emancipatory movements within colonial administrations, pro-democracy 'radicals' and corresponding societies, as well as more contemporary foes including National Action, Daesh, al Qaeda and paramilitaries associated with the Northern Ireland conflict. Such groups, of course, often share little beyond their apparent – or constructed – opposition to British norms, values or security as imagined at various historical junctures.

What emerges from our analysis, however, is that proscription is not just a consequential power, although it does have severe consequences in triggering significant criminal sanctions for designated organisations and their supporters. Rather, the power has (also) stood the test of time as a – if not the – principal means by which material threats to the state are *constituted* by Parliament, and then, of course, communicated to audiences from the British public to allied states and would-be belligerents. Clothed in the brutish logics of security, the formal process of proscription assumes a ritual form through which situated actors conjure up and perform a symbolic show of sovereignty. This involves, as we have seen, (re-)forging a vision of British identity, declaiming its enemies, and, in the process, conferring a permanent existence on the very entities this power is intended to make impermanent. Proscription and its antecedents have been used to such ends for centuries, having changed very little, if at all. For these reasons, proscription might be seen not so much as an unavoidable necessity, but an ancient and treasured privilege of British parliamentary sovereignty.

In the preceding pages, we have focused our attention primarily upon this power's contemporary manifestation following the TA 2000. This has enabled an exploration of proscription's enculturation as an important mechanism of parliamentary security politics today (see Neal 2019). Through proscription it is possible to access, in the first instance, a specific yet remarkably consistent framing of the British national identity – and, by extension, the identities of parliamentarians in the Lords or Commons – as a liberal, democratic, tolerant and just political space. Such a framing, of course, relies upon juxtaposition to specific (illiberal, anti-democratic, intolerant and unjust) terrorist others. It also builds on and feeds into rhetorical and political dynamics occurring in times, places and contexts not immediately related to counter-terrorism. Those contexts might be contemporary – the recent 'Remain' and 'Leave' Brexit campaigns, for example, made significant and contrasting plays of British national identity, traditions and heritage. They might also be historical or mnemonic in nature – for instance Enoch Powell's (1968) 'Rivers of Blood' speech which invoked the threat posed by political organisation within 'other' communities seeking to 'overawe' or 'dominate' the 'native' population:

> Here is the means of showing that the immigrant communities can organise to consolidate their members, to agitate and campaign against their fellow citizens, and to overawe and dominate the rest with the legal weapons which the ignorant and the ill-informed have provided. As I look ahead, I am filled with foreboding; like the Roman, I seem to see the River Tiber foaming with much blood.[1]

These historical and relational contexts shed additional light on the multiple significances of the UK's proscription regime. In the first instance – as argued in Chapter 2 – the UK's approach matters – or should matter – because of its influence in shaping other listing and proscription practices around the world. This influence is, of course, linked to the UK regime's longevity, which finds expression in significant – and, as yet, seriously under-researched – post-colonial ties. It also has its own temporal and spatial movements, appearing particularly acute at moments of rapid legislative action (such as in the post-2001 period), and in Commonwealth countries. Indeed, as we argue in Chapter 2, the United Nations appears to have held up the UK's membership offences as a best-practice model of anti-terrorism law-making in the aftermath of the 9/11 attacks. It is unsurprising, therefore – to take one example – that a 2001 amendment to Pakistan's Anti-Terrorism Act 1997 saw a direct emulation of the UK's proscription provisions set out in the TA 2000. This is a language, moreover, that has been mirrored in English-speaking countries across parts of Asia and Africa, and yet the logics that inspired the UK legislation had far more to do with its knotty history of hierarchical, organised paramilitary violence in Northern Ireland than with the disjointed, decentred networks of al Qaeda and equivalents.

The history of proscription and its ancillary powers is therefore not merely of scholarly interest. It reveals, as we discuss in Chapter 1, a genuinely international edifice of exclusionary politics that continues in operation today as a legacy of colonial administrations. It is not inconsequential, for instance, that laws enacted by colonial administrators in Malaysia in 1899 in order to consolidate British colonial rule[2] are today employed by the Malaysian government to outlaw opponents that attract its displeasure. In 2015, for instance, Malaysia's Registrar of Societies had rejected 38 per cent of all applications to form societies, which included the opposition Democratic Action Party's central executive committee and 120 party branches.[3] Nineteenth-century colonial provisions instituted in Hong Kong, similarly, remain in use today and are usually deployed to threaten the banning of organisations connected with Taiwan or foreign political organisations.[4] In September 2018 such provisions were employed to ban a pro-independence party, the Hong Kong National Party, via the publication of a short Societies Ordinance order:

> SOCIETIES ORDINANCE (Chapter 151) (Order under section 8(2))
>
> In exercise of the power conferred on the Secretary for Security by section 8(2) of the Societies Ordinance, I hereby order that the operation or continued operation of the Hong Kong National Party in Hong Kong be prohibited.

This order takes effect on publication in the Gazette.

24 September 2018 John K. C. LEE *Secretary for Security*[5]

On top of this, proscription – as we have seen – remains widely used within Britain, being drawn upon in high profile cases – such as that of Anjem Choudhary – despite attracting sporadic opposition amongst advocacy and campaign groups for its implications for citizenship, civil liberties, social 'cohesion' and beyond. A British campaign organisation – the Campaign Against Criminalising Communities – for instance, described the UK's proscription regime in a briefing paper on the UK's banning of the Kurdistan Workers' Party (PKK) in the following way:

> The UK government has been attempting to deter protest by migrant communities against oppressive regimes from which they have fled. A major weapon has been bans on 'terrorist' organisations. Through these bans, state terrorism abroad is represented as counter-terrorist activity, thus justifying and reinforcing the UK's alliance with those oppressive regimes. Such bans attack the right of national self-determination, as well as popular support for that right across countries. The bans are used selectively as an instrument of foreign policy.[6]

Although the number of prosecutions under the British regime remains relatively small, and proscription decisions may often attract considerable public support – as in the case of Choudhary, Daesh[7] or more recent prosecutions for membership of the far-right group National Action[8] – the implications for citizenship and associated liberties and protections are vital.

Moreover, and here lies the primary emphasis of our book, proscription and its use also tells us something important about the nature of security politics within ostensibly liberal democratic spaces and institutions. Our argument, elaborated in full in Chapter 7, is that the process of proscription – in its public, visible manifestation at least – functions as a form of political ritual that draws upon a recognisable cast of actors, who speak from a recognisable and enduring script culminating in an instantly recognisable – and, frankly, predictable – decision. In so doing, this ritual operates as a mode of ontological genesis. Deriving its illocutionary force from the authorising environment of a sovereign Parliament, the act of proscription is a reifying one in that it produces the material reality to which it purports to respond. This act of reification involves the constitution of (1) an organisation, which is now discursively and politically recognised and cemented (and 'banned') within the British political imagination, at least; which is also (2) ontologically terrorist, because the ritual makes it so in law.

In doing this, significantly, the ritual of proscription constitutes a performance of 'security', as much as – and, perhaps rather than – contributing in any objective sense to the improvement of national (or human) security within contemporary Britain. The proscription ritual is far from alone in doing this, of course. Strategic documents, executive speeches, the presence of security professionals (police officers, soldiers, border control guards) and technologies on our streets and at our airports, media headlines and beyond all offer familiar examples of the contemporary theatre of security (see, amongst many others, Campbell 1992; Buzan *et al.* 1998; Bigo 2002; Huysmans 2011). Moreover, as with these other performances, practices and acts, the proscription ritual not only expands security's remit by bringing additional organisations, individuals and the like into its purview. It also risks generating *in*security for individuals, communities and groups – including, for instance, diasporas who may find themselves at risk of association with specific organisations (as discussed further in Chapter 3). The politics of proscription, then, is fundamentally a politics of (in)security – one that involves producing and responding to threats – even if it is not a straightforward response to a (pre-)existing security challenge (see also Jarvis and Legrand 2017).

It is important to remember that the proscription ritual is not, either, immune to change or reinterpretation. As we saw in Chapter 7, minor transformations in its core script may be identified even in the two decades since its present instantiation. Nor is the ritual shorn of contestation, critical scrutiny, or challenge, despite the typicality of formal support from the official opposition at the ritual's outset. Indeed, a claim throughout this book has been that dissent and opposition – whether outright or via the questioning of the executive – form a vital part of this ritual itself for at least two reasons. First, because this sustains the ritual's appearance as a decision-making, deliberative exercise with an outcome that is to be decided by the ritual's arguments and participants. Second, and more importantly, such performances of dissent also serve to confirm and reproduce the identity claims upon which the ritual depends, whereby the UK is positioned as a liberal, democratic space governed by a cautious, moderate and reasonable legislative body. As we argued in Chapter 6, critics and advocates of specific proscription decisions within these debates alike rely upon and invoke the same construction of British identity, perceiving proscription to be either necessary (for advocates) or terminal (for critics) for the UK's rule of law and (liberal, democratic, tolerant, just) way of life.

Although it is not always as evident in the post-2000 period upon which we here focus, we might also note here that parliamentarians themselves are, at times, fully aware of these ritualistic dynamics. Indeed, if we briefly glance back to proscription's earlier incarnations within the UK it is possible to find multiple explicit examples of the language of ritual being used in debates on this power. In a debate on the Irish National Liberation Army, for instance, the Labour MP – and future opposition spokesman on Northern Ireland – Kevin McNamara (1979) asked of the House of Commons:

> This is a most regrettable occasion. We are going through a ritual denunciation of a terrorist organisation. We are passing two orders that will go through the House unopposed saying that this organisation should be proscribed. What will that mean? What positive, purposeful, courageous act are we taking that will somehow weaken this terrible organisation? I put it to the House that the answer is 'None at all'.

In December 1984, Peter Robinson MP similarly referred to this process as a ritual comprising repeated and predictable – but, here, necessary – activity in the safeguarding of security in Northern Ireland.

> I say, as I have said at six-month intervals since I became a Member, that the ritual of considering the Northern Ireland (Emergency Provisions) Act is likely to continue. The people of Northern Ireland have no joy in thinking of any legislation that limits or restricts their liberties. They recognise that the protection of an individual's rights must come second to the protection of a society. It is the society in Northern Ireland that is under attack. (Robinson 1984)

Future Secretary of State for Northern Ireland, Mo Mowlam, in 1995 employed similar language, if less sympathetically, in referring to the process of renewing the Northern Ireland (Emergency Provisions) Act as taking on an 'unfortunate ritual nature' (Mowlam 1995). Captain L.P.S. Orr, meanwhile, back in 1973, argued more forcefully still that the very ritual of proscription itself offered ample evidence of its lack of necessity:

> It has become almost a ritual when we embark upon a series of Northern Ireland orders at this time of night to make a complaint. I go through the ritual again simply to place upon the record the fact that we consider this a monstrous way of dealing with matters of such great importance. We are to deal tonight with an order concerning the life, limb and liberty of people, and an appropriation order concerning the whole range of Government expenditure in Northern Ireland. We are to do so while the staff of the House is depleted. We are left with the fag-end of the week, in the small hours of the morning possibly, debating these very serious matters at an inappropriate time.
>
> It is almost impossible to explain to anyone in Ulster how it comes about that, at what one might call a peak parliamentary time, on Monday next from 7 p.m. to 10 p.m., we are to debate the landscaping of New Palace Yard, but that we are dealing with matters of great importance to Ulster at the fag-end of the week.
>
> The hon. Member for Leeds, South (Mr. Merlyn Rees) has cogently and rightly argued against the case for proscription, and I agree with him. I think that on the whole I have steadily, over these debates on the subject, become convinced that there is no great value in proscription at all. I think the sooner it was ended the better. Proscription, as the hon. Gentleman rightly argued, does not achieve anything in the end. Proscription has proved in practice to have had no marked effect at all. (Orr 1973)

The Conservative MP, Ivor Stanbrook, finally, and more recently, condemned the proscription ritual as a substitute for more meaningful action, and an abrogation, therefore, of the public interest:

> The public insist on the defeat of terrorism. It is not enough to give them ritual denunciations of violence, and ritual avowals of dissociation from those who seek to achieve their political ends by violence. We have heard a great deal of that in this debate, and we have also heard people place considerable emphasis on civil liberties in this

> country as though they were endangered or threatened. Society needs to be able to defend itself by its own self-discipline, and must be given adequate weapons to do so. That is not the case yet. (Stanbrook 1991)

These very explicit references to the process of proscription as a form of political ritual stand in contrast to more contemporary debates where this framing tends to be absent. Taken together, they portray proscription as a ritual because of its recurrence and – in our opening example, at least – predictable conclusion. Many of these examples, moreover, decry this ritualistic character, seeing it, variously, as evidence of a lack of democratic scrutiny, a lack of seriousness on the part of Parliament, or, in our final example, as a lack of 'real' political activity.

While our analysis shares much with these understandings, we are less persuaded that this renders proscription or its equivalents in the UK and beyond (or, indeed, political ritual more generally) trivial, irrelevant or unnecessary. Indeed, our focus throughout this book has been on proscription's constitutive role in producing and reproducing those realities to which it ostensibly refers; whether terrorist organisations or parliamentary authority. Proscription, we argued, matters not only for its impact upon national security or human rights, as many authors, activists and journalists have already documented with great care and skill. It matters, too, because it contributes to the making of the socio-political world (with very real material consequences for individuals and organisations), re-drawing boundaries between self and other, and re-asserting the authority and legitimacy of established political practices.

One prominent, and significant, feature of this constitutive power is in proscription's contribution to the regulation of organised political activity within states such as the United Kingdom. Today, the proscription of terrorist organisations represents the exercise of a norm through which formal or informal forms of political organisation are prevented from undermining prevailing – sovereign – political authority. The violences (or advocacy or glorification thereof) of terrorism committed by some organisations, in this sense at least, serve in part to deflect or devalue questioning of either the functional or normative value of proscription (or, indeed, other counter-terrorism measures reliant upon similar designations). Yet we need not dig too deeply through the institutional archives to uncover a long-standing distrust of organised oppositional politics amongst

British elites. As we saw in Chapter 1, during the post-war administration of Britain's overseas colonies, administrators made wide use of 'Societies Ordinances' which regulated political organisations, outlawing those deemed 'prejudicial to peace, order, and good government'. The powers were deployed across Britain's colonies: Aden, Hong Kong, Malaysia (Sabah and Sarawak), Singapore and beyond. They were also heavily redolent of eighteenth-century Seditious Societies Acts, which forced all societies – with the explicit exception of Masonic Lodges, which counted many MPs amongst their membership – to register their existence, their membership, and so on.

In Parliament during the 1950s, societies ordinances were, on occasion, called into question although rarely with significant effect. Defending the outlawing of the Mwanza Branch of the Tanganyika African Union, Lennox-Boyd claimed the legislation was used 'to protect Africans from exploitation by unscrupulous society organisers'. In the colony of Aden (modern Yemen), the same ordinances were in place, according to Duncan Sandys MP, 'to secure better management of societies and to discourage the formation of bogus bodies or of societies organised from outside the Territory for objects contrary to the public interest' (Sandys 1962). Up to 1992, the same ordinances remained in place in Hong Kong, which according to the Hong Kong Human Rights Monitor 'provided for a draconian scheme of control and supervision inconsistent with international human rights standards'.[9] The UK government, however, has tended to rely on the same reasons to deny Parliament a full explanation: 'It is not always desirable in public to give all the reasons which lead a responsible official to come to a conclusion of that kind' (Lennox-Boyd 1955). What these actions have in common is that all were forms of political regulation: organisations had to seek approval from Britain's colonial authorities to lawfully operate and faced being outlawed without this. Today, this norm remains active, albeit less pronounced, in the Terrorism Act. Banned organisations, which have no means to resist or defend themselves against proscription, must attempt to demonstrate the legitimacy of their political organisation to the Home Secretary *after the fact of proscription*, and then before the Proscribed Organisations Appeal Committee or, ultimately, the Supreme Court.

Related to this is proscription's role in the regulation of political symbols; a further norm woven through British legislation and predicated on the institutionalised belief that organisational political power is acquired, legitimised, cemented and wielded through an orchestration of symbolisms either displayed, worn, performed or recited. This regulation of symbols, and their display, has been vital to proscription (and ancillary) legislation since, at least, the eighteenth century, as has the related prohibition upon public support for banned groups. Typically, this becomes manifest through a ban on the display of flags or the wearing of particular styles of, or insignia on, clothing implying membership of a banned group. As we have seen, this provision was innovated to quell the Jacobites amongst Scottish Clans, which outlawed tartan clothes, and continued in the Seditious Meetings Act 1819 ('flags, banners, ensigns, badges'); Northern Ireland's Civil Authorities (Special Powers) Act 1922 (which prohibited 'uniforms and badges'); and, the Public Order Act 1936 (which bans any form of uniform worn by political organisations).

This reasoning is evident, too, in the Societies Ordinances mentioned above that continue in force around the world today. Such laws allow for the seizure of 'books, accounts, writings, lists of members, seals, banners of insignia' suspected to be associated with designated 'unlawful societies' in Tanzania (the Societies Act 1954), Botswana (the Societies Act 1972), Zambia (the Societies Act 1958), Kenya (the Societies Act 1954) and Malaysia (the Societies Act 1966). And, as we noted in Chapter 1, in the UK today the TA 2000 provides that an individual commits a criminal offence if s/he '(a) wears an item of clothing, or (b) wears, carries or displays an article' that raises a reasonable suspicion that he or she supports a proscribed organisation. In these laws, clothes are understood as outward symbols of allegiance or dissent.[10]

Political symbols, however, are not only worn or displayed, they can also be performed or recited, hence proscription's interest in such practices too. Historically, we have seen the outlawing of declarations or oaths of allegiance to causes deemed antithetical to the British state. Kenyan Mau Mau oaths, for example, were constructed as 'part of a conscious attempt to transmit an ideology and directions for pragmatic action' (Green 2011, 82). And, we see similar efforts to regulate anti-establishment or oppositional discourse throughout legislation targeting radical nineteenth-century corresponding societies and labour movements; Irish republicanism in the Insurrection Act, 1796 (Ireland); in the Special Powers Act (1922); and in the 2006 extension of the UK's current proscription regime to include glorification offences.

If we take these together, we begin to see evidence of an institutionalised conviction persistent in British political institutions and cemented over centuries. This is a conviction that political organisations, and associated symbolisms (whether worn, performed or recited), are vital levers of oppositional power and influence. The fact of organised political cooperation has, in one form or another, remained subject to official approval both in the UK and in its ruled colonies. Symbolic activities associated with political organisation are deemed similarly dangerous: for the British state, symbols matter, which is why we see over the centuries repeated prohibitions on flags, uniforms, emblems, and the swearing of symbolic oaths. The Terrorism Act's proscription provisions, therefore, follow the precedents successively repeated by antecedent parliaments. And, as much as symbolic politics are deemed central to illegitimate organisations, symbolic politics is of course also made central to the legitimacy and authority of Parliament itself. The symbolisms denied to illegitimate entities are also those that help to constitute the legitimate citizen: the displaying or waving of a (national) flag; the wearing of (national) service uniforms; the singing of (national) anthems; and the recital of (national) oaths of loyalty.

From all of this, we might make two final points. In the first instance, making sense of proscription debates as a form of ritualised political activity may be less a challenge to the integrity of Parliament itself than it first appears. As Alan Finlayson (2017) has argued, (the function of) debate within Westminster has been conceptualised in a variety of ways, which he classifies as deliberation, oratory, opposition and spectacle. Although Parliament's deliberative role tends to dominate attention (and is manifestly apparent within some of the more critical denunciations of ritual noted above), discussion in the chamber has always done more than contribute to the decision-making process. If – continuing with Finlayson's (2017) typology – our case study shows few examples of impressive oratory, and perhaps fewer still of meaningful opposition, it does – we suggest – contribute to a repeated, familiar performance: an unspectacular spectacle, perhaps, of the British state doing its (liberal, democratic, cautious, responsible) work.

Second, let us not forget that if proscription – understood as an example of symbolic political activity – is inherently ritualistic, it is also inherently political. And it is political in at least two ways (see Jarvis 2009b, 196–197). First, the ritual, as we have seen, is political because it is productive. Proscription *produces* 'us', it produces 'them', and it produces proscription as an important political tool – serving as a moment of ontological institution or creation against an ultimately undecidable terrain. Proscription need not exist. Proscription offences need not be expanded. And proscription decisions – to ban specific actors – need not be made. And, yet, this all happens, and happens repeatedly, and happens, indeed, without wide recognition of this very contingency. Thus, as Jenny Edkins (1999, 2) has argued, both drawing on and citing Claude Lefort:

> 'the political' has to do with the establishment of that very social order which sets out a particular, historically specific account of what counts as politics and defines other areas of social life as *not* politics. For Claude Lefort, the political is concerned with the 'constitution of social space, of the form of society.' It is central to this process that the act of constitution is immediately concealed or hidden: Hence, 'the political is ... revealed, not in what we call political activity, but in the double movement whereby the mode of institution of society appears and is obscured'.

Proscription does not, however, only create or enable. It also – very visibly – excludes or forecloses. The power's central rationale is to deny the operation (and therefore, effectively, the existence) of specified groups within a designated territory. But the power's exclusionary force goes beyond this to militate against – amongst other things – dialogue or negotiation with banned organisations; alternative ways of countering terrorism; and, different conceptions of terrorism itself (both narrower, in the case of action-based definitions, and broader in discussions of state terrorism). Proscription is political, then, because it works against other forms of socio-political life and organisation, and perhaps against any recognition that other possibilities – of imagining the British identity; of engaging with antagonists; of countering terrorism – might even exist.

Notes

1 Enoch Powell, 'Rivers of Blood' speech, delivered to the Conservative Association meeting, Birmingham, 20 April 1968. Text republished in the *Daily Telegraph*, 6 November 2007. Available at: www.telegraph.co.uk/comment/3643823/Enoch-Powells-Rivers-of-Blood-speech.html (accessed 28 November 2019).

2 The Societies Enactment 1899, amended in 1913 to incorporate regulatory functions assigned to the 'Registrar of Society' and amended again 1927, 1947 and 1949.

3 Figures taken from Human Rights Watch World Report 2016. Available at: www.hrw.org/world-report/2016/country-chapters/Malaysia (accessed 18 February 2018).

4 'Hong Kong political bodies connected to foreign or Taiwan political orgs may be banned, says gov't', Hong Kong Free Press. Available at: www.hongkongfp.com/2017/07/05/hong-kong-political-bodies-connected-foreign-taiwan-political-orgs-may-banned-says-govt/ (accessed 18 December 2019).

5 Societies Ordinance (Chapter 151) (Order under section 8(2)). G.N. (E.) 52 of 2018. Available at: www.gld.gov.hk/egazette/pdf/20182244e/egn2018224452.pdf (accessed 27 September 2018).

6 CAMPACC (2010), cited in Crisis Balochistan (2010): https://crisisbalochistan.com/secondary_menu/news/campacc-launches-briefings-on-terrorist-bans.html (accessed 18 December 2019).

7 For example, in 2017 both Mohammed Abdallah and Samata Ullah were prosecuted for membership of Islamic State: www.cps.gov.uk/counter-terrorism-division-crown-prosecution-service-cps-successful-prosecutions-end-2006 (accessed 18 February 2018).

8 As we write, six individuals are being prosecuted for membership of National Action. The action is linked to a case involving an alleged plot to murder a Labour MP: www.theguardian.com/uk-news/2018/jun/12/man-pleads-guilty-to-plot-to-labour-mp-rosie-cooper (accessed 18 February 2018).

9 Memorandum submitted by the Hong Kong Human Rights Monitor: https://publications.parliament.uk/pa/cm199798/cmselect/cmfaff/710/8042820.htm (accessed 18 February 2018).

10 This sentiment is echoed in the various prohibitions placed on Nazi symbols in Germany today; and communist symbols in former Soviet bloc states such as Albania, the Czech Republic, Slovakia, Poland and Hungary.

References

Alao, A. (2006) *Mau-Mau Warrior*. Oxford: Osprey Publishing.

Alexander, J.C. (2006) 'Cultural pragmatics: social performance between ritual and strategy', in J.C. Alexander, B. Giesen and J.L. Mast (eds) *Social Performance: Symbolic Action, Cultural Pragmatics, and Ritual*. Cambridge: Cambridge University Press, pp. 29–90.

Allen, F.A. (1996) *The Habits of Legality: Criminal Justice and the Rule of Law*. New York: Oxford University Press.

Anderson, J. (1948) 'The politics of proscription', *The Australian Quarterly* 20(2): 7–15.

Aradau, C. (2004) 'Security and the democratic scene: Desecuritization and emancipation', *Journal of International Relations and Development* 7(4): 388–413.

Atkins, J. and A. Finlayson (2016) '"As Shakespeare so memorably said…": quotation, rhetoric, and the performance of politics', *Political Studies* 64(1): 1–18.

Baber, M. (1999) *The Terrorism Bill*. London: House of Commons Library.

Bachrach, P. and M.S. Baratz (1970) *Power and Poverty: Theory and Practice*. Oxford: Oxford University Press.

Bajc, V. (2007) 'Surveillance in public rituals: security meta-ritual and the 2005 US presidential inauguration', *American Behavioral Scientist* 50(12): 1648–1673.

Baker-Beall, C. (2016) *The European Union's Fight Against Terrorism: Discourse, Policies, Identity*. Manchester: Manchester University Press.

Balzacq, T. (2005) 'The three faces of securitization: political agency, audience and context', *European Journal of International Relations* 11(2): 171–201.

Balzacq, T. (2011) 'A theory of securitization: origins, core assumptions, and variants', in T. Balzacq (ed.) *Securitization Theory: How Security Problems Emerge and Dissolve*. Abingdon: Routledge, pp. 1–30.

Balzacq, T. (2015a) *Contesting Security: Strategies and Logics*. Abingdon: Routledge.

Balzacq, T. (2015b) 'Legitimacy and the "logic" of security', in T. Balzacq (ed.) *Securitization Theory: How Security Problems Emerge and Dissolve*. Abingdon: Routledge, pp. 1–10.

Barendt, E. (2005) 'Threats to freedom of speech in the United Kingdom', *University of New South Wales Law Journal*, 28(3): 895–899.

Barraclough, E. (2010) 'Inside outlawry in "Grettis saga Ásmundarsonar" and "Gísla saga Súrssonar": landscape in the outlaw sagas', *Scandinavian Studies* 82(4): 365–388.

Bartolucci, V. (2010) 'Analysing elite discourse on terrorism and its implications: the case of Morocco', *Critical Studies on Terrorism* 3(1): 119–135.

Beck, C.J. and E. Miner (2013) 'Who gets designated a terrorist and why?', *Social Forces* 91(3): 837–872.

Bell, C. (2011) *Ritual Theory, Ritual Practice*. Oxford: Oxford University Press.

Bigo, D. (2002) 'Security and immigration: toward a critique of the governmentality of unease', *Alternatives* 27(1): 63–92.

Blackbourn, J. (2008) 'Counter-terrorism and civil liberties: the United Kingdom experience, 1968–2008', *Journal of the Institute of Justice and International Studies* 8: 63–74.

Blackbourn, J. (2014) *Anti-Terrorism Law and Normalising Northern Ireland*. Abingdon: Routledge.

Blackstone, W. (1769) *Commentaries on the Laws of England. 1769*. 4 vols. Chicago: University of Chicago Press.

Blair, T. (2010) *A Journey: My Political Life*. London: Hutchinson.

Blakeley, R. (2009) *State Terrorism and Neoliberalism: The North in the South*. Abingdon: Routledge.

Booth, K. (2007) *Theory of World Security*. Cambridge: Cambridge University Press.

Bourne, A. (2015) 'Why ban Batasuna? Terrorism, political parties and democracy', *Comparative European Politics* 13(3): 325–344.

Bourne, A.K. and F. Casal Bértoa (2014) 'Prescribing democracy? Party proscription, militant democracy and party system institutionalization', paper presented at 42nd ECPR Joint Sessions of Workshops, University of Salamanca, 10–15 April 2014.

Bracton, H. (1968) *Bracton de Legibus Et Consuetudinibus Angliae* [*On the Laws and Customs of England*]. Translated by Samuel E. Thorne. Cambridge, MA: Belknap Press of Harvard University Press. A digital version is maintained at: http://amesfoundation.law.harvard.edu/Bracton/index.html. Volume 2. (Accessed 18 December 2019).

Bright, J. (2015) 'In search of the politics of security', *The British Journal of Politics and International Relations* 17(4): 225–256.

Bronitt, S. (2003) 'Australia's legal response to terrorism: neither novel nor extraordinary?', paper presented at the Castan Centre For Human Rights Law Conference, Melbourne.

Browning, C.S. and M. McDonald (2013) 'The future of critical security studies: ethics and the politics of security', *European Journal of International Relations* 19(2): 235–255.

Bubandt, N. (2005) 'Vernacular security: the politics of feeling safe in global, national and local worlds', *Security Dialogue* 36(3): 275–296.

Burke, J. (2003) *Al-Qaeda: Casting a Shadow of Terror*. London: IB Tauris & Company Limited.

Burnett, J. and D. Whyte (2005) 'Embedded expertise and the new terrorism', *Journal for Crime, Conflict and the Media* 1(4): 1–18.

Butler, J. (2010) 'Performative agency', *Journal of Cultural Economy* 3(2): 147–161.

Butler, S. (2002) *The Hand of Cicero*. Abingdon: Routledge.

Buzan, B., O. Wæver and J. de Wilde (1998) *Security: A New Framework for Analysis*. London: Lynne Rienner.

Byman, D. (2005) *Deadly Connections: States that Sponsor Terrorism*. Cambridge: Cambridge University Press.

Cameron, D. (2014) Remarks to the United Nations General Assembly 69th Session. Available at: https://undocs.org/pdf?symbol=en/A/69/PV.8 (accessed 24 May 2019).

Cameron, I. (2003) 'European Union anti-terrorist blacklisting', *Human Rights Law Review* 3(2): 225–256.

Campbell, D. (1992) *Writing Security: United States Foreign Policy and the Politics of Identity*. Minneapolis: University of Minnesota Press.

Campbell, D. (1998) *National Deconstruction: Violence, Identity, and Justice in Bosnia*. Minneapolis: University of Minnesota Press.

Cardwell, P. (2015) 'The legalisation of European Union foreign policy and the use of sanctions', *Cambridge Yearbook of European Legal Studies* 17: 287–310.

Carella, B. (2015) 'The earliest expression for outlawry in Anglo-Saxon law', *Traditio* 70: 111–143.

Carlile of Berriew, Lord QC (2010) *Report on the Operation in 2009 of the Terrorism Act 2000 and of Part 1 of the Terrorism Act 2006*. London: The Stationery Office.

Casier, M. (2010) 'Designated terrorists: the Kurdistan Workers' Party and its struggle to (re)gain political legitimacy', *Mediterranean Politics* 15(3): 393–413.

Chadwyck Healey, C.E.H. (ed.) (1897) *Somersetshire Pleas (civil and criminal), from the rolls of the itinerant justices (close of 12th century – 41 Henry III [1257])*. Somerset Record Society, volume 11. Available at: https://archive.org/stream/somersetshirepl00chadgoog/somersetshirepl00chadgoog_djvu.txt (accessed 3 April 2018).

Chou, W. (2015) 'Seen like a state: how illegitimacy shapes terrorism designation', *Social Forces* 94(3): 1129–1152.

Cole, M. (1999) 'Accountability and quasi-government: the role of parliamentary questions', *The Journal of Legislative Studies* 5(1): 77–101.

Cram, I. (2006) 'Regulating the media: some neglected freedom of expression issues in the United Kingdom's counter-terrorism strategy', *Terrorism and Political Violence* 18(2): 335–355.

Crenshaw, M. (2014) 'Terrorism research: the record', *International Interactions* 40(4): 556–567.

Crewe, E. (2005) *Lords of Parliament: Manners, Rituals and Politics*. Manchester: Manchester University Press.

Croft, S. (2006) *Culture, Crisis and America's War on Terror*. Cambridge: Cambridge University Press.

Cronin, A.K. (2003) *The FTO List and Congress: Sanctioning Designated Foreign Terrorist Organizations*. Library of Congress Washington, DC: Congressional Research Service.

Cronin, A.K. (2009) *How Terrorism Ends: Understanding the Decline and Demise of Terrorist Campaigns*. Princeton: Princeton University Press.

Davies, N. (2000) *The Isles: A History*. Basingstoke: Macmillan.

De Castella, K., C. McGarty and L. Musgrove (2009) 'Fear appeals in political rhetoric about terrorism: an analysis of speeches by Australian Prime Minister Howard', *Political Psychology* 30(1): 1–26.

De Goede, M. (2011) 'Blacklisting and the ban: contesting targeted sanctions in Europe', *Security Dialogue* 42(6): 499–515.

De Goede, M. (2018) 'Proscription's futures', *Terrorism and Political Violence* 30(2): 336–355.

de Lomnitz, L.A., R.S. Elena and I. Adler (2010) *Symbolism and Ritual in a One-Party Regime: Unveiling Mexico's Political Culture*. Tucson: University of Arizona Press.

Donohue, L.K. (2008) *The Cost of Counter-Terrorism: Power, Politics and Liberty*. Cambridge: Cambridge University Press.

Doty, R.L. (1993) 'Foreign policy as social construction: a post-positivist analysis of US counterinsurgency policy in the Philippines', *International Studies Quarterly* 37(3): 297–320.

Douglas, R.N. (2008) 'Proscribing terrorist organisations: legislation and practice in five English-speaking democracies', *Criminal Law Journal* 90(2): 90–99.

Dunn, K. (2006) 'Examining historical representations', *International Studies Review* 8(2): 370–381.

Durkheim, E. (2001) *The Elementary Forms of Religious Life*. Oxford: Oxford University Press.

Eburn, M. (2005) 'Outlawry in colonial Australia: the Felons Apprehension Acts 1865–1899', *Australia and New Zealand Law and History E-Journal [2005]*: 80–93.

Edelman, M. (1969) 'Escalation and ritualization of political conflict', *American Behavioral Scientist* 13(2): 231–246.

Edkins, J. (1999) *Poststructuralism & International Relations: Bringing the Political Back In*. London: Lynne Rienner.

Epstein, C. (2011) 'Who speaks? Discourse, the subject and the study of identity in international politics', *European Journal of International Relations* 17(2): 327–350.

Fekete, L. (2001) 'The Terrorism Act 2000: an interview with Gareth Peirce', *Race & Class* 43(2): 95–103.

Fenwick, H. (2002) 'Responding to 11 September: detention without trial under the anti-terrorism, crime and security Act 2001', *The Political Quarterly* 73(s1): 80–104.

Finlayson, A. (2017) 'What is the point of parliamentary debate? Deliberation, oratory, opposition and spectacle in the British House of Commons', *Redescriptions: Political Thought, Conceptual History and Feminist Theory* 20(1): 11–31.

Finnemore, M. and K. Sikkink (2001) 'Taking stock: the constructivist research program in international relations and comparative politics', *Annual Review of Political Science* 4(1): 391–416.

Fisher, K. (2013) 'Exploring the temporality in/of British counterterrorism law and law making', *Critical Studies on Terrorism* 6(1): 50–72.

Fisher, K. (2015) *Security, Identity and British Counterterrorism Policy*. Basingstoke: Palgrave.

Flyghed, J. (2002) 'Normalising the exceptional: the case of political violence', *Policing & Society* 13(1): 23–41.

Forcese, C. and K. Roach (2018) 'Yesterday's law: terrorist group listing in Canada', *Terrorism and Political Violence* 30(2): 259–277.

Foucault, M. (1986) *The Use of Pleasure: The History of Sexuality Volume Two*. London: Penguin.

Foucault, M. (2002) *Archaeology of Knowledge*. Abingdon: Routledge.

Franz, P. (1982) 'Unconstitutional and outlawed political parties: German-American comparison', *Boston College International and Comparative Law Review* 5(1): 51–90.

Freedman, B. (2010) 'Officially blacklisted extremist/terrorist (support) organizations: a comparison of lists from six countries and two international organizations', *Perspectives on Terrorism* 4(2): 46–52.

George, A. (ed.) (1991) *Western State Terrorism*. Cambridge: Polity Press.

Gerges, F.A. (2011) *The Rise and Fall of Al-Qaeda*. Oxford: Oxford University Press.

Girard, R. (1977) *Violence and the Sacred*. Translated by Patrick Gregory. Baltimore: Johns Hopkins University Press.

Gluckman, M. and C.D. Forde (1962) *Essays on the Ritual of Social Relations*. Manchester: Manchester University Press.

Goldsmith, A. (2007) 'Preparation for terrorism: catastrophic risk and precautionary criminal law', in A. Lynch, E. MacDonald and G. Williams (eds) *Law and Liberty and the War on Terror*. Sydney: Federation Press, pp. 59–74.

Goody, J. (1986) *The Logic of Writing and the Organization of Society*. Cambridge: Cambridge University Press.

Grice, A. (2014) 'Ed Miliband calls for "deradicalization" of Britons drawn into Islamic extremism abroad', *Independent*, 29 August. Available at: www.independent.co.uk/news/uk/home-news/ed-miliband-urges-west-to-unite-to-confront-isis-threat-at-home-and-abroad-9700803.html (accessed 24 May 2019).

Grierson, J., V. Dodd and J. Rodrigues (2016) 'Anjem Choudary convicted of supporting Islamic State', *Guardian*. Available at: www.theguardian.com/uk-news/2016/aug/16/anjem-choudary-convicted-of-supporting-islamic-state (accessed 24 May 2019).

Grimes, R.L. (2014) *The Craft of Ritual Studies*. Oxford: Oxford University Press.

Grob-Fitzgibbon, B. (2015) 'Britain's small wars: the empire strikes back, 1952–68', in R.D. Law (ed.) *The Routledge History of Terrorism*. Abingdon: Routledge, pp. 190–203.

Gross, J. (2010) 'Talking with terrorists: terrorist groups and the challenge of legitimization', *Journal of Public and International Affairs* 21: 93–114.

Gross, J. (2011) 'Proscription problems: the practical implications of terrorist lists on diplomacy and peacebuilding in Nepal', *Praxis* 26: 38–59.

Guardian (1934) 'Oswald Mosley's circus', 8 June 1934. Available at: www.theguardian.com/politics/1934/jun/08/thefarright.uk (accessed 18 December 2019).

Gunning, J. (2007) 'A case for critical terrorism studies?', *Government and Opposition* 42(3): 363–393.

Gusfield, J.R. and J. Michalowicz (1984) 'Secular symbolism: studies of ritual, ceremony, and the symbolic order in modern life', *Annual Review of Sociology* 10: 417–435.

Guzzini, S. (2000) 'A reconstruction of constructivism in international relations', *European Journal of International Relations* 6(2): 147–182.

Hansen, L. (2013) *Security as Practice: Discourse Analysis and the Bosnian War*. Abingdon: Routledge.

Harward, T. (1896) *Hereward, the Saxon Patriot: A History of His Life and Character, with a Record of His Ancestors and Descendants, A.D. 445 to A.D. 1896*. London: E. Stock.

Haspeslagh, S. (2013) '"Listing terrorists": the impact of proscription on third-party efforts to engage armed groups in peace processes – a practitioner's perspective', *Critical Studies on Terrorism* 6(1): 189–208.

Heartfield, J. and K. Rooney (2015) *Who's Afraid of the Easter Rising? 1916–2016*. Alresford: John Hunt Publishing.

Heath-Kelly, C. (2013) 'Counter-terrorism and the counterfactual: producing the "radicalisation" discourse and the UK PREVENT strategy', *The British Journal of Politics & International Relations* 15(3): 394–415.
Heath-Kelly, C. (2017) 'In memoriam: turning the anthropological gaze onto security ritual', *Critical Studies on Security* 5(2): 230–235.
Hocking, J. (2003) 'Counter-terrorism and the criminalisation of politics: Australia's new security powers of detention, proscription and control', *Australian Journal of Politics & History* 49(3): 355–371.
Hoffman, B. (1997) 'The confluence of international and domestic trends in terrorism', *Terrorism and Political Violence* 9(2): 1–15.
Hogg, R. (2008) 'Executive proscription of terrorist organisations in Australia: exploring the shifting border between crime and politics', in M. Gani and P. Mathew (eds) *Fresh Perspectives on the 'War on Terror'*. Canberra: ANU E Press, pp. 297–323.
Holland, J. (2010) 'Howard's war on terror: a conceivable, communicable and coercive foreign policy discourse', *Australian Journal of Political Science* 45(4): 643–661.
Holland, J. (2012) *Selling the War on Terror: Foreign Policy Discourses after 9/11*. Abingdon: Routledge.
Holland, J. (2013) 'Foreign policy and political possibility', *European Journal of International Relations* 19(1): 49–68.
Home Office (1998) Legislation Against Terrorism: A Consultation Paper. CM4178. London: The Stationery Office. Available at: https://assets.publishing.service.gov.uk/government/uploads/system/uploads/attachment_data/file/265689/4178.pdf (accessed 18 January 2018).
Home Office (2014). *Proscribed Terrorist Organisations*. Available at: https://assets.publishing.service.gov.uk/government/uploads/system/uploads/attachment_data/file/353993/20140820-List_of_Proscribed_organisations_WEBSITE_final.docx (accessed 19 December 2019).
Home Office (2017). Proscribed Terrorist Organisations. Available at: https://assets.publishing.service.gov.uk/government/uploads/system/uploads/attachment_data/file/670599/20171222_Proscription.pdf (accessed 18 January 2018).
Home Office (2019) Proscribed Terrorist Organisations. Available at: https://assets.publishing.service.gov.uk/government/uploads/system/uploads/attachment_data/file/795457/Proscription_website.pdf (accessed 24 May 2019).
Home Office and Northern Ireland Office (2000) Supplementary Memorandum by the Home Office and Northern Ireland Office, in Delegated Powers and Deregulation – Twelfth Report. Select Committee on Delegated Powers and Deregulation. House of Lords: Hansard. Available at: www.publications.parliament.uk/ pa/ld199900/ldselect/lddereg/57/5701.htm (accessed 3 June 2013).
Hopf, T. (1998) 'The promise of constructivism in international relations theory', *International Security* 23(1): 171–200.

Horgan, J. and J.F. Morrison (2011) 'Here to stay? The rising threat of violent dissident Republicanism in Northern Ireland', *Terrorism and Political Violence* 23(4): 642–669.

Horsman, S. (2005) 'Themes in official discourses on terrorism in Central Asia', *Third World Quarterly* 26(1): 199–213.

Hoskins, A. and B. O'Loughlin (2009) *Television and Terror: Conflicting Times and the Crisis of News Discourse*. Basingstoke: Palgrave.

House of Commons Information Office (2010) Parliamentary Questions: Factsheet P1 Procedure Series. Available at: www.parliament.uk/documents/commons-information-office/p01.pdf (accessed 17 March 2016).

Howe, M. (1937) 'Process of outlawry in New York: a study of the selective reception of English law', *Cornell Law Quarterly* 23(4): 559–579.

Husak, D.N. (1991) 'The orthodox model of the criminal offense', *Criminal Justice Ethics* 10(1): 20–23.

Huysmans, J. (2006) *The Politics of Insecurity: Fear, Migration and Asylum in the EU*. Abingdon: Routledge.

Huysmans, J. (2011) 'What's in an act? On security speech acts and little security nothings', *Security Dialogue* 42(4–5): 371–383.

Huysmans, J. and A. Buonfino (2008) 'Politics of exception and unease: immigration, asylum and terrorism in parliamentary debates in the UK', *Political Studies* 56(4): 766–788.

Innes, J. and A. Burns (2003) 'Introduction', in A. Burns, J. Innes and L. Roper (eds) *Rethinking the Age of Reform: Britain 1780–1850*. Cambridge: Cambridge University Press, pp. 1–70.

Jackson, R. (2005) *Writing the War on Terrorism: Language, Politics and Counter-Terrorism*. Manchester: Manchester University Press.

Jackson, R. (ed.) (2016) *The Routledge Handbook of Critical Terrorism Studies*. Abingdon: Routledge.

Jackson, R., J. Gunning and M. Breen-Smyth (eds) (2009) *Critical Terrorism Studies: A New Research Agenda*. Abingdon: Routledge.

Jackson, R., E. Murphy and S. Poynting (eds) (2010) *Contemporary State Terrorism: Theory and Practice*. Abingdon: Routledge.

Jackson, R., L. Jarvis, J. Gunning and M. Breen-Smyth (2011) *Terrorism: A Critical Introduction*. Basingstoke: Palgrave.

Jarvis, L. (2009a) 'The spaces and faces of critical terrorism studies', *Security Dialogue* 40(1): 5–27.

Jarvis, L. (2009b) *Times of Terror: Discourse, Temporality and the War on Terror*. Basingstoke: Palgrave.

Jarvis, L. (2012) 'Al Qaeda: a diminishing threat', in R. Jackson and S. Sinclair (eds) *Contemporary Debates on Terrorism*. Abingdon: Routledge, pp. 97–102.

Jarvis, L. (2016) 'Critical terrorism studies after 9/11', in R. Jackson (ed.) *Routledge Handbook of Critical Terrorism Studies*. Abingdon: Routledge, pp. 28–38.

Jarvis, L. (2019a) 'Terrorism, counter-terrorism, and critique: opportunities, examples, and implications', *Critical Studies on Terrorism* 12(2): 339–358.

Jarvis, L. (2019b) 'Toward a vernacular security studies: origins, interlocutors, contributions, and challenges', *International Studies Review* 21(1): 107–126.

Jarvis, L. and T. Legrand (2016) 'Legislating for otherness: proscription powers and parliamentary discourse', *Review of International Studies* 42(3): 558–574.

Jarvis, L. and T. Legrand (2017) '"I am somewhat puzzled": questions, audiences and securitization in the proscription of terrorist organisations', *Security Dialogue* 48(2): 149–167.

Jarvis, L. and T. Legrand (2018) 'The proscription or listing of terrorist organisations: understanding, assessment, and international comparisons', *Terrorism and Political Violence* 30(2): 199–215.

Jarvis, L. and M. Lister (2013) 'Vernacular securities and their study: a qualitative analysis and research agenda', *International Relations* 27(2): 158–179.

Jarvis, L. and M. Lister (2014) 'State terrorism research and critical terrorism studies: an assessment', *Critical Studies on Terrorism* 7(1): 43–61.

Jarvis, L. and M. Lister (2015) *Anti-Terrorism, Citizenship and Security*. Manchester: Manchester University Press.

Jarvis, L. and M. Lister (2016) 'What would you do? Everyday conceptions and constructions of counter-terrorism', *Politics* 36(3): 277–291.

Jones, D.M. and M.L. Smith (2009) 'We're all terrorists now: critical—or hypocritical—studies "on" terrorism?' *Studies in Conflict & Terrorism* 32(4): 292–302.

Jones, R. (2000) 'The unsolicited diary as a qualitative research tool for advanced research capacity in the field of health and illness', *Qualitative Health Research* 10(4): 555–567.

Jones, T. (2010) *Outlawry in Medieval Literature*. Basingstoke: Palgrave.

Joseph, J. (2011) 'Terrorism as a social relation within capitalism: theoretical and emancipatory implications', *Critical Studies on Terrorism* 4(1): 23–37.

Kanyinga, K. (2009) 'The legacy of the white highlands: land rights, ethnicity and the post-2007 election violence in Kenya', *Journal of Contemporary African Studies* 27(3): 325–344.

Kertzer, D.I. (1989) *Ritual, Politics, and Power*. New Haven: Yale University Press.

Kettell, S. (2013) 'Dilemmas of discourse: legitimising Britain's war on terror', *The British Journal of Politics and International Relations* 15(2): 263–279.

Laclau, E. (1990) *New Reflections on the Revolution of Our Time*. London: Verso.

Laclau, E. (1997) 'The death and resurrection of the theory of ideology', *Modern Language Notes* 112(3): 297–332.
Laclau, E. (2004) 'Introduction', in E. Laclau (ed.) *The Making of Political Identities*. London: Verso, pp. 1–8.
Laclau, E. and C. Mouffe (1987) 'Post-Marxism without apologies', *New Left Review* 1(166): 79–106.
Laclau, E. and C. Mouffe (2001) *Hegemony and Socialist Strategy: Towards a Radical Democratic Politics* (2nd edn). London: Verso.
Legrand, T. and L. Jarvis (2014) 'Enemies of the state: proscription powers and their use in the United Kingdom', *British Politics* 9(4): 450–471.
Lévi-Strauss, C. (1990) [1971] *The Naked Man*. Chicago: University of Chicago Press.
Lia, B. (2010) 'Al-Qaida's appeal: understanding its unique selling points', *Perspectives on Terrorism* 2(8): 3–10.
Linehan, T. (2007) '"On the side of Christ": fascist clerics in 1930s Britain', *Totalitarian Movements and Political Religions*, 8(2): 287–301.
Lloyd of Berwick, Lord (1996) *Inquiry into Legislation against Terrorism. Cm. 3420* (Vol. 1). London: The Stationery Office.
Lovenduski, J. (2012) 'Prime Minister's questions as political ritual', *British Politics* 7(4): 314–340.
Lukes, S. (1975) 'Political ritual and social integration', *Sociology* 9(2): 289–308.
Lum, C., L.W. Kennedy and A. Sherley (2006) 'Are counter-terrorism strategies effective? The results of the Campbell systematic review on counter-terrorism evaluation research', *Journal of Experimental Criminology* 2(4): 489–516.
Lynch, A., N. McGarrity and G. Williams (2009) 'The proscription of terrorist organisations in Australia', *Federal Law Review* 37(1): 1–40.
Lyttelton, O. (1963) *The Memoirs of Lord Chandos: An Unexpected View from the Summit*. New York: New American Library.
McDonald, M. (2008) 'Securitization and the construction of security', *European Journal of International Relations* 14(4): 563–587.
McDonald, M. (2015) 'Contesting border security: emancipation and asylum in the Australian context', in T. Balzacq (ed.) *Contesting Security: Strategies and Logics*. Abingdon: Routledge, pp. 154–168.
Macdonald, S. (2012) 'Understanding anti-terrorism policy: values, rationales and principles', *Sydney Law Review* 34: 317–395.
McCulloch, J. and S. Pickering (2009) 'Pre-crime and counter-terrorism imagining future crime in the "war on terror"', *British Journal of Criminology* 49(5): 628–645.
McGarr, P.M. (2010) '"A serious menace to security": British intelligence, VK Krishna Menon and the Indian High Commission in London, 1947–52', *The Journal of Imperial and Commonwealth History* 38(3): 441–469.

McGarrity, N. and G. Williams (2018) 'The proscription of terrorist organisations in Australia', *Terrorism and Political Violence* 30(2): 216–223.

McGreal, C. (2012) 'MEK decision: multimillion dollar campaign led to removal from terrorist list', *Guardian*, 21 September. Available at: www.guardian.co.uk/world/2012/sep/21/iran-mek-group-removed-us-terrorism-list (accessed 24 May 2019).

Mackintosh, K. and I. Macdonald (2013) 'Counter-terrorism and humanitarian action', *Humanitarian Exchange* 58: 23–25.

McSherry, B. (2004) 'Terrorism offences in the criminal code: broadening the boundaries of Australian criminal laws', *University of New South Wales Law Journal* 27(2): 354–372.

McWhinney, E. (1956) 'German federal constitutional court and the communist party decision', *Indiana Law Journal* 32(3): 295–312.

Martin, S. (2011) 'Parliamentary questions, the behaviour of legislators, and the function of legislatures: an introduction', *The Journal of Legislative Studies* 17(3): 259–270.

Milliken, J. (1999) 'The study of discourse in international relations: a critique of research and methods', *European Journal of International Relations* 5(2): 225–254.

Moore, S.F. and B.G. Myerhoff (1977) *Secular Ritual*. Assen: Uitgeverij Van Gorcum.

Mosley, O. (1933) *Fascism Explained: 10 Points of Fascist Policy*. [London]: Printed and published by B.U.F.

Muller, M. (2008) 'Terrorism, proscription and the right to resist in the age of conflict', *Denning Law Journal* 20(1): 111–131.

Nadarajah, S. and D. Sriskandarajah (2005) 'Liberation struggle or terrorism? The politics of naming the LTTE', *Third World Quarterly* 26(1): 87–100.

Neal, A.W. (2010) *Exceptionalism and the Politics of Counter-errorism: Liberty, Security and the War on Terror*. Abingdon: Routledge.

Neal, A.W. (2012) 'Terrorism, lawmaking, and democratic politics: legislators as security actors', *Terrorism and Political Violence* 24(3): 357–374.

Neal, A. (2019) *Security as Politics: Beyond the State of Exception*. Edinburgh: Edinburgh University Press.

Neumann, P. (2009) *Old and New Terrorism*. Cambridge: Polity.

Oren, I. and T. Solomon (2015) '"WMD, WMD, WMD": securitisation through ritualised incantation of ambiguous phrases', *Review of International Studies* 41(2): 313–336.

Paine, T. (1791) *Rights of Man*. London: Printed for J.S. Jordan.

Pantazis, C. and S. Pemberton (2009) 'From the "old" to the "new" suspect community: examining the impacts of recent UK counter-terrorist legislation', *British Journal of Criminology* 49(5): 646–666.

Pedahzur, A., W. Eubank and L. Weinberg (2002) 'The war on terrorism and the decline of terrorist group formation: a research note', *Terrorism and Political Violence* 14(3): 141–147.

Phillips, B.J. (2015) 'What is a terrorist group? Conceptual issues and empirical implications', *Terrorism and Political Violence* 27(2): 225–242.

Rai, S.M. (2010) 'Analysing ceremony and ritual in parliament', *The Journal of Legislative Studies* 16(3): 284–297.

Rai, S.M. (2014) 'Political performance: a framework for analysing democratic politics', *Political Studies* 63(5): 1179–1197.

Rai, S.M. and R. Johnson (eds) (2014) *Democracy in Practice: Ceremony and Ritual in Parliament*. Basingstoke: Palgrave.

Rappaport, R.A. (1999) *Ritual and Religion in the Making of Humanity*. Cambridge: Cambridge University Press.

Reid, R. (2017) *The Peterloo Massacre*. London: Windmill Books.

Rhodes, R.A.W. (2005) 'Everyday life in a ministry public administration as anthropology', *The American Review of Public Administration* 35(1): 3–25.

Richards, H.E. (1902) 'Is outlawry obsolete?', *Law Quarterly Review* 18(3): 297–304.

Richmond, O. and J. Franks (2005) 'Human security and the war on terror', in F. Dodds and T. Pippard (eds) *Human and Environmental Security: An Agenda for Change*. Sterling: Earthscan.

Ritchie, J. and L. Spencer (2002) 'Qualitative data analysis for applied policy research', in A. Humberman and M. Miles (eds) *The Qualitative Researcher's Companion*. London: Sage, pp. 305–330.

Robinson, N. (2012) 'Videogames, persuasion and the war on terror: escaping or embedding the military–entertainment complex?', *Political Studies* 60(3): 504–522.

Robinson, N. (2015) 'Have you won the war on terror? Military videogames and the state of American exceptionalism', *Millennium* 43(2): 450–470.

Roe, P. (2004) 'Securitization and minority rights: conditions of desecuritization', *Security Dialogue* 35(3): 279–294.

Roe, P. (2012) 'Is securitization a "negative" concept? Revisiting the normative debate over normal versus extraordinary politics', *Security Dialogue* 43(3): 249–266.

Rozenberg, Olivier, Olivier Chopin, Catherine Hoeffler, Bastien Irondelle and Jean Joana (2011) 'Not only a battleground: parliamentary oral questions concerning defence policies in four Western democracies', *The Journal of Legislative Studies* 17(3): 340–353.

Sageman, M. (2014) 'The stagnation in terrorism research', *Terrorism and Political Violence* 26(4): 565–580.

Salter, M. (2002) *Barbarians & Civilization in International Relations*. London: Pluto.

Salter, M. (2008) 'Securitization and desecuritization: a dramaturgical analysis of the Canadian Air Transport Security Authority', *Journal of International Relations and Development* 11(4): 321–349.

Salter, M. (2011) 'When securitization fails: the hard case of counter-terrorism programs', in T. Balzacq (ed.) *Securitization Theory: How Security Problems Emerge and Dissolve*. Abingdon: Routledge, pp. 116–132.

Saul, B. (2005) 'Attempts to define "terrorism" in international law'. *Netherlands International Law Review* 52(1): 57–83.

Schmid, A. (2011) 'The literature on terrorism', in *The Routledge Handbook of Terrorism Research*. Abingdon: Routledge, pp. 457–474.

Scrivener, M. (2000) 'John Thelwall's political ambivalence: reform and revolution', in M.T. Davis (ed.) *Radicalism and Revolution in Britain, 1775–1848*. Basingstoke: Palgrave, pp. 69–83.

Seal, G. (2011) *Outlaw Heroes in Myth and History*. London: Anthem Press.

Sentas, V. (2010) 'The violence of "terrorist organisation" bans', *Criminal Justice Matters* 82(1): 16–17.

Shapiro, J.B. (2007) 'Politicization of the designation of foreign terrorist organizations: the effect on the separation of powers', *The Cardozo Public Law, Policy & Ethics Journal* 6(3): 547–600.

Sharman, J.C. (2009) 'The bark is the bite: international organizations and blacklisting', *Review of International Political Economy* 16(4): 573–596.

Shephard, M. (2009) 'Parliamentary scrutiny and oversight of the British "War on Terror": from accretion of executive power and evasion of scrutiny to embarrassment and concessions', *The Journal of Legislative Studies* 15(2–3): 191–218.

Silke, A. (2004) 'The road less travelled: recent trends in terrorism research', in A. Silke (ed.) *Research on Terrorism: Trends, Achievements and Failures*. Abingdon: Routledge, pp. 194–195.

Singer, P. (2004) *The President of Good and Evil: Questioning the Ethics of George W. Bush*. London: Penguin.

Smith, B.L. and K.R. Damphousse (2009) 'Patterns of precursor behaviors in the life span of a US environmental terrorist group', *Criminology & Public Policy* 8(3): 475–496.

Solomon, T. (2012) '"I wasn't angry, because I couldn't believe it was happening": affect and discourse in responses to 9/11', *Review of International Studies* 38(4): 907–928.

Spencer, A. (2006) 'Questioning the concept of "new terrorism"', *Peace, Conflict and Development* 8: 1–33.

Spencer, A. (2010) *The Tabloid Terrorist: The Predicative Construction of New Terrorism in the Media*. Basingstoke: Palgrave.

Staal, F. (1996) *Ritual and Mantras: Rules without Meaning*. Delhi: Motilal Banarsidass Publishers.

Stampnitzky, L. (2013) *Disciplining Terror: How Experts Invented 'Terrorism'*. Cambridge: Cambridge University Press.

Stewart, S. (2016) 'Outlawry as an instrument of justice in the thirteenth century', in J.C. Appleby and P. Dalton (eds) *Outlaws in Medieval and Early Modern England*. Abingdon: Routledge, pp. 49–66.

Stiles, K.W. (2006) 'The power of procedure and the procedures of the powerful', *Journal of Peace Research* 43(1): 37–54.

Stockwell, A.J. (1993) 'A widespread and long-concocted plot to overthrow government in Malaya? The origins of the Malayan emergency', *The Journal of Imperial and Commonwealth History* 21(3): 66–88.

Stohl, M., and G. Lopez (eds) (1984) *The State as Terrorist: The Dynamics of Governmental Violence and Repression*. Westport: Greenwood Press.

Stohl, M. and G. Lopez (eds) (1988) *Terrible Beyond Endurance? The Foreign Policy of State Terrorism*. New York: Greenwood Press.

Stokes, D. (2005) *America's Other War: Terrorizing Colombia*. London: Zed.

Stokes, D. (2009) 'Ideas and avocados: ontologising critical terrorism studies', *International Relations* 23(1): 85–92.

Taylor, C. (2002) 'Modern social imaginaries', *Public Culture* 14(1): 91–124.

Tham, J.C. (2004) 'Possible constitutional objections to the powers to ban terrorist organisations', *University of New South Wales Law Journal* 27(2): 482–523.

T'Hart, P. (1993) 'Symbols, rituals and power: the lost dimensions of crisis management', *Journal of Contingencies and Crisis Management* 1(1): 36–50.

Torfing, J. (1999) *New Theories of Discourse: Laclau, Mouffe and Žižek*. Oxford: Blackwell.

Torfing, J. (2005) 'Discourse theory: achievements, arguments, and challenges', in D. Howarth and J. Torfing (eds) *Discourse Theory in European Politics: Identity, Policy and Governance*. Basingstoke: Palgrave, pp. 1–32.

Turner, V. (1967) *The Forest of Symbols: Aspects of Ndembu Ritual*. Ithaca, NY: Cornell University Press.

US Department of State (2012) *Country Reports on Terrorism 2012*. Available at: www.state.gov/j/ct/rls/crt/2012/209989.htm (accessed 24 May 2019).

Van der Bijl, N. (2017) *Mau Mau Rebellion: The Emergency in Kenya 1952–1956*. Barnsley: Pen and Sword.

Van der Valk, I. (2003) 'Right-wing parliamentary discourse on immigration in France', *Discourse & Society* 14(3): 309–348.

Van Dijk, T.A. (2000) Ideology and Discourse: A Multidisciplinary Introduction. English version of an internet course for the Universitat Oberta de Catalunya (UOC).

Van Dijk, T.A. (2004) 'Text and context of parliamentary debates', in P. Bayley (ed.) *Cross-Cultural Perspectives on Parliamentary Discourse*. Amsterdam: John Benjamins, pp. 339–372.

Van Houts, E. (2004) 'The vocabulary of exile and outlawry in the North Sea area around the first millennium'. In *Exile in the Middle Ages: Selected Proceedings from the International Medieval Congress, University of Leeds, 8–11 July 2002*, pp. 13–28.

Van Um, E. and D. Pisiou (2015) 'Dealing with uncertainty: the illusion of knowledge in the study of counterterrorism effectiveness', *Critical Studies on Terrorism* 8(2): 229–245.

Vittori, J. (2009) 'All struggles must end: the longevity of terrorist groups', *Contemporary Security Policy* 30(3): 444–466.

Vuori, J. (2008) 'Illocutionary logic and strands of securitisation: applying the theory of securitization to the study of non-democratic political orders', *European Journal of International Relations* 14(1): 65–99.

Vuori, J. (2011) 'Religion bites: Falungong: securitization/desecuritzation in the People's Republic of China', in T. Balzacq (ed.) *Securitization Theory: How Security Problems Emerge and Dissolve*. Abingdon: Routledge, pp. 186–211.

Waldron, J. (2003) 'Security and liberty: the image of balance', *Journal of Political Philosophy* 11(2): 191–210.

Walker, C. (1997) 'Constitutional governance and special powers against terrorism: lessons from the United Kingdom's Prevention of Terrorism Acts', *Columbia Journal of Transnational Law* 35(1): 1–62.

Walker, C. (2000) 'Briefing on the Terrorism Act 2000', *Terrorism and Political Violence* 12(2): 1–36.

Walker, C. (2006) 'Clamping down on terrorism in the United Kingdom', *Journal of International Criminal Justice* 4(5): 1137–1151.

Walker, C. (2018) '"They haven't gone away you know: the persistence of proscription and the problems of deproscription', *Terrorism and Political Violence* 30(2): 236–258.

Waylen, G. (2010) 'Researching ritual and the symbolic in parliaments: an institutionalist perspective', *The Journal of Legislative Studies* 16(3): 352–365.

Weitzer, R.J. (1990) *Transforming Settler States: Communal Conflict and Internal Security in Northern Ireland and Zimbabwe*. Oakland: University of California Press.

Wendt, A. (1998) 'On constitution and causation in international relations', *Review of International Studies* 24(5): 101–118.

Whaley, D. (2002) *Sagas of Warrior-Poets*. London: Penguin.

Wilkinson, P. (1997) 'The media and terrorism: a reassessment', *Terrorism and Political Violence* 9(2): 51–64.

Winkler, C. (2012) *In the Name of Terrorism: Presidents on Political Violence in the Post-World War II Era*. New York: SUNY Press.

Yong, C.F. and R.B. McKenna (1990) *The Kuomintang Movement in British Malaya, 1912–1949*. Singapore: NUS Press.
Young, J.K. and M. Findlay (2011) 'The promise and pitfalls of terrorism research', *International Studies Review* 13(1): 1–21.
Zulaika, Joseba and William Douglass (1996) *Terror and Taboo: The Follies, Fables, and Faces of Terrorism*. Abingdon: Routledge.

Parliamentary sources

Abbott, Diane (2016) *Hansard HC Deb* vol 618, col 773 (14 December).
Ahmad, Lord (2016) *Hansard HL Deb* vol 774, col 416–422 (14 July).
Ahmed, Lord (2002) *Hansard HL Deb* vol 640, col 252–256 (30 October).
Alderdice, Lord (2008) *Hansard HL Deb* vol 703, col 1351 (17 July).
Anelay, Baroness (2006) *Hansard HL Deb* vol 684, col 1610–1620 (24 July).
Archer, Lord (2008) *Hansard HL Deb* vol 702, col 1309 (23 June).
Ashton, Lord (2014) *Hansard HL Deb* vol 754, col 1099–1104 (27 November).
Attlee, Lord (2013) *Hansard HL Deb* vol 747, col 489–495 (11 July).
Bassam, Lord (2000) *Hansard HL Deb*, col 1431 (6 April).
Bassam, Lord (2005) *Hansard HL Deb* vol 674, col 490–496 (13 October).
Bates, Lord (2015) *Hansard HL Deb* vol 758, col 1500 (22 January).
Blears, Hazel (2005) *Hansard HC Deb* vol 437, col 466–482 (13 October).
Blunkett, David (2002) *Hansard HC Deb* vol 391, col 875–899 (30 October).
Blunt, Crispin (2010) *Hansard HC Deb* vol 506, col 1035–1051 (4 March).
Brake, Tom (2010) *Hansard HC Deb* vol 506, col 1035–1050 (4 March).
Brake, Tom (2011) *Hansard HC Deb* vol 521, col 965–974 (19 January).
Bridgeman, Viscount (2002) *Hansard HL Deb* vol 640, col 252–256 (30 October).
Brokenshire, James (2012) *Hansard HC Deb*, col 1020 (4 July).
Brokenshire, James (2013) *Hansard HC Deb* vol 566, col 456–468 (10 July).
Brokenshire, James (2014a) *Hansard HC Deb* vol 582, col 1280–1284 (19 June).
Brokenshire, James (2014b) *Hansard HC Deb* vol 588, col 1037–1046 (26 November).
Brokenshire, James (2015) *Hansard HC Deb* vol 594, col 1537–1540 (25 March).
Brown, Lyn (2016) *Hansard HC Deb* vol 607, col 912 (15 March).
Bryant, Chris (2006) *Hansard HC Deb* vol 449, col 490–510 (20 July).
Butler, [Mrs] (1956) *Hansard HC Deb* vol 553 col 58W (6 June).
Carmichael, Alistair (2005) *Hansard HC Deb* vol 437, col 466–482 (13 October).

Clarke, Charles (2000) *Hansard HC* Standing Committee D, col 56 (18 January).
Clegg, Nick (2007) *Hansard HC Deb* vol 462, col 1370–1379 (10 July).
Corbett, Lord (2008) *Hansard HL Deb* vol 702, col 1306 (23 June).
Corbyn, Jeremy (2011) *Hansard HC Deb* vol 521, col 963–979 (19 January).
Corbyn, Jeremy (2012) *Hansard HC Deb* vol 547, col 1020–1027 (4 July).
Davies, Lord (2016) *Hansard HL Deb* vol 777, col 1446 (15 December).
Dholokia, Lord (2005) *Hansard HL Deb* vol 674, col 490–495 (13 October).
Dholokia, Lord (2007) *Hansard HL Deb* vol 694 col 750–753 (24 July).
Dismore, Andrew (2002) *Hansard HC Deb* vol 391, col 875–899 (30 October).
Dismore, Andrew (2006) *Hansard HC Deb* vol 449, col 499 (20 July).
Dismore, Andrew (2007) *Hansard HC Deb* vol 462, col 1374 (10 July).
Dodds, Nigel (2014) *Hansard HC Deb 2014* vol 578, col 948–963 (2 April).
Doughty, Stephen (2014) *Hansard HC Deb* vol 588, col 1037–1046 (26 November).
Du Cann, Edward (1978) *Hansard HC Deb* vol 950, col 30–110 (15 May).
Ellwood, Tobias (2012) *Hansard HC Deb* vol 547, col 1020–1027 (4 July).
Falkner, Lord (2011) *Hansard HL Deb* vol 724, col 604–612 (20 January).
Field, Mark (2013) *Hansard HC Deb* vol 572, cols 205–206 (10 December).
Filkin, Lord (2002) *Hansard HL Deb* vol 640, col 252–256 (30 October).
Freer, Mike (2014) *Hansard HC Deb* vol 582, col 1294 (19 June).
Fuller, Richard (2013) *Hansard HC Deb* vol 566, col 456–468 (10 July).
Gapes, Mike (2014) *Hansard HC Deb* vol 582, col 1294 (19 June).
Gapes, Mike (2017) *Hansard HC Deb* vol 633, col 1006 (19 December).
Goodhart, Lord (2002) *Hansard HL Deb* vol 640, col 255 (30 October).
Goodman, Helen (2005) *Hansard HC Deb* vol 437, col 465 (13 October).
Gove, Michael (2006) *Hansard HC Deb* vol 449, col 490–510 (20 July).
Green, Damian (2011) *Hansard HC Deb* vol 521, col 963–979 (19 January).
Grieve, Dominic (2005) *Hansard HC Deb* vol 437, col 466–483 (13 October).
Grieve, Dominic (2007) *Hansard HC Deb* vol 462, col 1371 (10 July).
Hamwee, Baroness (2010) *Hansard HL Deb* vol 717, col 1635–1641 (4 March).
Hancock, Mike (2006) *Hansard HC Deb* vol 449, col 490–510 (20 July).
Hanson, David (2010) *Hansard HC Deb* vol 506, col 1035–1051 (4 March).
Harris, Baroness (2006) *Hansard HL Deb* vol 684, col 1611–1620 (24 July).
Harris, Lord (2011) *Hansard HL Deb* vol 724, col 605–606 (20 January).
Harris, Lord (2014) *Hansard HL Deb* vol 754, col 1012 (19 June).
Hayes, John (2016) *Hansard HC Deb* vol 613 col 306–311 (13 July).

Heath, David (2006) *Hansard HC Deb* vol 449, col 490–510 (20 July).

Hermon, Lady (2002) *Hansard HC Deb* vol 391, col 875–899 (30 October).

Hogg, Douglas (2002) *Hansard HC Deb* vol 391, col 875–899 (30 October).

Hopkins, Kris (2011) *Hansard HC Deb* vol 521, col 971 (19 January).

Hughes, Simon (2002) *Hansard HC Deb* vol 391, col 883 (30 October).

Jenkins, Roy (1974) *Hansard HC Deb* vol 882 col 634–752 (28 November).

Johnson, Diana (2012) *Hansard HC Deb* vol 547, col 1020–1027 (4 July).

Johnson, Diana (2014a) *Hansard HC Deb* vol 578, col 948–963 (2 April).

Johnson, Diana (2014b) *Hansard HC Deb* vol 582, col 1280–1298 (19 June).

Johnson, Diana (2014c) *Hansard HC Deb* vol 588, col 1037–1046 (26 November).

Johnson, Diana (2015) *Hansard HC Deb* vol 594, col 1537–1540 (25 March).

Kerr, Stephen (2017) *Hansard HC Deb* vol 633, col 1006–1021 (19 December).

Kingsland, Lord (2005) *Hansard HL Deb* vol 674, col 490–496 (13 October).

Kingsland, Lord (2008) *Hansard HL Deb* vol 76093, col 1349 (17 July).

Lennox-Boyd, Alan (1955) *Hansard HC Deb* vol 537 col 276–7W (2 March).

Letwin, Oliver (2002) *Hansard HC Deb* vol 391, col 875–898 (30 October).

Lewis, Julian (2005) *Hansard HC Deb* vol 437, col 466–482 (13 October).

Lyttelton, Oliver (1952) *Hansard HC Deb* vol 178 col 717 (16 October).

Lyttelton, Oliver (1953) *Hansard HC Deb* vol 515 col 368 (6 May).

Maclean, Rachel (2017) *Hansard HC Deb* vol 633, col 1006–1021 (19 December).

McDonnell, John (2005) *Hansard HC Deb* vol 437, col 466–482 (13 October).

McNamara, Kevin (1979) *Hansard HC Deb* vol 971 col 741–770 (25 July).

McNulty, Tony (2006) *Hansard HC Deb* vol 449, col 490–510 (20 July).

McNulty, Tony (2007) *Hansard HC Deb* vol 462, col 1369–1380 (10 July).

McNulty, Tony (2008) *Hansard HC Deb* vol 479, col 193–212 (15 July).

Mahmood, Khalid (2007) *Hansard HC Deb* vol 462, col 1371 (10 July).

Mahmood, Shabana (2011) *Hansard HC Deb* vol 521, col 963–979 (19 January).

Marllesford, Lord (2015) *Hansard HL Deb* vol 758, col 1498 (22 January).

Mercer, Patrick (2005) *Hansard HC Deb* vol 437, col 466–482 (13 October).

Mercer, Patrick (2006) *Hansard HC Deb* vol 449, col 490–510 (20 July).

Mercer, Patrick (2013) *Hansard HC Deb* vol 566, col 421–468 (10 July).

Mowlam, Mo (1995) *Hansard HC Deb* vol 261 col 501–547 (12 June).

Munster, Lord (1952) *Hansard HL Deb* vol 178 col 717–719 (16 October).

Neville-Jones, Baroness (2010) *Hansard HL Deb* vol 717, col 1635–1641 (4 March).
Neville-Jones, Baroness (2011) *Hansard HL Deb* vol 724, col 604–612 (20 January).
Ogmire, Lord (1952) *Hansard HL Deb* vol 178 col 1094 (29 October).
Orr, L.P.S. (1973) *Hansard HC Deb* vol 865 col 586–589 (6 December).
Price, Adam (2005) *Hansard HC Deb* vol 437, col 467 (13 October).
Redwood, John (2006) *Hansard HC Deb* vol 449, col 490–510 (20 July).
Rees, Meryl (1973) *Hansard HC Deb* vol 865 col 1585 (6 December).
Robinson, Peter (1984) *Hansard HC Deb* vol 70 col 575–650 (20 December).
Rosser, Lord (2011) *Hansard HL Deb* vol 724, col 609 (20 January).
Rosser, Lord (2014) *Hansard HL Deb* vol 754, col 1099–1104 (27 November).
Rosser, Lord (2016) *Hansard HL Deb* vol 777, col 1446 (15 December).
Rosser, Lord (2017) *Hansard HL Deb* vol 703, col 2297 (21 December).
Ruffley David (2008) *Hansard HC Deb* vol 479, col 193–212 (15 July).
Russell-Johnston, Lord (2006) *Hansard HL Deb* vol 684, col 1616 (24 July).
Sandys, Duncan (1962) *Hansard HC Deb* vol 669 col 29W (11 December).
Scotland, Baroness (2006) *Hansard HL Deb* vol 684, col 1611 (24 July).
Shannon, Jim (2016a) *Hansard HC Deb* vol 613 col 306–311 (13 July).
Shannon, Jim (2016b) *Hansard HC Deb* vol 618, col 773 (14 December).
Simpson, Alan (2005) *Hansard HC Deb* vol 437, col 466–482 (13 October).
Smith, Baroness (2012) *Hansard HL Deb* vol 740, col 2022 (22 November).
Smith, Baroness (2013) *Hansard HL Deb* vol 747, col 492 (11 July).
Smith, Baroness (2014) *Hansard HL Deb* vol 754, col 1008–1018 (19 June).
Smith, Baroness (2015) *Hansard HL Deb* vol 760, col 1550–1555 (26 March).
Smith, Baroness (2016) *Hansard HL Deb* vol 774, col 417–422 (14 July).
Stanbrook, Ivor (1991) *Hansard HC Deb* vol 187 col 21–71 (4 March).
Swinson, Jo (2008) *Hansard HC Deb* vol 479, col 193–212 (15 July).
Taylor, Dari (2010) *Hansard HC Deb* vol 506, col 1039 (4 March).
Taylor, Lord (2014) *Hansard HL Deb* vol 754, col 1008–1018 (19 June).
Tierney, George (1819) *Hansard HC Deb* vol 41, col 378–418 (29 November).
Tyler, Paul (2000) *Hansard HC Deb* vol 357, col 665–718 (27 November).
Vaz, Keith (2008) *Hansard HC Deb* vol 479, col 193–212 (15 July).
Vaz, Keith (2010) *Hansard HC Deb* vol 506, col 1035–1051 (4 March).
Vaz, Keith (2011) *Hansard HC Deb* vol 521, col 970–971 (19 January).
Vaz, Keith (2012a) *Hansard HC Deb* vol 547, col 1020–1027 (4 July).
Vaz, Keith (2012b) *Hansard HC Deb* vol 553, col 766 (22 November).
Vaz, Keith (2013) *Hansard HC Deb* vol 566, col 463 (10 July).
Vaz, Keith (2014a) *Hansard HC Deb* 2014 vol 578, col 948–963 (2 April).
Vaz, Keith (2014b) *Hansard HC Deb* vol 582, col 1280–1298 (19 June).

Vaz, Keith (2014c) *Hansard HC Deb* vol 588, col 1023 (26 November).

Vaz, Keith (2015) *Hansard HC Deb* vol 591, col 331 (21 January).

Vis, Rudi (2006) *Hansard HC Deb* vol 449, col 490–510 (20 July).

Waddington, Lord (2006) *Hansard HL Deb* vol 684, col 1610–1620 (24 July).

Wallace, Ben (2016) *Hansard HC Deb* vol 618, col 773–920 (14 December).

Wallace, Ben (2017) *Hansard HC Deb* vol 633, col 1006 (19 December).

Wallace, Lord (2008) *Hansard HL Deb* vol 703, col 1346–1352 (17 July).

Weir, Mike (2006) *Hansard HC Deb* vol 449, col 494 (20 July).

West, Lord (2008) *Hansard HL Deb* vol 703, col 1346–1352 (17 July).

Williams, Baroness (2017) *Hansard HL Deb* vol 787, col 2293 (21 December).

Winnick, David (2006) *Hansard HC Deb* vol 449, col 492 (20 July).

Wright, Tony (2000) *Hansard HC Deb* vol 357, col 665–718 (27 November).

Index